FREIREAN PEDAGOGY, PRAXIS, AND POSSIBILITIES

CRITICAL EDUCATION PRACTICE
VOLUME 19
GARLAND REFERENCE LIBRARY OF SOCIAL SCIENCE
VOLUME 1417

CRITICAL EDUCATION PRACTICE
SHIRLEY R. STEINBERG AND JOE L. KINCHELOE, *Series Editors*

Freirean Pedagogy, Praxis, and Possibilities

Projects for the New Millennium

edited by
STANLEY F. STEINER
Boise State University

H. MARK KRANK
Western Montana College of the
University of Montana

PETER MCLAREN
University of California at Los Angeles

ROBERT E. BAHRUTH
Boise State University

FALMER PRESS
A MEMBER OF THE TAYLOR & FRANCIS GROUP
NEW YORK & LONDON
2000

Published in 2000 by
Falmer Press
A member of the Taylor & Francis Group
19 Union Square West
New York, NY 10003

10 9 8 7 6 5 4 3 2 1

Library of Congress Cataloging-in-Publication Data is available from the
Library of Congress.

Permission to Reprint
*The following publications and publishers have released material for whose
original publication they were responsible. We are grateful for permission to
reprint work by the Pedagogy of the Oppressed Conference for McLaren,
Shepard, and Mayo; Z Magazine for Chomsky; Researcher: Journal for the
Northern Rocky Mountain Educational Research Assocation, Volume 11, Number 2, Dec. 1996 for Freire & Macedo, Reitz, Miller & Eleveld, Heaney, Dickar,
Gunter, Flores, and Burns-McCoy; from Cultural Circles, Fall 1997, Volume 1,
for Giroux, and Gabbard.*

Printed on acid-free, 250-year-life paper
Manufactured in the United States of America

This book is dedicated to
Paulo Freire and his followers
and to the words of change
which blow in the wind
like seeds.

Contents

A Pedagogy of Transformation: An Introduction

Like most edited volumes, this work is a product of both collective and individual efforts. The core of the work had three points of origin. For Stan Steiner and me, the work on this book began six years ago when we met at the annual Northern Rocky Mountain Educational Research Association (NRMERA) conference. Our resulting conversations were forays into uncharted territories as we struggled to find a way to give voice to the need to go beyond critique and find those spaces of hope Peter McLaren describes.

As our conversations continued over time, it became evident that many of our colleagues had a similar need to engage in a level of dialogue that was missing from traditional, pedantic academic discussions. Student nonengagement to a pedagogy that offered a democratic classroom, students struggling while finding voice, critical looks at the educational mainstream, careful analysis of what is missing in prescribed curricula, and institutional resistance to dialogical encounters within the power structure were common but often muted issues for many of us. At the same time, our systemic realities seemed intent on imposing an unbending intellectual orthodoxy. We became enthralled with the possibilities of going beyond our individual situations and problematizing common experiences with other colleagues. The seed had been planted and our interest grew.

In the fall of 1997 Stan and I accepted the task of coediting a special issue on critical pedagogy for *The Researcher,* NRMERA's journal. The response to our call for manuscripts went beyond our wildest expectations; the quality of the submissions was beyond our most optimistic hopes. Importantly, our call for manuscripts led to a collaboration with Peter McLaren. Through Peter we gained access to a set of papers gleaned from the University of Nebraska–Omaha Pedagogy of the Oppressed conference. Articles from both *The Researcher* and the Nebraska conference have found their way into this volume.

Shortly after connecting with Peter, we were joined by the powerful and articulate voice of Robert Bahruth. Our first work with Robert occurred at the 1997 NRMERA conference when he helped us facilitate a critical pedagogy symposium. Currently, he coedits *Cultural Circles,* a journal that focuses on educational issues of language minority students. His efforts netted the remaining manuscripts for this book. Beyond editorial expertise, his has been a wise counsel.

Though this set of essays is drawn from different points in time and place, each shares a common Freirean foundation. Clearly, the pedagogy of Paulo Freire is both explicitly and implicitly the focus of each element of this volume. Though many of our readers are intimately familiar with Freire's work and scholarship, a brief introduction is in order for the uninitiated. For those seeking additional information, a more detailed biography can be found in Peter McLaren's chapter. It goes without saying that it is an honor to include Paulo Freire in our list of authors.

Freire is a singularly important figure in the postmodern debate involving the constructs of teaching and learning. Although his seminal, theoretical scholarship developed out of experiences with the third world literacy movement in Brazil, Chile, and Guinea-Bissau, Freire's influence as a critical educational theorist has become worldwide. Humanization of society is the ultimate goal of his liberatory pedagogy.

Within Freire's system of pedagogy, an individual's ontological vocation is to be a subject who acts upon, and transforms, the world in order to become more fully human. This praxis, reflection and action, moves the individual towards ever new possibilities of a fuller and richer life through initial subjective reflection and the resulting rational and objective action. Critical pedagogy leaves no possibility of a neutral educational process. Education becomes either an instrument to help learners deal critically and creatively with reality in order to transform it through participatory action or an instrument to integrate learners into the present system by means of conformity. The result of the liberatory process will always be subjects who know and act. The result of the oppressive process will always be objects who are known and are acted upon. Freire defines any act that limits human potential as oppressive and dehumanizing.

Donaldo Macedo's work suggests traditional education intends to stupidify in an effort to conceal humanity's ability to transform the world and create history. Along with stupidification it resists dialogue, objectifies learners, domesticates thinking, immobilizes decision making, and fixates power. Liberating education poses problems, deconstructs, is founded in dialogue, requires critical thinking, requires creativity, stimulates action, and affirms changing reality. Freire views the teacher and teaching as democratic elements within liberatory education, where they are constantly being redefined by historical and cultural contexts.

This anthology proposes a number of themes to facilitate a Freirean transformation of education. Here, *transformation* will be defined as the continued utilization of purposeful critical reflection to establish a subjective frame of reference. This definition of transformation suggests critical reflection as a process rather than a destination.

Accordingly, the transformation of education will result in liberated learners actively involved in the humanization of their individual realities through subjective reflection and rational, objective action.

The transformational themes include, but are not limited to, dialogical encounters, cross-cultural explorations, and critical literacy. These essays also suggest transformation will be contingent on engaging students as liberatory learners during their educational experiences. Efforts to merely reform education through traditional power structures will predictably result in continued unequal social, political, and economic realities. There exists a clear distinction between educational institutions as sites for the critical facilitation of learning and sites for political activism. Political activism will only lead to reform; critical facilitation of learning will lead to a Freirean transformation.

Historically, educational institutions have followed an intellectual path of least resistance. Political expediency, rather than liberatory theory, has been the driving force behind educational practice. This work is based on the assumption that the generative facilitation of learning described by Freire is more than a theoretical construct. It is assumed the nonreductionistic, reflective facilitation of learning rather than a technocratic pedagogy is a practical, even necessary, artifact of cultural diversity during an era of reactionary educational reform.

Though it is acknowledged that Freire's conceptions of learning and teaching are both ephemeral and lofty, the purpose of this volume is to help build the case that education at all levels, contrary to past performance, is capable of having an impact on learners that is both generative and liberatory. In the past, education has succumbed to uninformed pressures to deliver a skills-driven product at the expense of fostering reflective, thoughtful, engaged learners. The result has been students unprepared to be proactive change agents during a time of needed change.

Students embedded in academic cultures for which they are unable to find personal referents are typically socially and intellectually inert. The time to adjust the culture of education to fit the learner has arrived. To do otherwise is an overt decision to marginalize the social and intellectual bounty offered by divergent perspectives. Educational institutions must treat all learners as valued others no matter their socioeconomic, cognitive, cultural, ethnic, racial, gender, or age-based mismatch to the norms of the dominant culture.

On our path as liberatory learners we must heed the words of Paulo: Donaldo, I don't want to be imported or exported. It is impossible to export pedagogical practices without reinventing them. Please tell your fellow American educators not to import me. Ask them to re-create and rewrite my ideas.

According to Freire, an open system, as a reflection of environmental reality, is the definition of rational. In contrast, a closed system is irrational because there are no phenomenological referents in environmental reality. Therefore, a rational act is any act that is inherently evolutionary, progressive, dynamic, or generative. It follows that an irrational act is any act that is inherently deterministic, static, or neutral. Any attempt to merely mimic Freire and his work is more than a disservice to his legacy, it is an irrational act.

From the start it was our intent that this set of essays be inclusive rather than exclusive. Within these pages you'll find the voices of internationally renowned professors, beginning assistant professors, community college instructors, public school teachers, and university graduate students. We hope you find the balance of articles and authors as enlightening as we did. For us, sharing the same concerns and thoughts serves as a means to continue the discussions. The greatest benefits to us resulting from this effort have been both the invigorating connections with new colleagues and friends and the richer personal connections to familiar colleagues and friends.

We would be remiss if we did not acknowledge the help and assistance of Joe Kincheloe, Shirley Steinberg, Michael Spurlock, Judy Ashkenaz, and particularly Donaldo Macedo. The support of each has been a boon during this process. It goes without saying that any fault found within these pages belongs to the editors and not the contributors.

H. Mark Krank
Western Montana College
m_krank@wmc.edu

Stanley F. Steiner
Boise State University
ssteine@boisestate.edu

About the Contributors

Robert E. Bahruth is a professor of bilingual education and a member of the Elementary Education and Specialized Studies Department at Boise State University.

Nancie Burns-McCoy completed her Ph.D. in English Education in December 1998 and currently teaches writing and literature for the University of Idaho's Department of English.

Noam Chomsky, Ph.D., is a professor of linguistics at the Massachusetts Institute of Technology. According to the *New York Times*, Noam Chomsky is "arguably the most significant intellectual alive." In addition to being a major figure in twentieth-century linguistics, he has published numerous books on contemporary political issues and has exerted considerable influence in various fields, including philosophy and psychology.

Maryann Dickar is currently completing her doctorate in American Studies at the University of Minnesota. She is living and teaching social studies in Brooklyn, NY.

Mark Roelof Eleveld teaches at Lewis University.

Paulo Freire (1921–1997) is a world-renowned educator and activist. His works are numerous, including *Pedagogy of the Oppressed*, and his legacy lives on in the lives of many, including the contributors to this book.

David A. Gabbard is an associate professor in the Department of Foundations, Research, and Reading at East Carolina University.

Henry A. Giroux is Professor of Education at Pennsylvania State University, where he currently serves as the director of the Waterbury Forum in Education and Cultural Studies.

Kimberly Kay Gunter is a doctoral candidate at the University of Illinois at Urbana-Champaign.

Thomas Heaney is an associate professor of adult education at National-Louis University, Chicago, and director of the Adult Education Doctoral Program.

Donaldo Macedo is a professor of English and a Distinguished Professor of Liberal Arts and Education at the University of Massachusetts, Boston. He directs the Bilingual and ESL Graduate Program at UMass.

Peter Mayo is lecturer at the Faculty of Education, University of Malta, where he coordinates the Adult Education Programme.

George David Miller teaches at Lewis University.

Peter McLaren is Professor of Education, Graduate School of Education and Information Studies, University of California, Los Angeles. He is an Associate of the Paulo Freire Institute, São Paulo, Brazil.

Charles Reitz teaches Ethics, Logic, and Multicultural Education at Kansas City Kansas Community College.

Scott Shepard completed his Ph.D. in Ethnic American Literatures at Bowling Green State University in Ohio. His dissertation focused on coming-of-age narratives by Japanese American women writers. He teaches Ethnic American and Contemporary World Literature at Richland College in Dallas, TX.

Stanley F. Steiner is an associate professor of literacy and a member of the Elementary Education and Specialized Studies Department at Boise State University.

CHAPTER 1

Paulo Freire's Pedagogy of Possibility

PETER McLAREN

> *I "played" so much at being a teacher when I was an adolescent that when I taught my first classes in an orientation course at the Osvaldo Cruz School of Recife, in the 1940s, I had a hard time distinguishing between the imaginary professor and the real one and I was happy in both worlds.*
>
> —PAULO FREIRE (IN PRESS)

> *[W]hat I have been proposing from my political convictions, my philosophical convictions, is a profound respect for the total autonomy of the educator. What I have been proposing is a profound respect for the cultural identity of students—a cultural identity that implies respect for the language of the other, the color of the other, the gender of the other, the class of the other, the sexual orientation of the other, the intellectual capacity of the other; that implies the ability to stimulate the creativity of the other. But these things take place in a social and historical context and not in pure air. These things take place in history and I, Paulo Freire, am not the owner of history.*
>
> —PAULO FREIRE (1997, PP. 307–308).

Paulo Freire was one of the first internationally recognized educational thinkers who fully appreciated the relationship among education, politics, imperialism, and liberation. Generally considered the inaugural philosopher of critical pedagogy, Freire was able to effectively recast pedagogy on a global basis in the direction of a radical politics of historical struggle, a direction that he expanded into a lifelong project. Long before his death on May 2, 1997, he was known to workers and theologians as well as scholars and researchers from numerous disciplinary traditions, for fomenting interest in the ways that education can serve as a vehicle for social and economic transformation. What is now termed "a politics of liberation" is a topic of pivotal significance among educational activists throughout the globe and one to which Freire had made important and pioneering contributions.

BIOGRAPHICAL SKETCH

Born Paulo Reglus Neves Freire on September 19, 1921, in Recife, in the northeast of Brazil, Freire has become a legendary figure in the field of education. A courageous scholar, social activist, and cultural worker admired for his integrity and humility, Freire became internationally renowned for developing an anti-imperialist and anticapitalist literacy praxis employed by progressive educators in Brazil.

In his early twenties Freire joined the faculty of law at the Universidade de Recife. His ten-year involvement with the Industry Council's social service organization in the regional department of Pernambuco and subsequently his general superintendency of that division and his participation in the Movement for Popular Culture of Recife helped to motivate him to devote his energies to the area of adult literacy. Shortly after his first case, he abandoned his vocation as a lawyer in order to study the relationships among pupils, teachers, and parents in working-class communities in the northeast of Brazil.

Freire completed his doctorate in 1959 (titled "Education and the Brazilian Reality"), and in 1961 he was invited by the Mayor of Recife to develop a literacy program for that city. As the newly appointed director of the Extension Service of the University of Recife, Freire began to work with new methods of teaching adult literacy. His approach to literacy was greatly influenced by his activities in the Catholic Action Movement and by Catholic collectivism, Communidades Eclesiales de Base (Basic Church communities), and a close association with the Bishop of Recife, Dom Helder Camara.

In 1962, in the town of Angicos, in Rio Grande de Norte, Freire's literacy program helped three hundred rural farm workers learn to read and write in forty-five days. The literacy worker, by living communally with groups of peasants and workers, was able to identify generative words according to their phonetic value, syllabic length, and social meaning and relevance to the workers. These words represented the everyday reality of the workers. Each word was associated with issues related to existential questions about life and the social factors that determined the economic conditions of everyday existence. Themes were then generated from these words (i.e., words such as *wages* or *government*) that were then codified and decodified by groups of workers and teachers who participated in groups known as "cultural circles."

Reading and writing thus became grounded in the lived experiences of peasants and workers and resulted in a process of ideological struggle and revolutionary praxis—or conscientization. As a result of this literacy process, workers and peasants were able to transform their "culture of silence" and become collective agents of social and political change. The success of this program—supported by the United States Agency for International Development—marked the beginning of what was to become a legendary approach in education.

In 1963, Freire was invited by President Joao Goulart and by the Minister of Education, Paulo De Tarso Santos, to rethink adult literacy programs on a national basis and to work with the national literacy program, the Movement for Basic Education. In 1964, twenty thousand cultural circles were designed to assist two million illiterate workers. However, all of that was brazenly interrupted by a military coup that year.

Freire's internationally celebrated work with the poor began in the late 1940s and continued unabated until 1964, when a right-wing military coup overthrew Goulart's democratically elected government. Freire was accused of preaching communism and was arrested. He was imprisoned by the military government for seventy days and exiled for his work in the national literacy campaign, of which he had served as director. According to Freire's leading biographer, Moacir Gadotti—also one of the founding members of the Partido dos Trabalhadores (Workers Party), Freire's Chief of Cabinet in the administration of São Paulo's Municipal Secretariat of Education—the Brazilian military considered Freire to be an international subversive, a traitor to Christ and the Brazilian people, and accused him of developing a teaching method similar to that of Stalin, Hitler, Peron, and Mussolini. He was furthermore accused of trying to turn Brazil into a Bolshevik country (Gadotti, 1994).

Freire's sixteen years of exile were tumultuous and productive times: a five-year stay in Chile as a UNESCO consultant with the Research and Training Institute for Agrarian Reform; an appointment in 1969 to Harvard University's Center of Educational and Developmental Studies associated with the Center for Studies in Development and

Social Change; a move to Geneva, Switzerland, in 1970 as consultant to the Office of Education of the World Council of Churches, where he developed literacy programs for Tanzania and Guinea-Bissau that focused on the re-Africanization of their countries; the development of literacy programs in some postrevolutionary former Portuguese colonies such as Angola and Mozambique, programs that were motivated by the work of Frantz Fanon, a reengagement with the works of Marx, and personal sympathy for Amilcar Cabral's Movimento Popular Libertacão de Angola (Popular Movement for the Liberation of Angola), Frente de Libertacao de Moccambique (Mozambique Liberation Front), and Partido Africans para Independencia de Guinea-Bissau e Cabo Verde (African Party for the Independence of Guinea-Bissau and Cabo Verde); assisting the governments of Peru and Nicaragua with their literacy campaigns; the establishment of the Institute of Cultural Action in Geneva in 1971; a brief return to Chile after Salvador Allende was assassinated in 1973, working in the area of agrarian reform and provoking General Pinochet to declare Freire a subversive; participation in literacy work in São Tome and Principe from 1975 to 1979; a brief visit to Brazil under political amnesty in 1979; and a final return to Brazil in 1980 to teach at the Pontificia Universidade Catolica de São Paulo and the Universidade de Campinas in São Paulo. Freire would go on to undertake literacy work in Australia, Italy, Angola, the Fiji Islands, and numerous other areas throughout the world.

In São Paulo, Freire witnessed growing resistance to the military government, such as the 1978 and 1979 strikes by the metalworkers of São Bernardo (an industrial region of São Paulo), and he joined the socialist democratic party, Partido dos Trabalhadores (Workers Party, or PT), which was formed in 1980. When the Workers Party won the 1989 municipal elections in São Paulo, Mayor Luiza Erundina appointed Freire Municipal Secretary of Education for São Paulo, a position he held until 1991. During his tenure as Secretary, Freire continued his radical agenda of literacy reform for the people of that city. Under Freire's guidance, the Secretariat of Education set up a literacy program for young people called MOVA-SP (Literacy Movement in the City of São Paulo), which contributed to strengthening popular movements and creating alliances between civil society and the state. Freire also created the Movimento de Reorientacão Curricular (Movement to Reorient the Curriculum), which attempted to create collective work through a decentralization of power and the fostering of school autonomy and the reconstruction of the curriculum around critical community issues.

What is remarkable about Freire's lifework is that while it is distinctly addressed to educators and literacy workers, it continues to be vigorously engaged by scholars in numerous disciplines: literary theory, composition, philosophy, ethnography, political science, sociology, teacher education, theology, and so on. He has given the word *educator* a new meaning, inflecting the term to embrace multiple perspectives: border intellectual, social activist, critical researcher, moral agent, radical philosopher, and political revolutionary. To a greater extent than any other educator of this century, Freire was able to develop a pedagogy of resistance to oppression. More than this, he lived what he taught. His life is the story of courage, hardship, perseverance, and unyielding belief in the power of love.

Reflecting upon his lifework and the circumstances and experiences associated with his exile that took him to so many countries around the world, Freire describes his professional mission as a search for unity between theory and practice. Freire writes:

> The experiences that I had in Africa, Asia, Europe, Latin America, the Caribbean, the United States, Mexico and in Canada, discussing with national educators fundamental problems in their educational systems; my participation in courses and seminars at North American, Latin American, African, European and Asian universities; my meetings with leaders of various liberation movements in Africa and Latin America, all of this is guarded in my memory, not as something of the past or something that has passed, that I remember with nostalgia. All of this, on the contrary, is quite alive and vivid. And when I think about all of this, something makes me believe that one of the most visible impressions on my professional trajectory is the consistent search for unity between theory and practice. It is in this sense that my books, good or bad, are theoretical chronicles of the "what was done," linked to the events in which I was involved.

FREIRE'S PHILOSOPHY OF PEDAGOGY: A PREFERENTIAL OPTION FOR THE POOR

Freire's life vehemently unveils the imprints of a life lived within the margins of power and prestige. Because his work centered around the issue of social and political change, Freire has always been considered controversial, especially by educational establishments in Europe and North America. Although he is recognized as one of the most significant philosophers of liberation and a pioneer in critical literacy and critical pedagogy, his work continues to be taken up mostly by marginal groups of educators working outside of the educational mainstream. The marginal status of Freire's followers is undoubtedly due to the fact that Freire firmly believed that educational change must be accompanied by significant changes in the social and political structure in which education takes place. It is a position most educators would find either politically untenable or hopelessly utopian. It is certainly a position that threatens the interests of those who are already well served by the dominant culture.

Freire's own personal contact early in his life with Brazilian peasants profoundly shaped his assent to popular revolts against economic exploitation in Latin America, Africa, and elsewhere. Given the basic contradictions facing a social order encapsulated in the exploitation of the vast majority of Brazilian society, the task or mission of Freire centered on the transformation of the relations of the production of social wealth (together with their ideological-political levels). Yet such an attempt to establish a new social order underwritten by a just system of appropriation and distribution of social wealth was to relegate Freire to the ranks of educators considered to be subversive to the state. For Freire, the very protocols of literacy and the act of "coming to know" must themselves be transformed in order to make a prominent place for issues of social justice and the struggle for emancipation. Freire taught that in order for the oppressed to materialize their self-activity as a revolutionary force, they must develop a collective consciousness of their own constitution or formation as a subaltern class, as well as an ethos of solidarity and interdependence. For Freire, a pedagogy of critical literacy becomes the primary vehicle for the development of "critical consciousness" among the poor, leading to a process of exploration and creative effort that conjoins deep personal meanings and common purpose. Literacy, for Freire, becomes that common "process" of participation open to all individuals. The problem of "critical consciousness" cannot be posed in abstraction from the significant historical contexts in which knowledge is produced, engaged, and appropriated.

Freire lamented the brute reality that witnessed the oppressed as always living as the detachable appendages of other people's dreams and desires. It seemed to Freire that the dreams of the poor were always dreamt for them by distant others who were removed from their daily struggles and who were either unable or unwilling to recognize the dreams that burned in the habitats of their hearts. Based on a recognition of the cultural underpinnings of folk traditions and the importance of the collective construction of knowledge, Freire's pedagogical project created a vivid new vocabulary of concern for the oppressed and revealed a new and powerful political terminology that enabled the oppressed to analyze their location within the privileging hierarchy of capitalist society and to engage in attempts to dislodge themselves from existing cycles of social reproduction. Literacy programs developed by Freire and his colleagues for disempowered peasants are now employed in countries all over the world. By linking the categories of history, politics, economics, and class to the concepts of culture and power, Freire managed to develop both a language of critique and a language of hope that work conjointly and dialectically and that have proven successful in helping generations of disenfranchised peoples to liberate themselves. Freire recognized that there is no way of representing the consciousness of the oppressed that escapes the founding assumptions of the culture and society in which the teacher or cultural worker is implicated (Freire, in press) Long before postmodernists brought us their version of "identity politics," Freire understood that the subjectivities of the oppressed are to be considered heterogeneous and cannot be represented extratextually, that is, outside of the discursive embeddedness of the educator's own founding value and epistemological assumptions (McLaren and Leonard, 1993).

Influenced by the work of Lucien Febvre, the French *nouvelle pedagogie* of Celestin Freinet and Edouard Claparede, and the writings of Leszek Kolakowski, Karel Kosik, Eric Fromm, Antonio Gramsci, Karl Mannheim, Teilhard do Chardin, Franz Fanon, Albert Memmi, Jean Piaget, Emilia Ferreiro, Madalena F. Weffort, Lev Vygotsky, Amilcar Cabral, and the Christian personalism theory of Tristiande Atiade and Emanuel Mounier (not to mention the classic works of Hegel, Marx, Rousseau, and Dewey), Freire's pedagogy was anti-authoritarian, dialogical, and interactive, and put power into the hands of students and workers. Most important, Freirean pedagogy put social and political analysis of everyday life at the center of the curriculum. The concise rendering of Freire's basic argument in *Pedagogy of the Oppressed* (1973) is that knowledge is a dialogical act—a political act of knowing. Freire's central importance in critical pedagogy can be traced to his model of emancipatory knowledge as praxis. Freire expresses this as a shift from "naive consciousness" to "critical consciousness." He is worth quoting at length:

> [T]rue dialogue cannot exist unless the dialoguers engage in critical thinking—thinking which discerns an indivisible solidarity between the world and the people and admits of no dichotomy between them—thinking which perceives reality as process, as transformation, rather than as a static entity—thinking which does not separate itself from

action, but constantly immerses itself in temporality without fear of the risks involved. Critical thinking contrasts with naive thinking, which sees historical time as a weight, a stratification of the acquisitions and experiences of the past, from which the present should emerge normalized and "well-behaved." For the naive thinker, the important thing is accommodation to this normalized "today." For the critic, the important thing is the continuing transformation of reality. (1973, p. 73)

Freire's writings exhibit a singular awareness that the oppressed will not recognize their oppression simply because somebody has pointed it out to them. They will come to recognize their oppression through their own daily experience of struggling to survive. Struggle and critical reflection are thus dialectically related. Daily struggle provides a reason for the oppressed to take seriously the type of self-reflection that empowers their daily efforts to fulfill their material needs and to be treated with dignity and respect. Engaged in Freirean praxis, people who suffer abuses take up the cause of liberation with increased courage and dynamism.

Freire understood that as the oppressed take more control of their own history, they assimilate more rapidly into society but on their own terms. He warrants the reputation as a preeminent critical educationalist in the way that he was able to foreground the means by which the pedagogical (the localized pedagogical encounter between teacher and student) is implicated in the political (the social relations of production within the global capitalist economy). Whereas mainstream educators often decapitate the social context from the self and then cauterize the dialectical movement between them, Freire stresses the dialectical motion between the subject and object, the self and the social, and social structure and human agency.

Educators who work within a Freirean-inspired critical pedagogy are more indebted to Freire's philosophical insights than to his commentaries on teaching methodologies (Taylor, 1995). Freire's working vocabulary of philosophical concepts enables the world of the oppressed to become visible, to inscribe itself as a text to be engaged and understood by the oppressed and non-oppressed alike. Freire's work does not reduce the world to a text but rather stipulates the conditions for the possibility of various competing and conflicting discourses or ways of making sense out of lived experiences. Freire interrogates the catharsis of value by urging educators to identify the aporias within their own philosophies of teaching and daily life.

In all of Freire's teachings, the concept of truth becomes vitiatingly unwounded as the truth becomes linked to one's own emplotment in the reigning narratives about truth. Of course, Freire's own work can be used against itself in this regard and interpreted as an epiphenomenon of the narratives that create the textual effects of his own work. In fact, Freire would most assuredly have encouraged readers to scrutinize his work in the same manner of ideology critique that he encouraged readers to interrogate other texts.

Freire often spoke against the authoritarian nostalgia that surrounds efforts by mainstream educational policy makers and their "authoritarian administrations" to reduce a highly complex world by means of simplistic answers (Freire, in press). Freire also opposed the destructive autodynamics of the economic system, its unequal distribution of advantages and disadvantages, and members of the well-heeled comprador landlord classes throughout the globe (McLaren and Lankshear, 1994). As a result, he remained scrupulously unwilling to allow his pedagogy to commit itself to a reproduction of the status quo social order.

He feared the consequences of the explosion of the international economy and the destructive efforts of deindustrialization. He was also critical of the depoliticized collectivization of civic agency most often associated with neoliberal state formations (Freire, in press). Freire's insights have been crucial for helping North American criticalists recognize that mainstream pedagogical efforts most often seen in their "democratic" schools were closely tethered to a liberal-capitalist social order that reproduces inequality at the ideological level through the Lockean social contract, in which asymmetrical relations of power are legitimated under the banner of autonomous agency and unfettered competition in the capitalist marketplace (Freire and Macedo, 1987). The economy is not a separate part of the lives of teachers and students. Market relations inform large facets of their lives, suffusing capital and everyday thoughts, dreams, and desires. Freire recognized that capitalism is complexly and heterogeneously embedded in the totalities of everyday life. Freire's pedagogical challenge betokens not only the current crisis in meaning but also the possibility for new ways of mobilizing pedagogy in the interests of a larger social transformation (McLaren, 1997).

One could argue convincingly that Freire's name functions emblematically to mark an epochal turning point in the way that educators have come to view knowledge as a political "act of knowing." Just as Whitehead was to pronounce that all philosophy was a series of footnotes on

Plato, some educators will undoubtedly make the claim that all criticalist endeavors in education owe their greatest debt to Freire. Although such an indebtedness is surely justified, it is also likely that Freire would reject the epochality of his own contribution to education, since to mark off his legacy as *la siecle Freirean* would be to affirm a general history of education, a perspective that brushed against the grain of Freire's own work.

FREIRE'S INFLUENCE ON NORTH AMERICAN CRITICAL PEDAGOGY

Discovering that pedagogy existed largely in pathologized conditions, Freire sought to advance new approaches to teaching and learning, carefully avoiding those "flesh-eating" varieties that separated mind from body, thought from action, and social critique from transformative praxis. For Freire, pedagogy has as much to do with the teachable heart as the teachable mind, and as much to do with efforts to change the world as it does with rethinking the categories that we use to analyze our current condition within history. In this way, Freire has pushed the debate over pedagogy out of familiar, well-worn grooves.

Freire's work has unarguably been the driving force behind North American efforts to develop critical pedagogy. Critical pedagogy is a way of thinking about, negotiating, and transforming the relationship among classroom teaching, the production of knowledge, the institutional structures of the school, and the social and material relations of the wider community, society, and nation-state (McLaren, 1993). Developed by progressive teachers attempting to eliminate inequalities on the basis of social class, it has sparked a wide array of antisexist, antiracist, and antihomophobic classroom-based curricula and policy initiatives.

Freirean-inspired critical pedagogies in North America have grown out of a number of theoretical developments such as Latin American philosophies of liberation (McLaren, 1993), critical literacy (Macedo, 1994; Lankshear and McLaren, 1993), the sociology of knowledge (Apple, 1985; Fine, 1990), the Frankfurt school of critical theory (Giroux, 1985; McLaren and Giarelli, 1995), adult education (Torres, 1988), bilingual and bicultural education (Moraes, 1996; Darder, 1991; Wink, 1997; Cummins, 1986), teacher education (McLaren, 1993), and neo-Marxist cultural criticism (McLaren, 1997a; Apple, 1996). In more recent years his work has been taken up by educators influenced by debates over postmodernism and poststructuralism (Kincheloe, 1993; Kanpol, 1992; Aronowitz and Giroux, 1995; Giroux and McLaren, 1989;

McLaren, 1995), cultural studies (Giroux and McLaren, 1994; Giroux et al, 1997), and multiculturalism (Sleeter and McLaren, 1995; McLaren, 1997b).

Yet even with such a divergent array of influences, at the level of classroom life Freirean pedagogy is often erroneously perceived as synonymous with whole-language instruction, adult literacy programs, and new "constructivist" approaches to teaching and learning based on Vygotsky's work. Not all such programs are necessarily Freirean, but need to be judged in relation to the contextual specificity of their philosophy and praxis.

Lankshear and McLaren have summarized six learning principles from Freire's work that have provided teachers with pivotal points of reference in the development of their pedagogical practices:

1. The world must be approached as an object to be understood and known by the efforts of learners themselves. Moreover, their acts of knowing are to be stimulated and grounded in their own being, experiences, needs, circumstances, and destinies.

2. The historical and cultural world must be approached as a created, transformable reality which, like humans themselves, is constantly in the process of being shaped and made by human deeds in accordance with ideological representations of reality.

3. Learners must learn how to actively make connections between their own lived conditions and being and the making of reality that has occurred to date.

4. They must consider the possibility for "new makings" of reality, the new possibilities for being that emerge from new makings, and become committed to shaping a new enabling and regenerative history. New makings are a collective, shared social enterprise in which the voices of all participants must be heard.

5. In the literacy phase learners come to see the importance of print for this shared project. By achieving print competence within the process of bringing their experience and meanings to bear on the world in active construction and reconstruction (of lived relations and practice), learners will actually experience their own potency in the very act of understanding what it means to be a human subject. In the postliteracy phase, the basis for action is print-assisted exploration of generative themes. Addressing the theme of "Western culture" as conceived by people like Hirsch and reified in prevailing curricula and pedagogies, and seeking

to transcend this conception in the kinds of ways elaborated in later chapters, involves exactly the kind of praxis Freire intends.
6. Learners must come to understand how the myths of dominant discourse are, precisely, myths which oppress and marginalize them—but which can be transcended through transformative action. (1993, pp. 43–44)

While critics often decry Freire's educational approach for its idealist vision of social transformation, its supporters, including Freire, have complained that critical pedagogy has often been domesticated and reduced to student-directed learning approaches devoid of social critique. Once considered by the faint-hearted guardians of the American dream as a term of opprobrium, critical pedagogy has become so completely psychologized, so liberally humanized, so technologized, and so conceptually postmodernized, that its current relationship to broader liberation struggles and to Freire's stress on revolutionary class struggle seems severely attenuated if not fatally terminated. Because Freire believed that the challenge of transforming schools should be directed at overcoming socioeconomic injustice linked to the political and economic structures of society, any attempt at school reform that claims to be inspired by Freire—but that is only concerned with social patterns of representation, interpretation, or communication, and that does not connect these patterns to redistributive measures and structures that reinforce such patterns—exempts itself from the most important insights of Freire's work.

Freire's approach stipulates a trenchant understanding of patterns of distribution and redistribution in order to transform—and not just interpret—the underlying economic structures that produce relations of exploitation. Freire was also concerned with practicing a politics of diversity and self-affirmation—in short, a cultural politics—not as a mere end in itself but in relation to a larger politics of liberation and social justice. Consequently, a Freirean pedagogy of liberation is totaling without being dominating in that it always attends dialectically to the specific or local "act of knowing" as a political process that takes place in the larger conflictual arena of capitalist relations of exploitation, an arena where large groups of people palpably and undeniably suffer needless privations and pain due to alienation and poverty. Thus, a pedagogy of the oppressed involves not only a redistribution of material resources, but also a struggle over cultural meanings in relation to the multiple social locations of student and teachers and their position within the global division of labor.

Has Freire's name become a floating signifier to be attached adventitiously to any chosen referent within the multistranded terrain of progressive education? To a certain extent this has already happened. Liberal progressives are drawn to Freire's humanism; Marxists and neo-Marxists are drawn to his revolutionary praxis and his history of working with revolutionary political regimes; left liberals are drawn to his critical utopianism; and even conservatives begrudgingly respect his stress on ethics.

No doubt his work will be domesticated by his followers—as selected aspects of his corpus are uncritically appropriated and decontextualized from his larger political project of struggling for the realization of a truly socialist democracy—in order to make a more comfortable fit with various conflicting political agendas. Consequently, it is important to read Freire in the context of his entire corpus of works, from *Pedagogy of the Oppressed* to his recent reflection on this early work, which he called *Pedagogy of Hope*.

FREIREAN PEDAGOGY: ITS SHORTCOMINGS

Those who have an important stake in the meaning of Freire's life and work will continue to disagree over how his politics and pedagogy should be interpreted. The assertive generality of Freire's formulations of and pronouncements on pedagogy can be highly frustrating, in that they index important concerns but do not fully provide the necessary theoretical basis for positing more progressive and programmatic alternatives to the theories and perspectives that he is criticizing. For instance, few accounts are provided as to how teachers are to move from critical thought to critical practice. Yet Freire's weakness is also a source of his strength and marks the durability of his thought. It is precisely his refusal to spell out alternative solutions that enables his work to be "reinvented" in the contexts in which his readers find themselves, thereby enjoying a contextually specific "translation" across geographic, geopolitical, and cultural borders. It also grants to Freire's corpus of works a universal character, as they are able to retain their heuristic potency (much like the works of Marx) such that they can be conscripted by educators to criticize and to counterpoint pedagogical practices worldwide. In fact, Freire urged his readers to reinvent him in the context of their local struggles. What could be retained in every instance of this reinvention process is Freire's constant and unstoppable ethics of solidarity and an unrepentant utopianism. Freire writes that "the progressive educator must always be moving out on his or her own, continually reinventing me and reinventing what it means to be democratic in his or her own specific cultural and historical context" (1997, p. 308). Some have assigned to Freire's work the Archimedian conceit of the idealist utopian view of society. However, such a criticism risks overlooking the practical utility of Freirean pedagogy, especially when one considers the success of the literacy campaigns that relied heavily on his work. Freire seizes on the occult presence of seeds of redemption at the center of a world gone mad. Yet his politics of liberation resists subsumption under a codified set of universal principles; rather, it animates a set of ethical imperatives that together serve as a precipitate of our answering the call of the other who is suffering and of a heavy heart. Such imperatives do not mark a naive utopian faith in the future; rather, they presage a form of active, irreverent, and uncompromising hope in the possibilities of the present.

The legacy of racism left by the New World European oppressor—that Blacks and Latino/as are simply a species of inferior invertebrates—was harshly condemned but never systematically analyzed by Freire. And while Freire was a vociferous critic of racism and sexism, he did not, as Kathleen Weiler (1996) points out, sufficiently problematize his conceptualization of liberation and the oppressed in terms of his own male experience.

From the perspective of North American critical pedagogy, Freire's politics of liberation partakes of its own political inertia consequent in the limited range of narratives out of which he constructs his praxis of hope and transformation. For instance, Freire failed to articulate fully his position on Christianity (Elias, 1994) and the male bias in his literacy method (Taylor, 1993). Freire rarely addressed the ways that oppression formed on the basis of ethnicity, class, and sexual orientation are intermingled. As a number of North American critics have pointed out, Freire failed to fully engage the issue of white male privilege (Ladson-Billings, 1997) or the interest and agency of African-Americans apart from a wider movement of emancipatory practices (Murrell, Jr. 1997). And when Freire did address this issue, he often retreated into mystical abstractions, thereby discounting the deep significance of patriarchy as a practice of oppression (Weiler, 1996).

The modality of theoretical envisioning deployed by Freire is decidedly modernist but, as I have argued elsewhere (McLaren, 1997b), some trappings of postmodernist discourses are immanent—yet barely registered—in Freire's articulation of human agency. Social theory identified as "postmodern" runs the serious risk of ignoring the brute reality that working people the world over share a common subjection to capitalist exploitation. The violent realities of the global economy are often dissipated within postmodern social theories. On the other hand, pedagogies of liberation such as Freire's, underwritten by modernist Marxian discourses, often seriously ignore issues of race, gender, and sexual orientation. Freire was aware of these omissions (Freire, 1977; Freire, in press) and had begun to address them in his most recent work. Despite the fact that deconstructionists such as Stuart Parker (1997) have revealed much of the work of the critical educational tradition—exemplified by the work of Freire—to be located within modernist assumptions of teacher autonomy, assumptions that essentially serve as "devices of enchantment" that can be deconstructed as discursive fictions, Freire's work holds vital importance. Freire's contribution remains significant not for its methodology of literary alone but in the final instance for its ability to create a pedagogy of practical consciousness that presages critical action (Taylor, 1993). Freire's primary achievement remains that of his role as the Vagabond of the Obvious, a term that he often used to describe his pedagogical role. The shortcomings of Freire's work constitute more than minor rhetorical fallout to be sure, but as Freire's aforementioned critics also acknowledge, they should not detract from Freire's central importance as a foundational educational thinker, a philosopher who ranks among the most important educators of our era.

The globalization of capital, the move toward post-Fordist economic arrangements of flexible specialization, and the consolidation of neoliberal educational policies demand not only a vigorous and ongoing engagement with Freire's work, but also a reinvention of Freire in the context of current debates over information technologies and learning, global economic restructuring, and the effort to develop new modes of revolutionary struggle.

The educational left in the United States is currently in a state of confusion and disarray, having itself been pulled into the ferocious orbit of capital. The globalization of labor and capital has brought about material shifts in cultural practices and the proliferation of new contradictions between capitalism and labor. The "free market revolution" and continuous capitalist accumulation have left the social infrastructure of the United States in tatters, and through their policies of increasing its military-industrial-financial interests, they continue to suck the lifeblood from the open veins of South America and other regions of the globe. The logic of privatization and free trade—where social labor is the means and measure of value and surplus social labor lies at the heart of profit—now odiously shapes archetypes of citizenship, manages our perceptions of what should constitute the "good society," and creates ideological formations that produce necessary functions for capital in relation to labor. As schools are financed more by corporations that function as service industries for transnational capitalism and as bourgeois think-tank profiteerism continues to guide educational policy and practice, the U.S. population faces a challenging educational reality. It is a reality that is witnessing the progressive merging of pedagogy to the productive processes within advanced capitalism. Education has been reduced to a subsector of the economy, designed to create cybercitizens within a teledemocracy of fast-moving images, representations, and lifestyle choices. Capitalism has been naturalized as commonsense reality—even as a part of nature itself—while the term "social class" has been replaced by the less antagonistic term "socioeconomic status." The focus of the educational left is now on asymmetrical gender and ethnic relations, and although this focus is important, class struggle is now seen as an outdated issue. When social class is discussed, it is usually viewed as relational, not as oppositional. In the context of discussions of "social status" rather than "class struggle," technoelite curriculum innovation has secured a privileged position that is functionally advantageous to the socially reproductive logic of entrepreneurial capitalism, private ownership, and the personal appropriation of social production. This neoliberal dictatorship of the comprador elite has resecured a monopoly on resources held by the transnational ruling class and their allies in the culture industry. The very meaning of freedom has come to refer to the freedom to structure the distribution of wealth and to exploit workers more easily across national boundaries by driving down wages to their lowest common denominator and by eviscerating social programs.

The new hidden curriculum, or "pedagogical unsaid," is the attempt to de-form knowledge into a discreet and decontextualized set of technical skills packaged to serve big business interests, cheap labor, and ideological conformity. School practices need to address more than ever before the objective, material conditions of the workplace and labor relations in order to prevent the further resecuring of the ideological hegemony of the neoliberal corporatist state. Schools in the United States need to provide students with a Freirean language of criticism and a language of hope. They should prepare students to conceptualize systematically and systemically the relationship among their private dreams and desires and the collective dreams of the larger social order.

They must further be capable of analyzing in Freirean fashion the social and material conditions in which dreams are given birth, realized, diminished, or destroyed. More importantly, students need to be able to recognize which dreams and which dreamers are dangerous to the larger society, and why this is the case. Schools need to foster collective dreaming, a dreaming that speaks to the creation of social justice for all groups, and the eventual elimination of classism, racism, sexism, and homophobia. This can only occur if schools help students analyze how their subjectivities have been ideologically formed within the exploitative forces and relations of globalized, transnational capitalism.

Schools also need to create "formations of affect" that can help to foster a critical praxis and eventually transform those social relations of production, ideological configurations, and material conditions that are responsible for exploiting the subordinate classes. Schools need to help citizens resist the American business plutocracy, which pursues speculative international financial markets at the expense of international democracy. Critical pedagogy in the United States must rededicate itself to the creation of classrooms designed to resist all forms of racist, classist, sexist, and ethnico-religious exclusionism. In all of these efforts, Freire's work can serve as an important guidepost.

As Freire's future hagiographers wrestle in the educational arena over what represents the "real" Freire and his legacy, Freire's work will continue to be felt in the lives of those who knew him and who loved him. Just as importantly, his work will continue to influence generations of educators, scholars, and activists around the world.

To the extent that the future of education is intimately connected to the ability of students and teachers to become more critically self-reflective in analyzing ways in which their own lives and those of their students have been inscribed by enchaining discursive practices and material social relations that support powerful elite groups at the expense of the majority of the population, Freire's work is indispensable to the progressive evolution of educational thought. Of course, the continuing advancement of critical pedagogy and Freirean praxis cannot be divorced from the crisis of the late bourgeois world, whose greatest symptom includes the logic of consumption as a regulating democratic ideal. Freire was always a revolutionary and as such never abandoned the dream of a radical transformation of the world. Freire writes: "As far as making the world, our world, a better place, there is no need to distinguish between modest or extravagant actions. Anything that can be done with competence, loyalty, clarity, perseverance, adding strength to the fight against the powers of non-love, selfishness, and evil is equally important" (Freire, in press).

Freire acknowledged that decolonization was a project that knows no endpoint, no final closure. It is a lifelong struggle that requires insight, honesty, compassion, and a willingness to brush one's personal history against the grain of "naive consciousness" or commonsense understanding. After the legacy of revolutionary struggles with the oppressed that has been bequeathed to us by Freire, it remains impossible to conceive of pedagogical practice evacuated of social critique. Freire has left stratified deposits of pedagogical insight upon which future developments of progressive education can be built. There is still reason to hope for a cooperative pedagogical venture among those who support a Freirean class-based pedagogical struggle, feminist pedagogy, or a pedagogy informed by queer theory and politics, which may lead to a revival of serious educational thinking in which the category of liberation may continue to have and to make meaning. The internationalization of the market and its border-crossing dimensions strongly suggest that in order to halt the continuing assaults of the market on human subjectivity, cultural workers must create alliances across national borders.

Freire's pedagogy of the oppressed is a clarion call to unhinge established structures of capitalist exploitation. It offers teachers a powerful context from which to consider rebuilding democracy and living and struggling for a qualitatively better life for the oppressed, for the non-oppressed, and for the generations to follow. Freirean pedagogy poses the challenge of finding new ways of facing up to our own frailty and finitude as global citizens while at the same time searching for the strength of will and loyalty to hope that will enable us to continue dreaming utopia into reality. With a liberating pedagogy such as Freire's, educators and cultural workers in the United States and elsewhere—both male and female, and from different ethnic backgrounds—have an opportunity to engage in a global struggle for transforming existing relations of power and privilege in the service of greater social justice and human freedom. Out of an historical context that was witnessing an agnostic contest between the mechanics of state regulation and bourgeois merchants of private entrepreneurship, Freire achieved far more than he had reason to expect, and he did so because he was able to give concrete shape to a pedagogy that enhanced personal and collective responsibility.

What sets Freire apart from most other leftist educators in this era of cynical reason is his unashamed stress on the importance and power of love. Love, he claims, is the most crucial characteristic of dialogue and the constitutive force that animates all pedagogies of liberation:

> Dialogue cannot exist, however, in the absence of a profound love for the world and for people. The naming of the world, which is an act of creation and re-creation, is not possible if it is not infused with love. Love is at the same time the foundation of dialogue and dialogue itself.

It is thus necessarily the task of responsible subjects and cannot exist in a relation of domination. Domination reveals the pathology of love: sadism in the dominator and masochism in the dominated. Because love is an act of courage, not of fear, love is commitment to others. No matter where the oppressed are found, the act of love is commitment to their cause—the cause of liberation. And this commitment, because it is loving, is dialogical. As an act of bravery, love cannot be sentimental: as an act of freedom, it must not serve as a pretext for manipulation. It must generate other acts of freedom, otherwise, it is not love. Only by abolishing the situation of oppression is it possible to restore the love which that situation made impossible. If I do not love the world, if I do not love people I cannot enter into dialogue. (1996, pp. 70–71)

The week after his unexpected death, Freire was scheduled to attend a ceremony in Cuba, where Fidel Castro was to present him with a major award for his contribution to education. According to his friends, this was to be the most important award in Freire's life.

During his last days, Freire was reported to say something to this effect: "I could never think of education without love and that is why I think I am an educator, first of all because I feel love . . ." As Marcia Moraes, who teaches in Rio de Janeiro State University and who was a friend of Freire, remarked to me recently, "Freire is not leaving the struggle, he has merely changed his location."

We will miss him.

REFERENCES

Apple, Michael. 1993. *The Politics of Official Knowledge.* New York and London: Routledge.

Aronowitz, Stanley, and Henry Giroux. 1991. *Postmodern Education.* Minneapolis: University of Minnesota Press.

Cummins, Jim. 1986. "Empowering Minority Students: A Framework for Intervention." *Harvard Educational Review, 56,* 18–36.

Darder, Antonia. 1991. *Culture and Power in the Classroom: A Critical Foundation for Bicultural Education.* Westport, CT: Bergin and Garvey.

Elias, John. 1994. *Paulo Freire: Pedagogue of Revolution,* Melbourne, FL: Krieger.

Ellsworth, Elizabeth. 1989. "Why Doesn't This Feel Empowering? Working Through the Repressive Myths of Critical Pedagogy." *Harvard Educational Review 59* (5), 297–324.

Fine, Michelle. 1990. *Framing Dropouts*. Albany: State University of New York Press.

Freire, Paulo. 1973. *Education for Critical Consciousness*. New York: Seabury Press.

Freire, Paulo. 1978. *Pedagogy in Process: The Letters to Guinea-Bissau*. New York: Seabury Press.

Freire, Paulo, 1985. *The Politics of Education: Culture, Power, and Liberation*. South Hadley, MA: Bergin and Garvey.

Freire, Paulo, and Donaldo Macedo. 1987. *Literacy: Reading the Word and the World*. South Hadley, MA: Bergin and Garvey.

Freire, Paulo, and Faundez, A. 1989. *Learning to Question: A Pedagogy of Liberation*. New York: Continuum.

Freire, Paulo, with Myles Horton, Brenda Bell, John Gaventa, and John Peters (Eds.). 1990. *We Make the Road by Walking: Conversations on Education and Social Change*. Philadelphia: Temple University Press.

Freire, Paulo. 1993. *Pedagogy of the City*. New York: Continuum.

Freire, Paulo. 1994. *Pedagogy of Hope: Reliving Pedagogy of the Oppressed*. New York: Continuum.

Freire, Paulo with Miguel Escobar, Alfredo L. Fernandez, and Gilberto Guerara-Niebla. 1994. *Paulo Freire on Higher Education: A Dialogue at the National University of Mexico*. Albany: State University of New York Press.

Freire, Paulo. 1996. *Letters to Christina: Reflections on My Life and Work*. New York: Routledge.

Freire, Paulo. 1997. *A Response*. In Paulo Freire with James W. Fraser, Donaldo Macedo, Tanya McKinnon, and Willian T. Stokes (Eds.). *Mentoring the Mentor: A Critical Dialogue with Paulo Freire*. New York: Peter Lang Publishers, pp. 303–329.

Freire, Paulo. 1996. *Pedagogy of the Oppressed*. New York: Continuum.

Freire, Paulo (in press a). *Politics and Education*. Trans. Pia Wong. Los Angeles: UCLA Latin American Center Publications.

Freire, Paulo. (in press b). *Teachers as Cultural Workers: Letters to Those Who Dare to Teach*. Trans. Donaldo Macedo, Dale Koike, and Alexandre Oliviera, Boulder: Westview Press.

Gadotti, Moacir. 1994. *Reading Paulo Freire: His Life and Work*. Albany: State University of New York Press.

Giroux, Henry, and Peter McLaren (Eds.). 1994. *Between Borders: Pedagogy and the Politics of Cultural Studies*. New York and London: Routledge.

Gore, Jennifer. 1993. *The Struggle for Pedagogies: Critical and Feminist Discourses as Regimes of Truth*. New York: Routledge.

Kanpol, Barry. 1992. *Toward a Theory and Practice of Teacher Cultural Politics: Continuing the Postmodern Debate*. Norwood, N.J.: Ablex Publications.

Kincheloe, Joe. 1993. *Toward a Critical Politics of Teacher Thinking: Mapping the Postmodern.* South Hadley, MA: Bergin and Garvey.

Ladson-Billings, Gloria. 1997. "I Know Why This Doesn't Feel Empowering: A Critical Race Analysis of Critical Pedagogy." In Paulo Freire et al. (Eds.), *Mentoring the Mentor,* pp. 127–141. New York: Peter Lang Publishers.

Lather, Patti. 1991. *Getting Smart: Feminist Research and Pedagogy within the Postmodern.* New York and London: Routledge.

Lankshear, Colin, and Peter McLaren, (Eds.). 1993. "Introduction." In Colin Lankshear and Peter McLaren (Eds.), *Critical Literacy: Politics, Praxis, and the Postmodern,* pp. 1–56. Albany: State University of New York Press.

Macedo, Donaldo. 1994. *Literacies of Power.* Boulder: Westview Press.

McLaren, Peter. 1997, "La Lucha Continua: Freire, Boal, and the Challenge of History 'In My Brothers and Sisters in Struggle." *Researcher,* 1 (2), 5–10.

McLaren, Peter. 1997a. "Freirean Pedagogy: The Challenge of Postmodernism and the Politics of Race." In Paulo Freire et al. (Eds.), *Mentoring the Mentor,* pp. 99–125. New York: Peter Lang Publishers.

McLaren, Peter. 1997b. *Revolutionary Multiculturalism: Pedagogies of Dissent for the New Millennium.* Boulder: Westview Press.

McLaren, Peter. 1997. *Critical Pedagogy and Predatory Culture.* New York and London: Routledge.

McLaren, Peter. 1993. *Life in Schools: An Introduction to Critical Pedagogy in the Social Foundations of Education.* White Plains, N.Y.: Longman.

McLaren, Peter, and Jim Giarelli, (Eds.). 1993. *Critical Theory and Educational Research.* Albany: State University of New York Press.

McLaren, Peter, and Peter Leonard, (Eds.). 1993a. *Paulo Freire: A Critical Encounter.* New York and London: Routledge.

McLaren, Peter, and Colin Lankshear, (Eds.). 1994. *Politics of Liberation: Paths from Freire.* New York and London: Routledge.

Moraes, Marcia. 1997. Personal Communication, Rio de Janeiro.

Moraes, Marcia. 1996. *Bilingual Education: A Dialogue with the Bahktin Circle.* Albany: State University of New York Press.

Murrel, Jr., Peter. 1997. "Digging Again the Family Wells: A Freirean Literacy Framework as Emancipatory Pedagogy for African American Children." In Paulo Freire et al. (Eds.), *Mentoring the Mentor,* pp. 19–58. New York: Peter Lang.

Parker, Stuart. 1997. *Reflective Teaching in the Postmodern World: A Manifesto for Education in Postmodernity.* Buckingham and Philadelphia: Open University Press.

Sleeter, Christine, and Peter McLaren, (Eds.). 1995. *Multicultural Education and Critical Pedagogy.* Albany: State University of New York Press.

Taylor, Paul. 1993. *The Texts of Paulo Freire.* Buckingham and Philadelphia: Open University Press.

Torres, Carlos. 1988. "An Analytical Framework for Adult Education in Alberta." *Alberta Journal of Educational Research, 34* (3), 269–286.

Weiler, Kathleen. 1996. "Myths of Paulo Freire." *Educational Theory, 46* (3), 353–371.

Weiler, Kathleen. 1988. *Women Teaching for Change: Gender, Class, and Power.* South Hadley, MA: Bergin and Garvey Publishing.

Wink, Joan. 1997. *Critical Pedagogy: Notes from the Real World.* White Plains, NY: Longman.

CHAPTER 2

Studying the Media
What Makes Mainstream Media Mainstream[1]

NOAM CHOMSKY

Part of the reason why I write about the media is because I am interested in the whole intellectual culture, and the part of it that is easiest to study is the media. It comes out every day. You can do a systematic investigation. You can compare yesterday's version to today's version. There is a lot of evidence about what's played up and what isn't and the way things are structured.

My impression is the media aren't very different from scholarship or from, say, journals of intellectual opinion—there are some extra constraints—but it's not radically different. They interact, which is why people go up and back quite easily among them.

You look at the media, or at any institution you want to understand. You ask questions about its internal institutional structure. You want to know something about their setting in the broader society. How do they relate to other systems of power and authority? If you're lucky, there is an internal record from leading people in the information system which tells you what they are up to (it is sort of a doctrinal system). That doesn't mean the public relations handouts but what they say to each other about what they are up to. There is quite a lot of interesting documentation.

Those are three major sources of information about the nature of the media. You want to study them the way, say, a scientist would study some complex molecule or something. You take a look at the structure and then make some hypothesis based on the structure as to what the

---

[1] From a talk at Z Media Institute, June 1997. This article is reprinted with permission from the October 1997 issue of *Z Magazine*.

media product is likely to look like. Then you investigate the media product and see how well it conforms to the hypotheses. Virtually all work in media analysis is this last part—trying to study carefully just what the media product is and whether it conforms to obvious assumptions about the nature and structure of the media.

Well, what do you find? First of all, you find that there are different media which do different things, like the entertainment/Hollywood, soap operas, and so on, or even most of the newspapers in the country (the overwhelming majority of them). They are directed to the mass audience.

There is another sector of the media, the elite media, sometimes called the agenda-setting media because they are the ones with the big resources, they set the framework in which everyone else operates. The *New York Times* and CBS, that kind of thing. Their audience is mostly privileged people. The people who read the *New York Times*—people who are wealthy or part of what is sometimes called the political class— they are actually involved in the political system in an ongoing fashion. They are basically managers of one sort or another. They can be political managers, business managers (like corporate executives or that sort of thing), doctrinal managers (like university professors), or other journalists who are involved in organizing the way people think and look at things.

The elite media set a framework within which others operate. If you are watching the Associated Press, who grind out a constant flow of news, in the mid-afternoon it breaks and there is something that comes along every day that says "Notice to Editors: Tomorrow's *New York Times* is going to have the following stories on the front page." The point of that is, if you're an editor of a newspaper in Dayton, Ohio, and you don't have the resources to figure out what the news is, or you don't want to think about it anyway, this tells you what the news is. These are the stories for the quarter page that you are going to devote to something other than local affairs or diverting your audience. These are the stories that you put there because that's what *The New York Times* tells us is what you're supposed to care about tomorrow. If you are an editor in Dayton, Ohio, you would sort of have to do that, because you don't have much else in the way of resources. If you get off line, if you're producing stories that the big press doesn't like, you'll hear about it pretty soon. In fact, what just happened at *San Jose Mercury News* is a dramatic example of this. So there are a lot of ways in which power plays can drive you right back into line if you move out. If you try to break the mold, you're not going to last long. That framework works pretty well, and it is understandable that it is just a reflection of obvious power structures.

The real mass media are basically trying to divert people. Let them do something else, but don't bother us (us being the people who run the show). Let them get interested in professional sports, for example. Let everybody be crazed about professional sports or sex scandals or the personalities and their problems or something like that. Anything, as long as it isn't serious. Of course, the serious stuff is for the big guys. "We" take care of that.

What are the elite media, the agenda-setting ones? The *New York Times* and CBS, for example. Well, first of all, they are major, very profitable, corporations. Furthermore, most of them are either linked to, or outright owned by, much bigger corporations, like General Electric, Westinghouse, and so on. They are way up at the top of the power structure of the private economy, which is a very tyrannical structure. Corporations are basically tyrannies, hierarchic, controlled from above. If you don't like what they are doing you get out. The major media are just part of that system.

What about their institutional setting? Well, that's more or less the same. What they interact with and relate to is other major power centers—the government, other corporations, or the universities. Because the media are a doctrinal system they interact closely with the universities. Say you are a reporter writing a story on Southeast Asia or Africa, or something like that. You're supposed to go over to the big university and find an expert who will tell you what to write, or else go to one of the foundations, like Brookings Institute or American Enterprise Institute, and they will give you the words to say. These outside institutions are very similar to the media.

The universities, for example, are not independent institutions. There may be independent people scattered around in them but that is true of the media as well. And it's generally true of corporations. It's true of Fascist states, for that matter. But the institution itself is parasitic. It's dependent on outside sources of support and those sources of support, such as private wealth, big corporations with grants, and the government (which is so closely interlinked with corporate power you can barely distinguish them); they are essentially what the universities are in the middle of. People within them, who don't adjust to that structure, who don't accept it and internalize it (you can't really work with it unless you internalize it, and believe it); people who don't do that are likely to be weeded out along the way, starting from kindergarten, all the way up. There are all sorts of filtering devices to get rid of people who are a pain in the neck and think independently. Those of you who have been through college know that the educational system is very highly geared to rewarding conformity and obedience; if you don't do that, you are a troublemaker. So, it is kind of a filtering device which ends up with people who really honestly (they aren't lying) internalize the framework of belief and attitudes of the surrounding power system in the society. The elite institutions like, say, Harvard and Princeton and the small upscale colleges, for example, are very much geared to socialization. If you go through a place like Harvard, most of what goes on there is teaching manners; how to behave like a member of the upper classes, how to think the right thoughts, and so on.

If you've read George Orwell's *Animal Farm,* which he wrote in the mid-1940s, it was a satire on the Soviet Union, a totalitarian state. It was a big hit. Everybody loved it. Turns out he wrote an introduction to *Animal Farm* which was suppressed. It only appeared 30 years later. Someone had found it in his papers. The introduction to *Animal Farm* was about "Literary Censorship in England" and what it says is that obviously this book is ridiculing the Soviet Union and its totalitarian structure. But he said England is not all that different. We don't have the KGB on our neck, but the end result comes out pretty much the same. People who have independent ideas or who think the wrong kind of thoughts are cut out.

He talks a little, only two sentences, about the institutional structure. He asks, why does this happen? Well, one, because the press is owned by wealthy people who only want certain things to reach the public. The other thing he says is that when you go through the elite education system, when you go through the proper schools and Oxford, you learn that there are certain things it's not proper to say and there are certain thoughts that are not proper to have. That is the socialization role of elite institutions and if you don't adapt to that, you're usually out. Those two sentences more or less tell the story.

When you critique the media and you say, look, here is what Anthony Lewis or somebody else is writing, they get very angry. They say, quite correctly, "Nobody ever tells me what to write. I write anything I like. All this business about pressures and constraints is nonsense because I'm never under any pressure." Which is completely true, but the point is that they wouldn't be there unless they had already demonstrated that nobody has to tell them what to write because they are going to say the right thing. If they had started off at the Metro desk, or something, and had pursued the wrong kind of stories, they never would have made it to the positions where they can now say anything they like. The same is mostly true of university faculty in the more ideological disciplines. They have been through the socialization system.

Okay, you look at the structure of that whole system. What do you expect the news to be like? Well, it's pretty obvious. Take the *New York Times*. It's a corporation and sells a product. The product is audiences. They don't make money when you buy the newspaper. They are happy to put it on the Worldwide Web for free. They actually lose money when you buy the newspaper. But the audience is the product. The product is privileged people, just like the people who are writing the newspapers, you know, top-level decision-making people in society. You have to sell a product to a market, and the market is, of course, advertisers (that is, other businesses). Whether it is television or newspapers, or whatever, they are selling audiences. Corporations sell audiences to other corporations. In the case of the elite media, it's big businesses.

Well, what do you expect to happen? What would you predict about the nature of the media product, given that set of circumstances? What would be the null hypothesis, the kind of conjecture that you'd make assuming nothing further. The obvious assumption is that the product of the media, what appears, what doesn't appear, the way it is slanted, will reflect the interest of the buyers and sellers, the institutions, and the power systems that are around them. If that wouldn't happen, it would be kind of a miracle.

Okay, then comes the hard work. You ask, does it work the way you predict? Well, you can judge for yourselves. There's lots of material on this obvious hypothesis, which has been subjected to the hardest tests anybody can think of, and still stands up remarkably well. You virtually never find anything in the social sciences that so strongly supports any conclusion, which is not a big surprise, because it would be miraculous if it didn't hold up given the way the forces are operating.

The next thing you discover is that this whole topic is completely taboo. If you go to the Kennedy School of Government, or Stanford, or somewhere, and you study journalism and communications or academic political science, and so on, these questions are not likely to appear. That is, the hypothesis that anyone would come across without even knowing anything—that is not allowed to be expressed, and the evidence bearing on it cannot be discussed. Well, you predict that too. If you look at the institutional structure, you would say, yeah, sure, that's got to happen because why should these guys want to be exposed? Why should they allow critical analysis of what they are up to to take place? The answer is, there is no reason why they should allow that and, in fact, they don't. Again, it is not purposeful censorship. It is just that you don't make it to those positions—that includes the left (what is called the left), as well as the right—unless you have been adequately socialized and trained so that there are some thoughts you just don't have, because if you did have them, you wouldn't be there. So you have a second order of prediction which is that the first order of prediction is not allowed into the discussion.

The last thing to look at is the doctrinal framework in which this proceeds. Do people at high levels in the information system, including the media and advertising and academic political science and so on, do these people have a picture of what ought to happen when they are writing for each other (not when they are making graduation speeches)? When you make a commencement speech, it is pretty words and stuff. But when they are writing for one another, what do people say about it?

There are basically three currents to look at. One is the public relations industry, you know, the main business propaganda industry. So what are the leaders of the PR industry saying? Second place to look is at what are called public intellectuals, big thinkers, people who write the "op eds" and that sort of thing. What do they say? The people who write impressive books about the nature of democracy and that sort of business. The third thing you look at is the academic stream, particularly that part of political science which is concerned with communications and information and that stuff which has been a branch of political science for the last 70 or 80 years.

So, look at those three things and see what they say, and look at the leading figures who have written about this. They all say (I'm partly quoting), the general population is "ignorant and meddlesome outsiders." We have to keep them out of the public arena because they are too stupid and if they get involved they will just make trouble. Their job is to be "spectators," not "participants."

They are allowed to vote every once in a while, pick out one of us smart guys. But then they are supposed to go home and do something else like watch football or whatever it may be. But the "ignorant and meddlesome outsiders" have to be observers, not participants. The participants are what are called the "responsible men" and, of course, the writer is always one of them. You never ask the question, why am I a "responsible man" and somebody else is in jail? The answer is pretty obvious. It's because you are obedient and subordinate to power and that other person may be independent, and so on. But you don't ask, of course. So there are the smart guys who are supposed to run the show and the rest of them are supposed to be out, and we should not succumb to (I'm quoting from an academic article) "democratic dogmatisms about men being the best judges of their own interest." They are not. They are terrible judges of their own interests, so we have [to] do it for them for their own benefit.

Actually, it is very similar to Leninism. We do things for you, and we are doing it in the interest of everyone, and so on. I suspect that's part of the reason why it's been so easy historically for people to shift up and back, from being sort of enthusiastic Stalinists to being big supporters of U.S. power. People switch very quickly from one position to the other, and my suspicion is that it's because basically it is the same position. You're not making much of a switch. You're just making a different estimate of where power lies. One point you think it's here, another point you think it's there. You take the same position.

How did all this evolve? It has an interesting history. A lot of it comes out of the First World War, which is a big turning point. It changed the position of the United States in the world considerably. In the 18th century the U.S. was already the richest place in the world. The quality of life, health, and longevity was not achieved by the upper classes in Britain until the early 20th century, let alone anybody else in the world. The U.S. was extraordinarily wealthy, with huge advantages, and, by the end of the 19th century, it had by far the biggest economy in the world. But it was not a big player on the world scene. U.S. power extended to the Caribbean Islands, parts of the Pacific, but not much farther.

During the First World War, the relations changed. And they changed more dramatically during the Second World War. After the Second World War the U.S. more or less took over the world. But after [the] First World War there was already a change, and the U.S. shifted from being a debtor to a creditor nation. It wasn't huge, like Britain, but it became a substantial actor in the world for the first time. That was one change, but there were other changes.

The First World War was the first time there was highly organized state propaganda. The British had a Ministry of Information, and they really needed it because they had to get the U.S. into the war, or else they were in bad trouble. The Ministry of Information was mainly geared to sending propaganda, including huge fabrications about "Hun" atrocities, and so on. They were targeting American intellectuals on the reasonable assumption that these are the people who are most gullible and most likely to believe propaganda. They are also the ones that disseminate it through their own system. So it was mostly geared to American intellectuals, and it worked very well. The British Ministry of Information documents (a lot have been released) show their goal was, as they put it, to control the thought of the entire world, a minor goal, but mainly the U.S. They didn't care much what people thought in India. This Ministry of Information was extremely successful in deluding hot-shot American intellectuals into accepting British propaganda fabrications. They were very proud of that. Properly so, it saved their lives. They would have lost the First World War otherwise.

In the U.S., there was a counterpart. Woodrow Wilson was elected in 1916 on an antiwar platform. The U.S. was a very pacifist country. It has always been. People don't want to go fight foreign wars. The country was very much opposed to the First World War and Wilson was, in fact, elected on an antiwar position. "Peace without victory" was the slogan. But he was intending to go to war. So the question was, how do you get the pacifist population to become raving anti-German lunatics so they want to go kill all the Germans? That requires propaganda. So they set up the first and really only major state propaganda agency in U.S. history. The Committee on Public Information it was called (nice Orwellian title), called also the Creel Commission. The guy who ran it was named Creel. The task of this commission was to propagandize the population into a jingoist hysteria. It worked incredibly well. Within a few months there was a raving war hysteria, and the U.S. was able to go to war.

A lot of people were impressed by these achievements. One person impressed, and this had some implications for the future, was Hitler. If you read *Mein Kampf,* he concludes, with some justification, that Germany lost the First World War because it lost the propaganda battle. They could not begin to compete with British and American propaganda which absolutely overwhelmed them. He pledges that next time around they'll have their own propaganda system, which they did during the Second World War. More important for us, the American business community was also very impressed with the propaganda effort. They had a problem at that time. The country was becoming formally more democratic. A lot more people were able to vote and that sort of thing. The country was becoming wealthier and more people could participate and a lot of new immigrants were coming in, and so on.

So what do you do? It's going to be harder to run things as a private club. Therefore, obviously, you have to control what people think. There had been public relations specialists but there was never a public relations industry. There was a guy hired to make Rockefeller's image look prettier and that sort of thing. But this huge public relations industry, which is a U.S. invention and a monstrous industry, came out of the First World War. The leading figures were people in the Creel Commission. In fact, the main one, Edward Bernays, comes right out of the Creel Commission. He has a book that came out right afterwards called *Propaganda.* The term *propaganda,* incidentally, did not have negative connotations in those days. It was during the Second World War that the term became taboo because it was connected with Germany, and all those bad things. But in this period, the term *propaganda* just meant information or something like that. So he wrote a book called *Propaganda* around 1925, and it starts off by saying he is applying the lessons of the First World War. The propaganda system of the First World War and this commission that he was part of showed, he says, it is possible to "regiment the public mind every bit as much as an army regiments their bodies." These new techniques of regimentation of minds, he said, had to be used by the intelligent minorities in order to make sure that the slobs stay on the right course. We can do it now because we have these new techniques.

This is the main manual of the public relations industry. Bernays is kind of the guru. He was an authentic Roosevelt/Kennedy liberal. He also engineered the public relations effort behind the U.S.-backed coup which overthrew the democratic government of Guatemala.

His major coup, the one that really propelled him into fame in the late 1920s, was getting women to smoke. Women didn't smoke in those days and he ran huge campaigns for Chesterfield. You know all the techniques—models and movie stars with cigarettes coming out of their mouths and that kind of thing. He got enormous praise for that. So he became a leading figure of the industry, and his book was the real manual.

Another member of the Creel Commission was Walter Lippmann, the most respected figure in American journalism for about half a century (I mean serious American journalism, serious think pieces). He also wrote what are called progressive essays on democracy, regarded as progressive back in the 1920s. He was, again, applying the lessons of the work on propaganda very explicitly. He says there is a new art in democracy called manufacture of consent. That is his phrase. Edward Herman and I borrowed it for our book, but it comes from Lippmann. So, he says, there is this new art in the method of democracy, "manufacture of consent." By manufacturing consent, you can overcome the fact that formally a lot of people have the right to vote. We can make it irrelevant because we can manufacture consent and make sure that their choices and attitudes will be structured in such a way that they will always do what we tell them, even if they have a formal way to participate. So we'll have a real democracy. It will work properly. That's applying the lessons of the propaganda agency.

Academic social science and political science come out of the same thing. The founder of what's called communications and academic political science is Harold Lasswell. His main achievement was a book, a study of propaganda. He says, very frankly, the things I was quoting before—those things about not succumbing to democratic dogmatism—that comes from academic political science (Lasswell and others). Again, drawing the lessons from the war time experience, political parties drew the same lessons, especially the Conservative party in England. Their early documents, just being released, show they also recognized the achievements of the British Ministry of Information. They recognized that the country was getting more democratized, and it wouldn't be a private men's club. So the conclusion was, as they put it, politics has to become political warfare, applying the mechanisms of propaganda that worked so brilliantly during the First World War towards controlling people's thoughts.

That's the doctrinal side, and it coincides with the institutional structure. It strengthens the predictions about the way the thing should work. And the predictions are well confirmed. But these conclusions, also, are not allowed to be discussed. This is all now part of mainstream literature, but it is only for people on the inside. When you go to college, you don't read the classics about how to control people's minds.

Just like you don't read what James Madison said during the constitutional convention about how the main goal of the new system has to be "to protect the minority of the opulent against the majority," and has to be designed so that it achieves that end. This is the founding of the constitutional system, so nobody studies it. You can't even find it in the academic scholarship unless you really look hard.

That is roughly the picture, as I see it, of the way the system is institutionally, the doctrines that lie behind it, the way it comes out. There is another part directed to the "ignorant, meddlesome" outsiders. That is mainly using diversion of one kind or another. From that, I think, you can predict what you would expect to find.

CHAPTER 3

Scientism as a Form of Racism

PAULO FREIRE AND DONALDO MACEDO

Macedo: If it were not for the amnesia prevalent within U.S. society, it would be very easy to understand that the present cruel and frontal attack on affirmative action, immigrants, and unwed mothers and so forth is a mere continuation of a historical context where Blacks were "scientifically" relegated to a subhuman existence that, in turn, justified the irrationality of their alienating reality as slaves. After the abolition of slavery and with it the eradication of laws that protected the existence of slavery, the dominant white ideology resorted to "science" as a means not only to demonize but also to dehumanize Blacks in the United States. These race-based ideological mechanisms were very prominent during the Reconstruction, as succinctly described by a Black historian of the era, W. E. B. DuBois:

The South proved by appropriate propaganda the Negro government was the worst ever seen and that it threatened civilization. They suited their propaganda to their audience. They had tried the accusation of laziness but that was refuted by a restoration of agriculture to the prewar level and beyond it. They tried the accusation of ignorance, but this was answered by the Negro schools.

It happened that the accusation of incompetence impressed the North . . . because the North had never been thoroughly converted to the idea of Negro equality . . .

Did the nation want blacks with power sitting in the Senate and the House of Representatives, accumulating wealth and entering the learned professions? Would this not eventually and inevitably lead to social equality. . . ? Was it possible to contemplate such eventualities? Under such circumstances, it was much easier to believe the accusations of the South and to listen to the proof by which biology and social science hastened to adduce the inferiority of the Negro. The North seized upon the new Darwinism, the "survival of the fittest," to prove that what they had attempted in the South was an impossibility; and they did this in the face of the facts before them, the examples of Negro efficiency, of Negro brains, of phenomenal possibilities of advancement.[1]

Sadly, after over a century, the United States continues to be embroiled in the debate centered on the false notion of the genetic inferiority of Blacks. The publication of the book *The Bell Curve,* authored by Charles Murray and Richard J. Herrnstein, once more presents "evidence" in support of genetic inferiority. This book has not only activated what had appeared to be a dormancy of racism in the United States after the enactment of the civil rights laws, but it also has resurrected an old form of intellectual lynching that, unfortunately, has been embraced by ever more powerful representatives of the far right and, with some exception, by liberals through a form of silence. Paulo, can you comment on the reemergence of the legitimization of racism through pseudoscientific methods?

Freire: When I am confronted with the problem of racial discrimination, independently of the insidious explanations that a racist pretends to give in order to maintain his or her attitude that negates the existence and equal rights of the other, my first reaction is one of anger mixed with pity. By *pity* I am not referring to the victims of discrimination. I pity those who discriminate. I pity their lack of human sensibility. I pity their exaggerated arrogance with respect to the world and their lack of humility.

These expressions of both anger and pity are obviously understood by those who discriminate, particularly those who use pseudoscience to legitimatize their racism, as empty platitudes, empty and incompetent discourses. But, for me, the use of science to prove the inferiority of Blacks is also an incompetent discourse. Between these two incompetent discourses, I prefer the humanism and humility that exist in my position.

I remember very well when I was at Harvard and a professor there published an infamous and highly controversial article in the

Harvard Education Review. In this article, the author, Arthur Jensen, argued that he would be more than happy to say that there is no racial inferiority between races, but science would not permit him to do so since, according to his calculations, Blacks are inferior, even though they excel in their ability as runners. When I think about the reaction I had when I read his argument, I feel the same way today when the authors of *The Bell Curve* strive to resurrect the mechanism of dehumanization parading, once again, under the veil of science.

Another thing that I want to point out is that when I oppose these pseudoscientists and their scientism for their cruel and racist approach to scholarship, I remain unafraid of being criticized for not having a scientific basis upon which to make such a claim. I would like to say here, to proclaim, if you will, that there is no other basis upon which to judge one another, than upon the basis of membership in the human race. I am not interested in going to a laboratory in an effort to attempt to prove that Blacks are inferior to whites, or vice versa; I find this pseudoscientific endeavor absurd. It is absurd to claim the inferiority of human beings because of their historical accident of birth along the lines of race, gender, and ethnicity. If there is one thing that distinguishes humans from animals, as François Jacoby notes, it is our innate ability to learn. This is, in my view, scientific affirmation. It is not a mere dream to say that we are beings who are programmed to know and to learn. Jensen, Murray, Herrnstein, and others would have to demonstrate that Blacks are programmed to know and learn less than whites. I would argue otherwise. Even if their claim were to be scientifically true, there would have to be no exceptions to the rule. In other words, we could not have a W. E. B. DuBois, a Martin Luther King, Jr., a Toni Morrison, or a Nelson Mandela among a constellation of great Black leaders and intellectuals in the world. If the claim of inferiority were to be true, all Blacks in the world would have to be inferior in all domains and respects, in both time and space. They would have to be inferior ethically, aesthetically, physically, and so forth. In fact, this never is the case. If, in fact, Blacks were genetically inferior, Amilcar Cabral, the leader of the movement for the independence of Guinea-Bissau and Cape Verde, would not have created so many problems for the Portuguese government and, indirectly, its supporter, the United States. Amilcar Cabral and his Black army defeated completely the Portuguese white army. When I say Amilcar Cabral, I also have in mind other African leaders and their people who also defeated the European colonizers. It was the African intelligence and its ethical conscience that enabled the indigenous population to reacquire not only its land but also its human dignity by removing the yoke of a vicious colonialism. It is this intelligence that triumphed over the human exploitation, the dehumanization, the cowardice, and deceitful attitudes of the European colonizers. The Africans won the war, and the Europeans had to flee.

Macedo: Let me interrupt you for a moment. I think it is important not only to point out the Africans' intelligence in devising battlefield strategies that led to the defeat of European colonialism, but it is also crucial that the ethical and moral issues involved in the struggle for independence be analyzed. In other words, how can the Europeans who, according to these pseudoscientists, are holders of superior intelligence, this civilization, justify the dehumanizing effects of colonialism and the barbaric and cruel atrocities committed by them in their pursuit of ways to satiate their greed. As supposedly superior and more civilized beings, how can Europeans justify their quasi-genocide inherent in the process of colonialization designed to secure and help them consolidate European cultural hegemony. If the white race is intellectually superior and, in turn, it supposedly represents the bastion of civilization, how can these pseudoscientists justify the worldwide human exploitation engineered by whites, the mass killings of the elderly, women, and children by our Western-developed smart bombs, the mass killing and raping of women, including children as young as five years old in Bosnia, as Western civilization watches from the sidelines? The supposed white European superiority is directly compromised in the following historical observation:

> If you were a colonist, you knew that your technology was superior to the Indians: You knew that you were civilized, and they were savages. . . . But your superior technology proved insufficient to extract anything. The Indians, keeping to themselves, laughed at your superior methods and lived from the land more abundantly and with less labor than you did . . . And when your own people started deserting in order to live with them, it was too much . . . so you killed the Indians, tortured them, burned their villages, burned their corn fields. It proved your superiority, in spite of your failures. And you gave similar treatment to any of your own people who succumbed to their savage ways of life. But you still did not grow much corn.[2]

How can Charles Murray and his cultural legionnaires justify the superiority of the white race, when technology and military intelligence fashioned by whites lead American GIs to commit horrendous crimes against humanity, as described by Vietnam veterans themselves:

The girls were unconscious at that point [after repeated rapes]. When they finished raping them, three of the Gls took hand flares and shoved them in the girls' vaginas. . . . No one needed to hold them down any longer. The girls were bleeding from their mouths, noses, faces and vaginas. Then they struck the exterior portion of the flares and they exploded inside the girls. Their stomachs started bloating up and they exploded. The stomachs exploded and their intestines were just hanging out of their bodies.[3]

If Murray, Herrnstein, and Jensen, among others, were to be true to the claim of the objectivity of their science, they would factor in why the higher white IQ predisposed the white civilization to commit grotesque, barbaric, and horrendous crimes against humanity, as has been the case throughout history. It is precisely because of these pseudoscientists' selective selection of historical facts in their determination of IQ that we need to keep dangerous historical memories alive as reminders of the consequences of all forms of dehumanization, particularly the type of dehumanization sanctioned by science. It is for this reason that for each Museum of Fine Arts we build in a given city, we should also build a museum of slavery with graphic accounts of the dehumanization of African-Americans, when entire families were split and sold on the block to the highest bidder and where pictures of lynching would remind us of our racist fabric. For each museum of science built in a given city, we should also build a museum of the quasi-genocide of American Indians, their enslavement, the raping and killing of their women, and the appropriation of their land. Although we have built a Holocaust Museum in Washington, D.C.—fifty years after the Nazis' horrendous crimes against Jews, Gypsies, and Communists—we also need to build a Vietnam War Museum along with the Vietnam Memorial, where graphic accounts of rape and killing of Vietnamese women, children, and innocent elderly by Western-heritage-trained GIs would be described, thus keeping the dangerous memories of My Lai alive.

Although the existence of these museums would represent historical truths, I doubt very much that our society is willing to confront its demons, as exemplified in the watering down and rewriting of history in the case of the exhibition of the Enola Gay at the Smithsonian. After ferocious protests by veterans' groups, the exhibition not only brooks no historical analysis, it also suppressed historical truths, rendering the exhibition to a mere presentation of artifacts without any connection with historical analysis.

For me, more important than proving white IQ superiority, is the design of scientific studies that engage students in the archaeology of a white genetic map that may be responsible for the barbaric crimes committed against humanity through colonialism, slavery, and the Holocaust, among other historical atrocities. It is only through our willingness to confront the demon in us that we become willing to stop demonizing and dehumanizing the other.

Freire: I agree, Donaldo. You see, for me it is far more important to study the interrelationship between white supremacy and dehumanization than to spend time and energy to maintain white supremacy through the enactment of a pseudoscience that attempts to prove Black inferiority dislodged from the sociocultural conditions that may, in fact, hinder normal intellectual development. For instance, the ignorance laws that made it a crime for slaves to learn how to read and write certainly represent a socially constructed context for lack of reading ability. You cannot isolate in a scientific study the genes that seemingly are responsible for Black inferior intellectual capacity while ignoring the material conditions that adversely affect cognitive and intellectual development. What is needed is not another study like *The Bell Curve* designed to rationalize the further abandonment of Blacks. What is needed is the courage to transcend the deficit orientation supported by a suspect and racist scholarship hidden under the guise of scientism, so we can move beyond the pipe dream of a democratic education and create the reality. However, in order to make education democratic, we must simultaneously make the society within which it exists democratic as well. We cannot speak of democracy while promoting racist policies.

Macedo: Well put. Democracy in a racist society is an oxymoron.

Freire: Exactly. Thus, the humanization and the democratization of society must imply the necessary transformation of an oppressive and unjust apparatus that guides and shapes society. Since racism is a form of oppression, you can never achieve any substantive humanization by accommodating to racist structures. For me, there can never be any humanistic dimension in oppression, nor is there dehumanization in true liberation. The fact that Blacks in the United States continue to be dehumanized means their liberation from slavery is compromised, as indicated in W.E.B. DuBois's pronouncements.

In order to maintain new forms of slavery, the dominant white class must attempt to eliminate Blacks' capacity to think. An attempt such as this can be characterized as nothing less than an aggression against nature and against humanity. It is for this reason that authors such as Murray and Herrnstein have so attempted, with technology and "science" at their disposal, to generate dubious studies like those published in *The Bell Curve*.

Donaldo, when I am confronted with the arguments in *The Bell Curve*, I say strongly and loudly that we should not respect these arguments scientifically or humanistically.

Macedo: The near euphoric embracing of the debate generated by *The Bell Curve* puts your reaction against its racist propositions in the minority. In fact, *The Bell Curve* has been embraced not only by right-wing ideologues who have been impatiently waiting for science to legitimize their racism, it also has been embraced willfully by the media, which gave many authors space to shape and define the agenda on race issues in the United States. Even when the media would contest the racist propositions presented in *The Bell Curve*, it nonetheless facilitated wide dissemination of these propositions which, in turn, reinforced the racist fabric of our society that is presently launching frontal attacks on affirmative action and immigrants. As David Duke, a presidential candidate in 1992, put it, "America is being invaded by hordes of dusty third-world peoples, and with each passing hour our economic well-being, cultural heritage, freedom and racial roots are being battered into oblivion."[4] One could argue that David Duke represents the fringe, but I find little substantive difference between the unveiled racism of David Duke and the scientifically veiled racism of Charles Murray and Richard Herrnstein. In fact, one could easily consider Charles Murray as a David Duke in academic regalia. Given that a major portion of the data used to provide the basis for the main arguments in *The Bell Curve* was funded by The Pioneer Fund, an organization with a long history of association with Nazi groups, and the fact that

Murray, in his youth, flirted with the burning of the cross, should have been a wake-up call for those who profess to combat racism. Instead, Charles Murray has appeared in all major media outlets from conservative to the so-called liberal media such as *Nightline, MacNeil/Lehrer Hour,* NPR's *All Things Considered,* the *New York Times Book Review,* to mention only a few. The question remains as to whether or not the media would give an antiracist book that indicts our racist society equal time. Given our society's preponderance to oppose an open debate concerning our ethical posture in the Enola Gay exhibition and given the marginalization of major dissident scholars like Noam Chomsky, even though he is considered the most influential intellectual alive in the world today, we can easily understand the celebration of questionable scholars such as Charles Murray and society's complicity with his racist tirades. Although on the surface it may be hard to comprehend that our so-called democratic society is obviously in complicity with racism, upon further analysis it becomes less difficult to unveil the racist structures that continually debilitate our ever more fragile democracy, as demonstrated by John Sedgwick, who writes: "It shouldn't be hard to find, in a country where blacks are far more likely than whites to grow up poor, fatherless, malnourished, badly educated, and victimized by crime and drugs. Then there is the matter of racism in America, which, like bloodstains on the hands of Lady Macbeth, cannot be washed away."[5] Charles Murray and Richard Herrnstein's book, *The Bell Curve,* represents the bloodstain of American racism. It cannot be washed away without the total transformation of the present oppressive racist structures that characterize our democracy in crisis.

NOTES

[1] Derrick Z. Jackson, "Reconstruction Part Two," *Boston Globe,* July 5, 1995, p. 15.

[2] Howard Zinn, *A People's History of the United States* (New York: Harper Perennial, 1980), p. 184.

[3] James W. Gibson, *The Perfect War* (New York: Vintage Books, 1988), pp. 202–203.

[4] David Duke, *Boston Globe,* October 24, 1991.

[5] John Sedgwick, "Inside the Pioneer Fund," in Russell Jacoby and Naomi Glaubeman (Eds.), *The Bell Curve Debate* (New York: Times Books, 1995), p. 158.

CHAPTER 4

Liberating the Critical in Critical Theory
Marcuse, Marx, and a Pedagogy of the Oppressed: Alienation, Art, and the Humanities[1]

CHARLES REITZ

> *"Truth is ugly. We possess art lest we perish of the truth."*
> —FRIEDRICH NIETZSCHE, *THE WILL TO POWER* #822

What is the truth about learning and art and political education as these relate to the human condition and human flourishing? Philosophers from Confucius and Aristotle to John Dewy and Paulo Freire have investigated, as the axial human problem, how education is to help us in accomplishing our own humanization. The contemporary search for a genuinely critical theory and an authentically democratic society continues that project. But what can make theory critical, education liberating, society democratic? These questions continue to confront each of us as we enter into our daily pedagogical tasks and the general historical process as public schoolteachers (at state universities, community colleges, and at the K–12 level) in civic and educational solidarity with our students.

It is necessary to critically theorize about our society if we are to have a vehicle for correctly informed transformative practice. The problem is that much of what is called critical theory today is very often rooted specifically in the thought of Herbert Marcuse, and it is usually limited to the work of a particular set of philosophers: the Frankfurt School (Horkheimer, Benjamin, Fromm, Adorno, Habermas, Gadamer) and the Western Marxists (Korsch, Lukács, Gramsci, Althusser, Sartre). What I want to argue here is that Marcuse has formulated a particular approach to aesthetic education and a unique version of a philosophical humanism that he then presents as critical theory against the debilitating fragmentation of consciousness and profound numbing of the senses that he considers to be the major sources of our current cultural alienation. In this paper I want to pose Marcuse's formulation of critical theory as a problem and investigate some of the questionable implications of his philosophy for an emancipatory theory of education.

In this paper I use the term *critical theory* in a technical sense to refer to the theories of Marcuse, the Frankfurt School, Western Marxism, and their deconstructionist and postmodernist philosophical progeny.[2] When I wish to speak more generically, I shall use the terms *critical thinking* or *critical theorizing*.

Marcuse's continued appeal stems especially from his Marxist-like work on the problems of knowledge and the political implications of education, particularly his critique of the prevailing mode of schooling in the United States as education to alienation and to single-dimensionality. It also arises from his emphasis on the emancipatory and dis-alienating potential of art and the humanities. These topics are closely connected to the original concerns articulated by Max Horkheimer and Theodor W. Adorno, who, together with Marcuse, attempted in the 1930s to delineate the epochal difficulties and contradictions of the era around World War II. They viewed that period as a time of incredible scientific-technological achievement, but also as a time indelibly marked by militarist oppression and genocide. In their estimation the entire century (from World War I to the bombing of Hiroshima and the Vietnam War) represented the simultaneous culmination and twilight of civilization. Human dignity and barbarism were inextricably interlocked, a condition they came to accept as a truth that tragic art could help us understand. Their increasingly pessimistic vision of our culture and history held science and technology to be largely responsible for the epoch's troubles. Already utilizing what were to become central tenets of postmodern theory, especially what are taken to be the illusions of progress, reason, and scientific objectivity, they rejected the political-economic categories of the Enlightenment, positivist social science, and traditional Marxist thought as they sought to understand fascism, world war, repression, and alienation.

It must be admitted from the start that Marcuse's analysis is unusually absorbing. Even those who strongly disagree with certain of his formulations, as I do, will find in him (as in other critical theorists, Western Marxists, deconstructionists, and postmodernists) sources of immense insight into philosophical traditions largely eclipsed in the usual forms of U.S. higher education, a familiarity with which is indispensable for breadth and depth of theoretical development in philosophy and the social sciences.

Marcuse philosophizes about education under conditions of oppression and alienation, and this concern and activity has been central to his entire intellectual effort. His work communicates the vibrancy of his German intellectual sources and an appreciation for much of the real stress and tension in our lives, which, as he finds, are continually torn in the conflicts between sensuousness and reason, longing and gratification. The essential connection of education to the attainment of the social potential of the human race is an integral part of his general theoretical discourse. Marcuse's final book, *The Aesthetic Dimension* (*AD*, 1978), deals importantly with the sources of our wisdom and learning and with the theory of literary art. His relatively recently (1977) published doctoral dissertation, *The German Artist Novel* (originally completed in 1922) concerns itself with the education of the artist as this is depicted in modern German fiction. Thus, it is no wonder that the most current scholarship on Marcuse displays a new emphasis on his aesthetic philosophy (Katz, 1982; Lukes, 1985, 1994; Nicholson, 1994; and Becker, 1994).

I add two points to this discussion. First, a positive one: that Marcuse's unique emphasis on the humanities as a foundation for critical theory has an unintended relevance today, as right-wing commentators carry out their culture wars with regard to the literary canon, the place of values in schooling, and the role and function and future of the arts and humanities in higher education.[3] Second, I want to underscore not only the gains to be made from a familiarity with Marcuse's philosophy of education, but also the theoretical limitations of his approach.[4] The philosophical foundations of his work remain to be accurately identified—and transcended. Although his work is thought to be grounded in Hegel, Marx, and Freud, I find that his theory owes more to Nietzsche, Dilthey, and Heidegger. I find myself troubled, in particular, by the way Marcuse's theories of art, alienation, and the humanities displace Marx's structural analysis of social life to such an extent that his work also ultimately takes on ironically conservative political overtones. There is much to gain by casting Marcuse's uniquely developed analytical categories into relief, comparing them to those of the classical Marxist theory he sought to come to terms with throughout his career. I hold that the philosophical difficulties of Marcuse's theories of art and education hinge upon his reformulation of the analysis of alienation, veering attention toward a concept of reification (as *Verdinglichung*) taken out of the materialist context of the Marxist economic analysis. In what follows I want to show why I consider this philosophical shift to debilitate our efforts to understand ourselves and extricate us from the oppressive conditions of our social lives.

In 1972, Marcuse wrote: "The inner dynamic of capitalism . . . necessitates the revival of the radical rather than the minimal goals of socialism" (*Counterrevolution and Revolt*, p. 5). Ultimately, however, his critical theory turns away from this position. *Eros and Civilization* (1955) centered on Schiller and aesthetic education, emphasizing beauty as the key to political emancipation. This occurred within the context of a blistering critique of the highly administered oppression characteristic of the contemporary U.S. social and economic order. By the time of his final book, *The Aesthetic Dimension* (*AD*, 1978), though, Marcuse seems to be speaking as an aesthetician in the most classical and abstract sense. The book underscores the primacy of the aesthetic form and aesthetic autonomy and favorably reevaluates such notions as "art as art" and the liberating potential of mental labor separated from manual labor. In so doing, Marcuse retreats to a restatement of arguably the most well-established elements of the idealist aesthetic tradition. He develops a love/hate relationship to a materialist and historical approach to aesthetics. "In all its ideality art bears witness for the truth of historical materialism—the permanent non-identity of subject and object, individual and individual" (*AD*, 29). The longstanding utopian element in Marcuse's thought now becomes an explicit philosophical idealism. Ideality is now the method by which to access and understand reality: "The truth of art lies in this: the world really is as it appears in the work of art" (*AD*, xii).

The insights of historical materialism—the formulation of a dialectics of history and matter and the social relations of production—were taken as sources of inspiration and causes for disdain by Marcuse during a lifetime of writing and teaching. He nonetheless importantly interacted with members of the radical and international student movement of the 1960s (Angela Davis, Rudi Dutschke), even as these efforts were accompanied by a political distancing, an intensifying interest in art, and the emancipatory potential of a liberal education, classically conceived. Like Marx and Freire, Marcuse turned his attention to the essentially pedagogical dimensions of intellectual activity preparatory to revolution. Known during the 1960s as "the philosopher of the student revolts," his writings of that period were thought to embody a philosophy of protest within higher education itself. He considered higher education to be qualitatively higher only where the humanities fulfilled their potential to work against alienation: as a critique of positivism, conformity, and repression, and also as a means to political engagement. Marcuse stressed the educational value of the arts because of the qualitative difference he found between the multidimensional kind of knowledge produced by the aesthetic imagination against the unidimensional kind of knowledge attributed to the controlled and repressive rationality (the *Leistungsprinzip*) of action geared to the socially established goals of achievement, performance, conformity/success, and domination.

The restoration of the aesthetic dimension as a source of guiding principles of cultural critique, political activism, and the social organization of the future is the educational goal Marcuse proposes. In his estimation, our technological mindlessness and social fragmentation have to be educationally remediated through a broadened philosophy of the human condition—emphasizing particularly the aesthetic roots of reason—if we are ever to accomplish our own liberation. Marcuse's understanding of alienation and oppression is linked to art and the aesthetic dimension in two major ways: Marcuse has indicated that art may either act against alienation and oppression or act to preserve them. In the former context, in *Eros and Civilization,* Marcuse makes reference to the aesthetic dimension's power to counteract the alienation that comes from the bureaucratization and mechanization of one-dimensional society. The standardization of "competencies" and "performances" in the economic milieu of advanced industrial society is thought to lead quite directly to regimentation and to unthinking and unfeeling forms of social interaction. Meaning and fulfillment are eradicated from a society that is so highly engineered that it stands beyond freedom and dignity. He utilizes the aesthetic categories of pleasure and beauty as criteria by which to condemn the existing order as well as to create an alternative one. Orpheus and Narcissus are offered as aesthetic symbols of a nonrepressive Eros that can pursue gratification and peace through artistry and beauty. These ideals are thought capable of effecting the reconciliation of humanity and nature in a sensuous totality. In "An Essay on Liberation" he advocates the development of an aesthetic rationality and an aesthetic ethos that can secure and consummate an aesthetic world.

Alienation is understood as anaesthetization—a deadening of the senses that makes repression and manipulation possible. Thus, art can act against alienation as a revitalizing, rehumanizing force. But Marcuse acknowledges that art can also contribute to an alienated existence. *Alienation* is understood in this second sense as a freely chosen act of withdrawal. It represents a self-conscious bracketing of certain of the practical and theoretical elements of everyday life for the sake of achieving a higher and more valuable philosophical distance and perspective. Marcuse contends that artists and intellectuals (especially) can utilize their own personal estrangement to serve a future emancipation. Art and philosophy (i.e., the humanities) can, by virtue of their admittedly elitist critical distance, oppose an oppressive status quo and furnish an intangible, yet concrete, telos by which to guide emancipatory social practice. Marcuse is attracted to the humanities because their subject matter and methodology are thought to focus upon questions of the meaning of human experience, rather than on the sheer description of data (this latter procedure being rejected as the "nonphilosophical" approach of behaviorism and the physical sciences). He regards classical learning by means of discourse and reflection on philosophy, literature, drama, music, painting, sculpture, and so forth as liberating insofar as it is thought to impel humanity beyond the "first dimension," the realm of mere fact, to the world of significance and meaning. As Marcuse sees it, the very form of beauty is dialectical. It unites the opposites of gratification and pain, death and love, repression and need, and therefore can authentically represent what he takes to be the conflicted, tragic, and paradoxical substance of human life. In Marcuse's view, the insights provided by these liberal studies are "transhistorical" and are considered the precondition to any political transformation of alienated human existence into authentic human existence. The liberal arts and humanities are not seen simply to transmit or to preserve (or, as he says, to "affirm") culture. They make possible the very development of a "critical theory" and human intelligence itself. Here the arts relate to higher education and advanced forms of knowledge, not merely in terms of "arts instruction," but as the very basis of a general educational theory.

Much of this is an immensely valuable philosophical excursion into a discussion of the nature of emancipatory education, which is usually absent in the United States, even in academic circles, and swamped by nationalism and conservative moralism at the hands of William Bennett and others. The problem here, as I see it, is that despite Marcuse's valuable attention elsewhere to issues of class, race, and gender, he ultimately articulates a concept of literary-aesthetic education standing in disjunction from much sociological and historical methodology as well as the philosophical categories generally associated with a dialectical or historical materialism. Political, historical, and educational issues are, from here on in, considered better understood out of art itself and out of art alone. This aspect of Marcuse's approach, drawn from Dilthey, as well as the cultural radicalism of Nietzsche, asserts a logical and political-philosophical priority over his treatment of the thought of Hegel, Marx, and Freud and comes to define Marcuse's characteristic understanding of aesthetic education as the foundation of a critical theory.

I believe we need to examine carefully the epistemological underpinnings of this intellectual position. To do so we must come to understand more fully what I take to be the philosophical cornerstone of the critical theory of the Frankfurt School and Western Marxism, namely their central analysis of alienation as reification. This involves a particular theorization of the concept of reification, as involving a faulty projection of reality that is caused by an intellectual deficiency that may be remediated only through the deconstructive and reconstructive power of a philosophical critique grounded in the aesthetic imagination. This notion of reification has also been a major influence on certain literary tendencies within much postmodern and deconstructionist cultural commentary over against the more sociological and historical postmodernist tendencies.

Reification, in Marcuse's sense, as will be shown, goes back ultimately to Kant. It surfaced more recently in philosophical discussion during the era around World War I, in various ways within the related outlooks of existentialism, phenomenology, and hermeneutics. Aspects of each of these theoretical perspectives find eclectic expression in Marcuse's work, along side his Marxist analysis. Thus, Marcuse's 1941 *Reason and Revolution* (*RR*) provides a brief Marxist explication of this concept, initially treating reification as a fetishization or worship of capitalist exchange transactions and private accumulation within the productive apparatus of advanced industrial society. The emphasis in *RR*, however, comes to be placed on an ostensibly deeper elucidation of the idea of reification in terms consistent with a basic neo-Kantian concern. It becomes an insight of unique methodological significance that can supposedly redeem social philosophy from its alleged reduction to objectivistic, mechanistic, or deterministic modes. In Marcuse's estimation, it is precisely the proper explication of the phenomenon of reification—as *Verdinglichung*—that can achieve what he holds to be the necessary intellectual condition for liberation in which economic theory would be transformed into a critical theory. This is an extremely important point to which I shall return. First, it is necessary to review some background material on the philosophical analysis of alienation and art.

COMPETING THEORIES OF ALIENATION—RIVAL PHILOSOPHIES OF ART

Marx's contribution to a contemporary theory of alienation was to consider alienation as the exploitative outcome of the capitalist economic appropriation process hidden in the exchange of commodities, specifically the sale of labor power as a commodity by workers in exchange for

wages. For Marx, alienation is understood (in the economic and philosophical manuscripts of 1844) as the seizure of wealth during the social
process of production that alienates (divests) property in the form of the
surplus product of labor from the laborers themselves. Power is structured in such a manner that the work force is further alienated from control over the labor process, from other laboring people, and from ever
being able to attain the (political-economic, sensual, and aesthetic) potential of the human species itself. In *Das Kapital*, the core concern of
capitalism with the private appropriative gains to be made from production for profit and exchange-value rather than use-value is termed *commodity fetishism.* Marx argued that capitalism as an economic system
tended toward an obsession with private accumulation at the expense of
public well-being. Social life and social consciousness tend to become
commercialized and commodified—or reified—as exchange relationships come to predominate in society. This pivotal cultural warp is illus-
trated by a striking citation from Marx's *The Poverty of Philosophy:*

> . . . everything, which up to now has been considered as inalienable, is
> sold as objects of exchange, of chaffering. It is the time in which ob-
> jects, which earlier have been conveyed, but never exchanged, have
> been given away but never offered for sale, have been acquired but
> never been bought: virtue, love, conviction, knowledge, consciousness
> and so on, the time which, in a word, everything has been transformed
> into a commercial commodity. It is the time of general corruption, of
> universal bribery or, in the language of economics, it is the time when
> each object, physical as well as moral, is put on the market as an object
> of exchange to be taxed at its correct value.[5]

Marx's economic and philosophical criticism, here, is clearly aimed at
the indiscriminate capitalist reduction of even the most intimate interpersonal relationships into alienating, market modes. Marx's analysis in
Das Kapital shows that private accumulation is immensely enhanced
when exchange relationships multiply and predominate in society as a
whole, and because of this, social relationships oriented toward the non-
commercial fulfillment of human needs are thought to be increasingly
eliminated. Where these needs and relationships are not simply abandoned, they are coerced into inverted and exploitable social phenomena,
subject to capitalism's conventions of commodity exchange. Alienation
occurs here because genuinely social attitudes and interests in people
and toward people get driven out by business relationships. Exchange in

the capitalist market is thought to evoke: ". . . sachliche Verhältnisse der Personen und gesellschaftliche Verhältnisse der Sachen"[6] (matter-of-fact and impersonal attitudes towards persons, but social concern for mere matters of business). The essential activity of labor, involuntarily transformed into work for wages under capitalist conditions, is restricted and distorted into an item for sale, barter, or exchange. "Free" labor, in fetishized legalistic terms, is in fact exploited and oppressed through the capitalistic accumulation process.

The remarks on the commodity fetish from Marx's *Poverty of Philosophy* were perhaps first cited with reference to matters in the philosophy of art by historical materialist theoretician, George Plekhanov. In his 1912 essay "Art and Society," he writes:

> While combating philistinism verbally, our contemporary bourgeois aesthetes worship the golden calf as much as any bourgeois philistine. "They imagine there is a movement in the sphere of art," says Mauclair, "while in reality the movement is only in the picture market, where speculation goes on also in undiscovered genius."[7]

Similarly, Mikhail Lifshitz devoted the two concluding chapters of his *The Philosophy of Art of Karl Marx* (1933) to a consideration of culture and the commodity fetish. He notes sardonically that, "Viewed from the standpoint of the objective relations of capitalist society, the greatest work of art is equal to a certain quantity of manure."[8]

Plekhanov and Lifshitz, as dialectical materialist commentators on aesthetic problems, emphasize that modern art stands under the influence of objective social relations, including those of commodity exchange and private appropriation, which can adversely affect it, even in devastating ways. In their estimation, not only the capitalist economy, but also the sphere of art, remained to be liberated from these cultural constraints. They contended that unless the commodity fetish were eradicated (along with the productive system that sustained it), the affective and cognitive potential of art would remain obstructed. I shall indicate how Suchodolski and Meszáros view the relevant educational implications of this position. They hold that the core cultural potential of humanity is decisively blocked by the reification rooted in the capitalist commodity fetish.

Such are the main parameters of the Marxist notion of reification. Mitchell Franklin points out, however, that "a collision in regard to the theory of reification"[9] has emerged between the outlooks of existentialism and historical materialism. The existentialist theory of reification centers, in contrast, on the notion of a loss of identity that results when an individual is treated as an object, in a depersonalized fashion, regardless of the economic questions of appropriation, profit, or need. Franklin links this nonappropriative meaning of reification to the work of Karl Mannheim and Max Weber and their conceptions of the inevitably and permanently alienating effects of bureaucracy and scientific rationalization. This formulation of the theory of reification is especially pertinent to Georg Lukács's 1923 redefinition of fetishization as *Verdinglichung*. This concept is utilized by Lukács to signify a profound fragmentation and paralysis of consciousness within the working-class movement, involving a restriction of mental activity to calculative and deductive modes that makes individuals comfortable only when handling facts and things. Lukács's German-language work cites no primary source in the writings of Marx for his use of the term *Verdinglichung*. He elaborates, however, on this very concept in the chapter on reification from *History and Class Consciousness:* "Die Verdinglichung und das Bewuátsein des Proletariats"—Reification and the Consciousness of the Proletariat. Lukács's major contribution to the emerging lexicon of Western Marxism was the conceptual dyad of "reification" and "totality." These were understood with special reference to the problem of epistemological reductionism, which he considered to have marred what he then dismissed as "orthodox" Marxism. To Lukács the real historical world was much too complex to be understood in terms of a mechanical materialism or economic determinism that he said (inaccurately, in my estimation) characterized philosophical Marxism. His vision of the theoretical task at hand involved a reassertion of the dialectic in Marxist philosophy. In Lukács's view, dialectics must insist on the concrete unity of the whole. Without this, "fetishized" relationships between parts are thought to prevent consciousness from ever finding meaning. "Totality" is seen as the revolutionary philosophical category that governs historical reality, whereas reification as *Verdinglichung* represents a rigid and reductionist fragmentation of consciousness that afflicts both the bourgeois and the proletarian. The concepts of totality and reification are thought to be more germane to this "Western" Marxist analysis than the primacy of economic factors in historical explanation. Lukács admonishes Engels for supposedly involving Marxist philosophy with the mechanical correspondence theory of truth. Although space does not permit the defense that Engels' position deserves against this unwarranted attack, it should be recalled that Engels wrote in the *Dialectics of Nature:*

The world is not to be comprehended as a complex of ready made things but as a complex of processes, in which the things apparently stable no less than their mind images in our heads, the concepts, go through uninterrupted change of coming into being and passing away, in which, in spite of all seeming accidentality and of all temporary retrogression, a progressive element asserts itself in the end . . .[10]

Nature is in motion according to Engels and historical materialism. Their concept of a dialectics of nature, society, and thought attempts to account for this and in so doing tries to preserve the "rational kernel" of classical German idealism. Western Marxism, critical theory, and existentialism, however, will not accept that objective tendencies, contending social forces, and conflicted structural relationships are discernible within this motion that science can discover. For Horkheimer and Adorno (as well as later for Derrida and Lyotard), objective grounds for science and philosophy are considered illusory fabrications of a reductionist naturalism or mechanical materialism made possible by forgetting truth. The "loss of memory is the transcendental condition for science. All objectification is a forgetting. . . . Dominant practice and its inescapable alternatives are not threatened by nature, which tends rather to coincide with them, but by the fact that nature is remembered."[11] The concept of totality here breaks with that utilized by Hegel. Neither the Frankfurt School nor Western Marxism view totality in the Hegelian sense of concrete scientific appreciation of progressive motion of the world historical whole. One of Adorno's most cited epigrams is "the whole is the untrue."[12] If this meant the phenomenal whole or the empirical whole, this would be consistent with Hegel. But for Adorno and the Frankfurt School, the intellectual or theoretical whole, as a product of a "dialectical imagination," is a subjective fiction every bit as much as is any fragmentary perception. Deconstruction for Nietzsche, as for the late Wittgenstein and Derrida, means realizing that all words or concepts are ultimately groundless, except in the multiple ways they may enhance a feeling of power and sustain life. With regard to knowledge, no progressive element is thought to assert itself in the end. Advancement in learning is impossible. "Knowledge" becomes fictive political narrative and arbitrary interpretative choice. As Nietzsche contends, not truth but the value for life determines in the end what one will believe.

For Martin Heidegger, Marcuse's one-time mentor at Freiburg, art is seen as a human act of bringing forth meaning in life from the meaningless realm of becoming. Thought and language ultimately derive from the creative fixation of form out of formlessness and meaning through human efforts at poesis and *Dichtung* (literary art in the broadest sense). Hence, the "problem of the thing" emerges as centrally important in both his alienation theory and his theory of art. Likewise, Horkheimer, Adorno, and Marcuse all come to prefer the *Verdinglichung* theory of reification in their subsequent analyses of alienation as primarily a form of false consciousness and conduct.

Reification in this sense is viewed as the result of illegitimately concretizing that which defies concretization.[13] It also means illegitimately conceptualizing that which is said to defy conceptualization. It defines the problem of truth in terms of a process where some fundamentally "un-thinglike" condition is erroneously consigned to a "thingified" mode of existence and represents an unwarranted "thingification." Our concepts and things are considered to be the product of subjective reification. Being, in its truest sense, while held to be actual, is unthinged. Sometimes equated with flux, flow, force, energy, will, becoming, or process, the actual world is in itself also unknowable. Here is where Heidegger, Dilthey, and Nietzsche take us back through Schopenhauer to Kant. We subjectively form the unformed, artificially halting the irrepressible motion of the world.

It is in this vein that Heidegger recapitulates his underlying interest in the methodological problems of reification as *Verdinglichung* on the last page of *Being and Time:*

> It has long been known that ancient ontology works with "thing-concepts" and that there is a danger of "reifying consciousness." But what does this "reifying" signify? Where does it arise? Why does Being get "conceived" "proximally" in terms of the present at hand . . . Why does this reifying always keep coming back to exercise its domination?[14]

According to Heidegger, human beings are "worldly" in a nonobjective way: our "being-in" is not of the "reified," spatial sort (as when a book might be said to be "in" a briefcase), but of an "unreified," existential sort. Existence that is authentically human is held to infuse its world with meaning, at the same time as it opens itself up to an understanding of being. In Heidegger's estimation, alienated human beings are "with" one another merely "onticly," as closed things, while authentic human beings are "with" one another "ontologically," as open potentialities or communicative projects within the field of being as such. In a vivid turn of phrase, Heidegger contends that things can never "touch" other things, "even if the space between them should be equal to zero."[15] Objective entities are considered to be "worldless" finalities, without the open and projective "ontological" dimension that is said to distinguish humanity (Dasein). In addition, Heidegger flatly rejects science, which he undialectically equates with positivism and reification, maintaining bluntly that "science does not think."[16]

To Marcuse, reification as *Verdinglichung* is thought to describe a reductionist and distorting activity of the alienated human consciousness that gives a natural appearance to social institutions and a rigid unhistorical cast to cultural phenomena. If this were taken as a key insight into legitimation theory, in which the social is ideologically regarded as the natural in order to perpetuate itself, this would be consistent with Marx's analysis of the problem. But Marcuse takes the concept further in his version of philosophical idealism. Reification is held to be responsible for the objective, material "semblance" (*RR*, 281) adhering to the social arrangements of human civilization. According to Marcuse:

> Marx's early writings are the first explicit statement of the process of reification (Verdinglichung) through which capitalist society makes all personal relations between men take the form of objective relations between things. (*RR*, 279)

> Economic relations only seem to be objective because of the character of commodity production. As soon as one delves beneath this mode of production, and analyzes its origin, one can see that its natural objectivity is mere semblance while in reality it is a specific historical form of existence that man has given himself. Moreover, once this content comes to the fore, economic theory would turn into critical theory. (*RR*, 281)

Although the text of *RR* was initially published in English, Marcuse inserts the German word, *Verdinglichung,* into the statement cited. In several other places Marcuse also ascribes *Verdinglichung* to Marx. It is improbable that Marx ever employed the term *Verdinglichung* himself, however. Marcuse nowhere cites a text from Marx with regard to the use of this concept, and other published scholarship on this issue is inadequate, even contradictory.[17] For my part, diligent comparative readings of the German-language texts of both Marx's essay "On Alienated Labor" and his subsection of *Capital* in "The Secret of the Fetish Character of Commodities" disclose no instance of Marx's use of this term.

Certainly, if *Verdinglichung* represented merely a terminological change with reference to a concept of alienation whose content remained the same, this shift would not be a matter of much analytical concern. I have endeavored to show that this alteration is by no means an inconsequential semantic variation of the original notion of reification as fetishization as this appears in Marx's writings. This is a philosophically, socially, and politically substantive shift. Marcuse (on the basis of the writings of Lukács and Heidegger) ultimately allows the economic phenomena of commodity fetishism and the dynamics of capital accumulation to recede into the deep background of his analysis. Instead, he conceives of alienation and reification almost exclusively as a sclerosis of thought and action, as a subordination of philosophical method to mechanistic and objectivistic principles. By the time he wrote his final book, Marcuse claims the following (echoing Horkheimer and Adorno's statement in *Dialectic of Enlightenment*): "'All reification is a forgetting,' Art fights reification by making the petrified world speak, sing, perhaps dance" (*AD,* 73). Art is thought to preserve a liberating memory that the social and cultural worlds are not the inevitable products of nature, nor are they fixed or static. Fundamentally dynamic and nonobjective, social forces and social structure nonetheless become factors secondary to and derived from the tentative, creative, and productive ideational acts of human objectification. Reification occurs when this is forgotten, and thus alienation also takes on connotations of amnesis and cultural depersonalization.

Marx, to the contrary, has no quarrel with the independent objectivity of social forces and social structure, nor with the existence of production goods as things. Wood worked into a table "continues to be that common everyday thing, wood. But as soon as it steps forth as a commodity, it is changed into something transcendent."[18] For Marx, production goods become inappropriately dematerialized and idealized when they are elevated through a system of exchange transactions into objects of worship because they bring the blessings of accumulation to the owners of capital, above and beyond the good's worth in terms of societal use value. Obviously, Marx wants to overcome this fetish or idolization and restore the "human dimension" to the reified, structured social practices and ideologies that serve to replicate the social order and heighten the accumulation of capital. Here the philosophical working out of a demystifying social analysis was required, not aesthetic reminiscence. Marx certainly did not dispute the objective character of social relationships and their reality independent of the perceiving subject in this critique of the commodity fetish. Rather, he criticized the ultimate rationale and justice of those specific sets of objective economic, social, and cultural interactions, which, as structured sets of human relations, were maintained in order to pursue profit under capitalism. Marx protested not against any general philosophical treatment of human beings as things, but against the reduction of humanity to a certain kind of thing, namely a commodity, whose social function is disclosed only through a dialectical and materialist philosophy. Likewise, there was for Marx no question that social relationships are always dynamic, material, and objective; his point was that these need not continue forever to reproduce the commodity form. Marcuse, however, criticizes the objectivity of economic relations rather than their subjugation to the commodity form: "Economic relations only seem to be objective . . . objectivity is mere semblance . . ." (*RR*, 281). Likewise, Marcuse rejected scientific objectivity as a conceptual model for "critical" theory in his 1937 article on "Philosophy and Critical Theory" (*CT*):

> Scientific objectivity as such is never a sufficient guarantee of truth, especially in a situation where the truth speaks as strongly against the facts and is as well hidden behind them as today. (*CT*, 156)

> Theory can invoke no facts in confirmation of the theoretical elements that point toward future freedom. (*CT*, 145)

Much like Heidegger, then, Marcuse's *CT* rejected a reification, or fetishism, of objectivity, science, facts, and things in a manner far beyond Marx's discussion in *Capital* of the fetishism of commodities. Near the conclusion, he sums up significantly: "Thus the fateful fetishism of science is avoided here in principle" (*CT*, 156). Marcuse has largely deflected the philosophical focus from Marx's original target, that is, the commodification and commercialization of social life and culture under capitalism, and redirected it toward a Heideggerian critique of the inauthentic "thing-character" of objects and social relationships, as such, and the supposedly "reified" nature of their scientific study. Ultimately, Marcuse's *Reason and Revolution* would ascribe to Marx even a "repudiation of any fetishism concerning the socialization of the means of production" (*RR*, 294), thus indicating the full measure of his non-Marxist reinterpretation of alienation and reification as *Verdinglichung*.

As we have seen, *Verdinglichung* is said to describe a dehumanization of thought and conduct that is necessarily encountered wherever

theory or practice appear in society to be structured objectively or organized around "things," and consequently as improperly separated from
subjective human activity. This approach to reification is characteristic of
the kind of critical theory that informs much of critical pedagogy. Thus,
Paulo Freire writes in a similar fashion, warning against treating people
as things:

> In order to achieve humanization, which presupposes the elimination
> of dehumanizing oppression, it is absolutely necessary to surmount the
> limit-situations in which people are reduced to things.

> Problem-posing education affirms men and women as beings in the
> process of becoming—as unfinished uncompleted beings in and with a
> likewise unfinished reality.

> . . . problem posing education . . . roots itself in the dynamic present
> and becomes revolutionary.[19]

Freire and Marcuse interpret the revolutionary political potential of
philosophy as stemming from a Kantian rehumanization of philosophy
itself. Disalienation through conscientization (Freire) or the aesthetic dimension (Marcuse) is held to be situated logically and chronologically
prior to social and political emancipation. In the case of Marcuse, the
treatment of reification as *Verdinglichung* is the pivotal theoretical revi-
sion he utilizes to recast the formerly scientific (in the Hegelian and
Marxist sense) connection of reason to revolution, and to subjectify it.
Where Hegel and Marx emphasize the role of science, dialectically conceived, Marcuse increasingly looks to an ontology of art located in the
subjective but universally human condition. Marcuse considers the aesthetic dimension to be the most authentic preserve of a liberating negation and critique of the empirical or phenomenal world, becoming the
soundest foundation for an emancipatory social theory. It is my contention, then, that aesthetic theory ultimately emerges, in Marcuse's estimation, as the most critical theory of all, providing him with a new
foundation for his social philosophy and a new theoretical standard for
critique.

The Frankfurt School substituted this ontological aesthetic, developed upon the basis of classical German idealism following Kant,
Schopenhauer, Nietzsche, Dilthey, and Heidegger, for the progress-
oriented philosophy of history of Hegel and Marx and called it critical

theory. In accordance with a prominent motif in this tradition, Marcuse holds that education through art provides the best impetus to philosophical and political education. As ingenious and thought-provoking as the rational kernel of this theory is in this regard, it is not without its problems. In my view, the most important of these defects is its reduction of social and educational philosophy to aesthetic philosophy. Marcuse's theory of art-against-alienation converts abruptly into a theory of art-as-alienation. Thus it oscillates in a fashion that can furnish no ground for the supersession of alienation. He postpones an end to the alienation of the artist and intellectual "until the millennium which will never be" (*CR*, 103). The very permanence of this alienation makes his account antidialectical in the Hegelian and Marxist sense.

There can be no question that the truths made sensuously apparent in the humanities do present warrants for political critique and action. The debate is about what exactly does form the ground of reason in art? This is the truly profound question raised by Marcuse's aesthetic philosophy even while his attempts at answers must be transcended. What is it about art, as a medium of intellectual insight as well as affective understanding, that can help us perfect our freedom and our humanity? Marcuse's abstract philosophical humanism is grounded in a depth-dimensional ontology of sensuousness that the aesthetic imagination ostensibly captures as the eternal interplay and opposition of Eros and Thanatos, desire and destruction, gratification and alienation. At this level of analysis it is a version of philosophical anthropology that utilizes the humanities as a means of understanding what are held to be the universal characteristics of human needs, conditions, and conflicts. But how can we understand the social, cultural, and economic diversity of the human experience today? Can we understand this multidimensional reality with the undifferentiated essentialist ontology furnished by Marcuse in both his philosophy of art and theory of alienation? Even if Marcuse and the Frankfurt School were correct in analyzing human beings at the level of a philosophical anthropology, we, and they, still need to account for human sociocultural specificity and the historical aspects of economic oppression. This diversity and its manifestations in the arts is the product of a number of mediations—economic, cultural, social, and so forth—that would require an extension and transcendence of the structure and movement of Marcuse's aesthetic theory. The issue here is really one of working with an ontological or a dialectical materialist aesthetic and educational philosophy. The foundations of the latter have been provided by Marx.

Two paradigms for theories of art and alienation emerge from my discussion, each with distinctive criteria for critical insight. The ontological or hermeneutic paradigm is subjectively self-contained and considers meaning in self-referential terms. For Marcuse this means interpreting the internal turmoil and distress supposedly inherent in the depth dimension of the human condition (with Eros and Thanatos as the core sensual forces). This conflict is revealed, enclosed, and preserved by the aesthetic form, and its truth is untethered to societal and historical particulars. The limits of such a position are noted by feminist literary critic, Aeron Haynie, who has written, "It is important not to posit an essential, pre-existing sexuality-as-truth."[20] Following Edward Said, Michel Foucault, and Gayatri Spivak, she contends, through an analysis of mid-Victorian literary art, that an adequate interpretation of such art requires a recontextualizing of a work's supposedly inherent meaning in terms of the historical and political impact of imperialism. In my view, the historical materialist paradigm gains greater explanatory power and retains a malleability and freedom from apriori categorization because it remains externally referential. Because it continually implicates art and knowledge in a structural and historical analysis of social life, it possesses a capacity to construct and engage that context in many ways in accordance with several appropriate intellectual interests. It can also raise the problems and possibilities of intervention against the material structure of oppression in ways the ontological-hermeneutical approaches never have.

Marxism does not wish to sever the bond between its critique of political economy and its analysis of the humanities and social science. Rather, it strives to maintain this interconnection through the distinctive philosophy of history (which does not necessarily involve either mechanical materialism nor economic determinism) initially developed by Hegel and extended through Marx. To my mind, it is the paradigm that allows us to adequately develop an underpinning for the social sciences and the humanities. In contrast, Dilthey's theory of the humanities and social sciences (*Geisteswissenschaften*) rests upon what Makkreel[21] calls a poetics of history or an aesthetics of history that clashes with the Marxian philosophy of art as a social history of art.

It is necessary at this point also to ask by what criteria can we measure the advance of educational philosophy toward the goals of a pedagogy of the oppressed? Hegel's classic treatment in the *Phenomenology* of the consciousness of those who serve and the consciousness of those who are served discloses something of immense importance here for critical pedagogy. For Hegel, only the oppressed have the power to recognize the dialectic of interdependence that binds the "autonomous" subjectivity of the master to the subjugated condition of the servant. The social power imbalance prevents the master from recognizing this truth, but disposes the servant toward it. A serving consciousness becomes aware, through labor, that those served are dependent on it and that the master is not absolutely independent or free. The liberation of consciousness for both the master and servant requires this dialectification of consciousness, which I would also call, following Findlay,[22] a socialization of consciousness. The very concept of selfhood is grounded in this social interdependence and social relationality. Knowing ourselves begins when each of us sees that we are who we are through our own doing and the doing of others, and that this reciprocal doing is objectively structured. Alienation is obviated when we come to understand that self-awareness is more than awareness of "self," it is seeing ourselves in others, even in those who fail to acknowledge our work or our worth but who could not exist without us. It is through struggle, Hegel indicates, that the polarities of master and servant may be obviated and canceled, liberated and restructured, with a progressive element moving along a middle path toward our self-awareness as *zoon politikon*. This is the disalienating education that emancipates, empowers, and humanizes.

As Freire and Marx clearly recognize, liberation is a historical and not merely a mental act, requiring active involvement in social movements and within social organizations. What have been called the civilizing forces of our age, the organized popular struggles against racism, sexism, poverty, war, and imperialism, have educated this nation about oppression, power, and empowerment. The professoriate, as such, certainly did not lead in this educational effort, although many individual college teachers played important roles. No philosophy of teaching or learning is sufficient that does not more fully empower students to be coinvestigators with us into the political-economic dimension of the class, race, and gender problems with which we continue to cope and seek to overcome.

Marxism's classical educational aims require the agency of dialectical philosophical knowledge, as this knowledge is gleaned from the interdisciplinary studies of social history, natural history, art history, and intellectual history. Education is never to be considered merely an affair of inwardness or the supposedly unchanging nature of the human essence or condition. Education means apprehending the dialectic of the historical and material world and the changing social condition of humanity within it. It aims at an understanding of the principles of action required for human beings, as living labor, to grasp theoretically and possess politically the productive process that, though now alienated, ultimately is our own. As even Marcuse has acknowledged, part of the dilemma of education today requires the transformation of the frayed academic credo of liberation through the arts into a more philosophically advanced form of educational theory. For the classical Marxist, human intelligence is emergent from material, historical, and cultural (aesthetic and ethical) sources. At the center of this inherently political process is debate and struggle around the key problems of labor, oppression, and democracy. Contrary to Marcuse's pessimistic conclusion that art as art "can do nothing to prevent the ascent of barbarism" (*CR,* 121), classical Marxism argues that much of the best art (from *Jane Eyre* and *Madame Butterfly* to *The Grapes of Wrath*) actually achieves its eminence precisely by commenting on oppressive material and cultural conditions and by eliciting a sense of moral and political right.

Critical theory, on the other hand, in many venues comes to equate praxis with philosophical and literary criticism and the development of an aesthetic taste for cosmic ironies. Operating fully within the conventional division of mental from physical labor and the relations of power that these divisions represent in monopoly capitalist society, critical theory is largely divested of a dimension of defiance and the power of transformation. Martin Jay points out how rapidly the struggle dimension of the work of the Frankfurt School atrophied.[23] The legacy of Marcuse, Horkheimer, and Adorno threatens to transform the Marxist dialectics of nature, society, and thought into a mere *Geisteswissenschaft*, an academic rather than a transformative practice. Similarly, postmodernists such as Lyotard also leave the world exactly as it is while they condemn theory as but a reified nest of ungrounded propositions that serves only to rigidify discourse. Like much of critical theory, postmodernism profoundly castigates social science that seeks an analysis of social structure, stressing instead methodological empathy, social interactionism, and the unavoidable ambiguities of interpretation. Irigaray simplistically calls for new forms of writing and thinking that counter reification by being open, fluid, and nonlinear. Meaning is seen as a free aesthetic or literary choice effected through the acts of reading and the interpretation of texts.

Marcuse does acknowledge the need for action: "In a situation where the miserable reality can be changed only through radical political praxis, the concern with aesthetics demands justification" (Marcuse at

AD, 1). Yet, the epistemological assertions he makes about *Verdinglichung*, as well as similar claims from Lukács to Lyotard, reviewed earlier, serve only to encapsulate us within the aesthetic dimension. They displace the needed economic analysis and disarm our ability to overcome alienation. While appreciating the unique contributions Marcuse's discourse furnishes critical theorizing, the critical potential of social and political philosophy must be liberated from the constraints of aesthetic theory. I would like to rephrase the Nietzschean epigram that began this essay, in terms of the Hegelian insights discussed previously. If the truth is ugly, we have political education and revolutionary praxis that we may not perish of the truth. Labor's political self-education to critical consciousness and collective moral action can humanize and sustain our lives, building upon the real insights that the history of art also furnishes for this effort. The dialectic is to be liberated from a restriction solely to the aesthetic form as art is liberated from the commodity fetish. Our natural and social materiality must be liberated from the philosophy of mere sensuousness (and postmodernism's preoccupation with life-world and the body). Truth needs liberation from both empiricism and dematerialization.

The advancement of educational philosophy involves the solution of basic problems of economics and power as well as those of pedagogy and art. Marx himself emphasized the dialectical nature of revolutionary activity as an educative practice: "We say to the workers: 'you will have to go through fifteen or twenty or fifty years of civil wars and international wars, not only to change extant conditions, but in order to change yourselves and render yourselves fit for political dominion'"[24] According to Polish educational theorist, Bogdan Suchodolski,[25] the advance of education is tied inextricably to the advance of the working class in the direction of its self-abolition as an oppressed class (through its own increasingly emancipatory class consciousness and revolutionary class action). A labor movement that is aware of itself and its power is thought to make possible the initiation of a culture more nearly adequate to the universal political and aesthetic potential of what Schiller and Marx called the human *Gattungswesen* (species being). István Meszáros[26] argues that genuine aesthetic education will involve an explicitly socialist educational strategy predicated upon the international elimination of the political economy of capitalism.

Marcuse's work, sometimes even in spite of itself, did encourage the U.S. antiwar movement, the student antiracist movement, and the women's movement during his more militant middle period. He asked us to take theory and higher learning as seriously as activism. In certain ways his work does represent a theoretical advance: specifically, his concepts of repressive desublimation and repressive tolerance as well as his insights into the emancipatory potential of Eros and art.

If we still find fault with Marcuse we need also to examine ourselves: our illusions about liberal education, our passivity. Are we practicing a critical pedagogy? How are we grounded, philosophically speaking? Does our practice reflect the notion that resistance, not simply criticism, is the driving force of history? Even if the world is not necessarily as it appears in the work of art, do we know how art may strengthen our classroom practice? How well have we thought through the philosophical foundations and political implications of our teaching and learning such that our educational activity can actually lead to the goals we seek?

This essay has drawn attention to a collision of opposing arguments about what makes critical theorizing critical. It has presented what I believe are key, but underrepresented, philosophical considerations with regard to alienation, art, and the development of an emancipatory political consciousness and an authentically democratic social system. I believe that there is a kind of education that can help the individual overcome a sense of powerlessness in the face of global and local structures of alienation. In my estimation this is found in the rational kernel of the *pædagogia perennis*: a world-historical, international, and multicultural perspective that examines the emergence of various standards of ethical criticism, logical criticism, social criticism, and so forth as a foundation for critical thinking and critical theorizing.

Plato asked to what extent we were enlightened or unenlightened about our being. The Greeks acknowledged that this was a public and not merely a private concern and that societal support was the precondition for the classical flowering of philosophy and art. Philosophers of education like Meszáros and Suchadolski have updated this view. Educational institutions in oppressive societies, however, essentially replicate our alienation. None of us, not even the oppressor, is capable of "knowing ourselves" through the agency of those educational institutions committed fundamentally to the reproduction of an oppressive social division of labor. It is through practical opposition to currently (and historically) established oppressor systems that critical theorizing emancipates itself from even the most beautiful oppressor-system ideals. This is how our humanity may come into possession of itself. By struggling to learn in spite of these institutions of domination, and by coming to understand the history of competing warrants for knowledge claims, moral judgments, and political goals, we, who begin life oppressed and alienated, equip ourselves with a comparative and critical view of the multidimensional experience of being human and being oppressed. This is the source of a social intelligence that inspires the political ingenuity and the action required to advance toward the nonalienated character, conscience, and culture that we have yet to achieve.

NOTES

[1] The current form of this essay owes much to the thoughtful commentary of Morteza Ardebili, Stephan Spartan, Tamara Agha-Jaffar, Fred Whitehead, and Roena L. Haynie.

[2] Marcuse's work is also indicative of a more contemporary tradition that has developed on the basis of the technical philosophical innovations of the Frankfurt School and Western Marxism (Wellmer, Schroyer, Agger, Freire, Giroux, and others). In addition, the legacy of this form of critical theory, especially its aestheticized, Nietzschean challenge to objectivist theory of knowledge, is felt within the more contemporary and related theoretical perspectives of deconstructionism and postmodernism (Derrida, Foucault, Lyotard) and also the relativist epistemologies of some forms of feminist philosophy (Irigaray). It is imperative that we analyze and transcend certain of the epistemological implications of this kind of critical theory, especially with regard to the notion of alienation, if we wish to pursue our own critical theorizing to its highest levels.

[3] Allan Bloom, for example, seeks to "rescue" university programs in the humanities from the perils of political protest and value relativism in *The Closing of the American Mind*. Although higher education in the humanities is generally thought of as pursuing universally human aims and goals, Bloom is unwilling to admit that a cultural politics of class, a cultural politics of race, and a cultural politics of gender have historically set very definite constraints upon the actualization of the humane concerns of a liberal arts education. Marcuse and the critical theorists, on the other hand, have made some important contributions to the critical analysis of such problems as anti-Semitism, the alienation of labor, patriarchy and male authority, and the class character of higher education and high art, even as they sought universalizable insights through philosophy. Bloom, however, attributes a decline of the humanities, and U.S. culture in general, to the supposedly inane popularization of German philosophy in the United States today, especially the ideas of Nietzsche, Heidegger, and Marcuse. These philosophers are regarded as nihilistic and demoralizing, in part, because they urge U.S. students to question nationalist commitments. Bloom asserts that we have imported

"a clothing of German fabrication for our souls, which . . . cast doubt upon the Americanization of the world on which we had embarked" (p. 152). In a typically superficial remark, he dismisses Marcuse, saying he "began in Germany in the twenties by being something of a serious Hegel scholar . . . [who] . . . ended up here writing trashy culture criticism with a heavy sex interest" (p. 226). No hint from Bloom that Marcuse's prime contribution to the critical analysis of American popular culture is his notion of "repressive desublimation"—how the unrestrained use of sex and violence by the corporate mass media and other large-scale commercial interests accomplishes social manipulation and control in the interest of capital accumulation. Or that Marcuse (in some ways very much like Bloom) valued high art and the humanities precisely because they teach the sublimation of the powerful urge for pleasure, which, in other contexts, threatens destruction. The uninformed and unremitting conservative backlash to the progressive and radically democratic educational reform efforts of the 1960s and 1970s is now in full swing, and Marcuse knows this tradition more critically than it knows itself.

4 It is here that certain of Paulo Freire's critical concepts also are problematic to me: the economically unanalyzed notions of oppression and dehumanization, the ahistorical Aristotelian approach to humanization and conscientization, not to mention his generalized appeal to love.

[4] It is here that certain of Paulo Freire's critical concepts also are problematic to me: the economically unanalyzed notions of oppression and dehumanization, the ahistorical Aristotelian approach to humanization and conscientization, not to mention his generalized appeal to love.

[5] Marx in Joachim Israel, *Alienation From Marx to Modern Sociology* (Boston: Allyn and Bacon, 1971), p. 44.

[6] Karl Marx, *Das Kapital* (Stuttgart: Alfred Kroener Verlag, 1965), p. 52.

[7] George Plekhanov, *Art and Society & Other Papers* (New York: Oriole Editions, 1974), p. 63.

[8] Mikhail Lifshitz, *The Philosophy of Art of Karl Marx* (London: Pluto Press, 1973), p. 93.

[9] Mitchell Franklin, "On Hegel's Theory of Alienation and Its Historic Force," *Revolutionary World,* No. 10, 1974, p. 25. (Originally published in Tulane Studies in *Philosophy,* Vol. 9, 1960).

[10] Engels in James Lawler, "Heidegger's Theory of Metaphysics and Dialectics," *Philosophy and Phenomenological Research,* V. 35, N. 3, March 1975, p. 364.

[11] Max Horkheimer and Theodor W. Adorno, *Dialectic of Enlightenment* (New York: Herder and Herder, 1972), pp. 230, 255.

[12] Adorno in Martin Jay, *The Dialectical Imagination* (Boston: Little, Brown, 1973), p. 277.

[13] Donald Palmer, *Looking at Philosophy* (Mountain View, CA: Mayfield, 1994), p. 389.

[14] Martin Heidegger, *Being and Time* (New York: Harper and Row, 1962), p. 487.

[15] Ibid., p. 81.

[16] Martin Heidegger, in Richard Wisser (ed.), *Martin Heidegger im Gespräch* (Freiburg: Verlag Karl Alber, 1970), p. 71.

[17] For example, P. Berger and S. Pullberg, in "The Concept of Reification," *New Left Review*, No. 35, 1966, pp. 56–71, attribute "reification" and *Verdinglichung* to Marx. Paul Piccone and Alexander Delfini concur that Marx also used the term *Verdinglichung*, and they ascribe the use of this term also to Husserl in their "Herbert Marcuse's Heideggerian Marxism," *Telos*, No. 6, Fall 1970. Other scholars claim, with greater warrant in my estimation, that *Verdinglichung* is a term introduced after Marx by Lukács. See, for example, Andrew Feenberg, "Reification and the Antinomies of Socialist Thought," *Telos*, No. 10, Winter 1971. Also see Joachim Israel, *Alienation from Marx to Modern Sociology* (Boston: Allyn and Bacon, 1971).

[18] Karl Marx, *Capital*, Vol. I (New York: The Modern Library, n.d.), p. 82.

[19] Paulo Freire, *Pedagogy of the Oppressed* (New York: Continuum, 1993), pp. 84, 65.

[20] Aeron Haynie, *Imperialism and the Construction of Femininity in Mid-Victorian Fiction* (Gainesville: University of Florida, Ph.D. dissertation, 1994). Aeron Haynie argues that women's roles and sexuality do not merely symbolize the deferential domesticity of a colonized land or people, but also become emblematic of colonial ambitions and colonial authority. Constructions of femininity are traced to the commodification of culture and issues of overproduction ("surplus" women being advised to emigrate to the colonies) as well as to the presumed moral superiority of the female-centered colonial ruler, Queen Victoria, vis-à-vis the ostensible barbarism of colonial insurrectionism.

[21] Rudolf Makkreel, *Dilthey: Philosopher of the Human Studies* (Princeton: Princeton University Press, 1975).

[22] J. N. Findlay, *Hegel: A Re-examination* (New York: Collier, 1958), p. 93.

[23] Martin, op. cit., p. 286.

[24] Marx in Otto Rühle, *Karl Marx* (New York: The New Home Library, 1943), p. 176.

[25] Bogdan Suchodolski, *Einführung in die marxistische Erziehungstheorie* (Kln: Pahl-Rugenstein Verlag, 1972).

[26] István Maszáros, *Marx's Theory of Alienation* (New York: Harper and Row, 1970), pp. 290–293.

REFERENCES

1932 *HM* "The Foundation of Historical Materialism," *Studies in Critical Philosophy* (Boston: Beacon, 1973).

1933 *CL* "On the Philosophical Foundation of the Concept of Labor in Economics," *Telos* No. 16, Summer 1973.

1937 *CT* "Philosophy and Critical Theory," *Negations, Essays in Critical Theory* (Boston: Beacon, 1968).

1941 *RR Reason and Revolution, Hegel and the Rise of Social Theory* (Boston: Beacon, 1960).

1955 *EC Eros and Civilization, A Philosophical Inquiry into Freud* (Boston: Beacon, 1966).

1964 *OD One-Dimensional Man, Studies in the Ideology of Advanced Industrial Society* (Boston: Beacon, 1964).

1972 *CR Counterrevolution and Revolt* (Boston: Beacon, 1972).

1978 *AD The Aesthetic Dimension, Toward a Critique of Marxist Aesthetics* (Boston: Beacon, 1978).

Becker, Carol. "Surveying the Aesthetic Dimension at the Death of Postmodernism," in Bokina and Lukes, op. cit., pp. 170–186.

Bokina, John, and Timothy J. Lukes, eds. *Marcuse: From the New Left to the Next Left* (Lawrence: University of Kansas Press, 1994).

Kátz, Barry. *Herbert Marcuse: Art of Liberation* (London: Verso, 1982).

Lukes, Timothy J. *The Flight into Inwardness* (Selinsgrove, PA: Susquehanna University Press, 1985).

Nicholsen, Shierry Weber. "The Persistence of Passionate Subjectivity: Eros and Other in Marcuse, by Way of Adorno," in Bokina and Lukes, op. cit., pp. 149–169.

CHAPTER 5

Multiculturalism[1] and the Politics of Nationalism in the Global Age

HENRY A. GIROUX

INTRODUCTION

Global changes have provided the conditions for the emergence of new theoretical discourses that pose a powerful challenge to modern assumptions regarding the unity of nationalism and culture, the state and the nation, and national identity and the universal imperatives of a common culture. The historic and spatial shifts that have, in part, produced new forms of theorizing about globalization, the politics of diaspora, immigration, identity politics, multiculturalism, and postcolonialism are as profound intellectually as they are disruptive politically.[2] Judith Squire captures the scope of these changes while expressing some reservations about what they have come to mean as they are rapidly absorbed into new theoretical discourses:

> The global economy is a given in our life now: transnational corporations cross borders to maximize productivity and transnational intellectuals cross academic boundaries to maximize knowledge. The academic discipline, along with the national state, is subject to powerful forces of change. And, as we might acknowledge the failings of the old model of state sovereignty and hegemonic nationalism but nonetheless remain deeply skeptical about the gains to be had from the free movement of international capital around the globe in pursuit of profit, so we must be attuned to the benefits of jettisoning the status of empirical area studies, the constricting patriarchal academic canons and oppressive hierarchical department structures, but also the pitfalls.[3]

Originally published in *Cultural Circles*, Vol. 1, Fall 1997.

The pitfalls to which Squires refers are the lack of specificity and theoretical blurriness that sometimes accompany the scholarly rush to take up issues of the politics of globalization, diaspora, multiculturalism, and postcolonialism.[4] I am particularly concerned here with a position that does not attempt to differentiate among radical, liberal, and conservative forms of multiculturalism, or refuses to address within a social vocabulary in which issues of identity and culture are linked to questions of power.[5] Within the politics of the nation-state, such generalizations often recycle or reproduce colonialist discourse. What must be resisted is the assumption that the politics of national identity is necessarily complicitous with a reactionary discourse of nationalism and has been superseded by theories that locate identity politics squarely within the discourses of postnational, diasporic globalism or what Arjun Appadurai calls the "search for nonterritorial principles of solidarity."[6]

This is not to suggest that diverse nationalisms can be addressed outside of their transnational links or that the mechanisms of a dominant and oppressive politics of assimilation can be abstracted from the pain, anguish, and suffering experienced by those diasporic groups who define themselves through nonnational identities and aspirations.[7] What I am resisting is the claim that nationalism can only be associated with ethnic conflict, that nationalism is witnessing its death knell, or that the relationship between nationalism and national identity can only be framed within a transnational discourse that cancels out nationalism as a viable force within what Gayatri Spivak calls "configurations of globality today."[8] The importance of such arguments must be acknowledged, but at the same time it is important to recognize in the context of the current conservative ideological offensive in the United States that it is crucial for critical educators and others to locate our theorizing in the grounded sites of cultural and political resistance within the United States, on the one hand, and to guard against the tendency to overgeneralize the global current of so-called nomadic, fragmented, and deterritorialized subjectivity.[9]

I want to argue that nationalism is crucial to understanding the debates over identity and multiculturalism in the United States and that as important as the discourse of globalization might be, it cannot be used to overlook how national identity reasserts itself within new discourses and sites of learning. More specifically, I want to argue that rather than dismissing the politics of identity as another essentialist discourse, progressives need to address how the politics of identity and difference are being constructed around new right-wing discourses and policies, and how the pedagogical implications of such discourses are shaping both new identities and policy formations that have domestic and international consequences. Central to the construction of a right-wing nationalism is the project of defining national identity through an appeal to a common culture that displaces any notion of national identity based upon a pluralized notion of culture with its multiple literacies, identities, and histories and erases histories of oppression and struggle for the working class and minorities. Stuart Hall is right in arguing that the 1990s is witnessing the return of recharged nationalism in big and small societies that serves to restore national culture as the primordial source of national identity.[10] But this should not suggest that the relationship between nationalism and culture manifests itself exclusively in terms of oppression or domination or that any attempt to develop an insurgent multiculturalism through an appeal to radical democracy necessarily assumes or leaves intact the boundary of the nation as an unproblematic historical, political, and spatial formation. At stake here is the need to both acknowledge the existence of the nation-state and nationalism as primary forces in shaping collective identities while simultaneously addressing how the relationship between national identity and culture can be understood as part of a broader struggle around developing national and transnational forms of democracy.

The relationship between culture and nationalism always bears the traces of those historical, ethical, and political forces that constitute the often shifting and contradictory elements of national identity. To the degree that the culture of nationalism is rigidly exclusive and defines its membership in terms of narrowly based common culture, nationalism tends to be xenophobic, authoritarian, and expansionist; hence, the most commonly cited example of a nationalism is one steeped in the practices of ethnic cleansing, genocide, or imperialist aggression. On the other hand, nationalism moves closer toward being liberal and democratic to the degree that national identity is inclusive and respectful of diversity and difference while at the same time expanding economic and political equality. And yet, a civic nationalism that makes a claim of respecting cultural differences does not guarantee that the state will not engage in coercive assimilationist policies, nor does it guarantee that cultural politics will be linked to political parity.[11] In other words, democratic forms of nationalism cannot be defended simply through a formal appeal to abstract, democratic principles. How nationalism and the nation-state embrace democracy must be determined, in part, through the access that diverse cultural groups have to shared structures of power that organize commanding legal, economic, state, and cultural institutions on the local, state, and national level.[12]

Cultural differences and national identity stand in a complex relationship to each other and point to progressive as well as totalitarian elements of nationalism that provide testimony to its problematic character and effects. On the negative side, recent history bears witness to the Second World War steeped in forms of national identity that mobilized racial hatred and supported right-wing, antidemocratic governments in Germany, Italy, and Japan. Following 1945, one of the most flagrant legacies of such a poisonous nationalism was evident in the long-standing apartheid regime that, until recently, dominated South African politics as well as in the continuing attempt on the part of Turkey to deny the Kurds any status as a national group.

Representations of national identity constructed through an appeal to racial purity, militarism, anti-Semitism, and religious orthodoxy have once again surfaced aggressively in Western Europe and can be seen in the rise of neo-Nazi youth movements in Germany, the neo-Fascist political parties that won the recent election in Italy, and the ethnic cleansing that has driven Serbian nationalism in the former Republic of Yugoslavia. This highly selective list merely illustrates how national identity can be fashioned around appeals to a monolithic cultural identity that affirms intolerance, bigotry, and an indifference to the precepts of democratic pluralism. Needless to say, these forms of demagogic nationalism emerge from a diverse set of conditions and circumstances, the roots of which lie in a complex history of racial conflict, the unstable economic conditions that have gripped Europe, and the dismantling of the Soviet Union and its empire. As a social construction, nationalism does not rest upon a particular politics, but takes its form within rather than outside of specific historical, social, and cultural contexts.

The more positive face of nationalism has emerged in a number of countries through a legacy of democratic struggles and can be seen not only in various anticolonialist struggles in Asia and Africa, but also in diverse attempts on the part of nation-states to mobilize popular sentiment in the interest of expanding human rights and fighting against the encroachments of undemocratic social forces. Although many of these movements of national struggle are far from unproblematic, particularly during periods in which they assume state control, they do provide credibility to the emancipatory power of nationalism as a defining principle in world politics.[13] Equally important is the need to develop a politics of difference and multiculturalism that combines the most progressive elements of nationalism with a notion of border crossing, diasporic politics, and postnationalism that recognizes the transits, flows, and social formations being produced on a global scale. It is precisely in the interaction between the national and the global that a borderline space exists for generating new forms of transnational literacy, social relations, and cultural identities that expand the meaning of democratic citizenship beyond national borders.

MYTHIC NATIONAL IDENTITY

For many Americans, questions of national identity seem to elude the complex legacy of nationalism and take on a mythic quality. Informed by the powerful appeal to assimilation and the legitimating discourse of patriotism, national identity often operates within an ideological register untroubled by the historical and emerging legacies of totalitarianism. Rather than being viewed cautiously as a potential vehicle for undermining democracy, national identity in the United States has been defined more positively in commonsensical terms as deeply connected to the mythic march of progress and prosperity at home and the noble effort to export democracy abroad. Hence, national identity has all too often been forged within popular memory as a discourse that too neatly links nation, culture, and citizenship in a seamless and unproblematic unity. Invoking claims to the past in which the politics of remembering and forgetting work powerfully to legitimate a notion of national belonging that "constructs the nation as an ethnically homogeneous object,"[14] national identity is rewritten and purged of its seamy side. Within this narrative, national identity is structured through a notion of citizenship and patriotism that subordinates ethnic, racial, and cultural differences to the assimilating logic of a common culture, or, more brutally, the "melting pot." Behind the social imagery that informs this idea of national identity is a narrowly defined conception of history that provides a defense of the narratives of imperial power and dominant culture and legitimates an intensely narrow and bigoted image of what it means to be an American.

In an era of recharged nationalist discourse in the United States, the populist invocation of national identity suggests that social criticism itself is antithetical to both the construction of national identity and the precepts of patriotism. Of course, national identity, like nationalism itself, is a social construction that is built upon a series of inclusions and exclusions regarding history, citizenship, and national belonging. As the social historian Benedict Anderson has pointed out, the nation is an imagined political community that can only be understood within the intersecting dynamics of history, language, ideology, and power. In other words, nationalism and national identity are neither necessarily reactionary nor necessarily progressive politically; thus, they give rise to communities that, as Anderson points out, are to be distinguished, not by their falsity/genuineness, but by the style in which they are imagined.[15]

The insight that national identity must be addressed according to the ways in which it is imagined signals for me the importance of pedagogical practices to current controversies around questions of identity that characterize much political debate in the United States. It is the pedagogical processes at work in framing the current debates on national identity that interest me most. More specifically, the questions I want to raise are: what forms of address, images, texts, and performances are being produced and used in popular discourses to construct what it means to be an American? and what are the implications of these dominant representations for extending or undermining a substantive plural democracy?

The current debate over national identity represents not only a conservative backlash fueled by the assumption that those common values and consensual freedoms that have defined the American way of life, circa Norman Rockwell,[16] are now under attack by racial, sexual, and political minorities. Moreover, the current conservatism produces a new nationalism rooted in an imaginary construction of national identity that is dangerous to any viable notion of democracy. This is not meant to suggest that the discourse of national unity voiced through an appeal to shared language of difference (not the assimilationist language of a common culture) should be summarily dismissed as Eurocentric, racist, or patriarchal. National identity steeped in a shared vision of social justice and a respect for cultural differences is to be applauded. At the same time, the healing grace of a national identity based on a respect for lived cultures in the plural[17] should not be confused with a politically reactionary notion of national identity whose primary purpose is to restrict the terms of *citizenship* and *community* to a discourse of monoculturalism and nativism. National identity in the service of a common culture recognizes cultural differences only to flatten them out in the conservative discourse of assimilation and the liberal appeal to tolerance.[18] However, the linkage between national identity and nationalism is not bound by any particular politics, and nationalism is not by definition intrinsically oppressive. Hence, it is both important and necessary as part of a progressive politics of national identity to provide a theoretical space to address the potential of both a pedagogy and politics that can pluralize cultural differences within democratic relations of power as part of an effort to develop an emancipatory politics of national identity and nationalism. This is especially important at a time in the United States when the discourses of nationalism and national identity have taken a decidedly reactionary political turn.

The appropriation of national identity as a vehicle to foster racism, nativism, and political censorship is not unique to the 1990s, but has a long history in the United States.[19] However, the conditions, contexts, and content through which the discourse of national identity is being produced and linked to virulent forms of nationalism are new. For example, media culture with its new cable technologies coupled with the proliferation of radio and television talk channels have created a public sphere that vastly expands the intrusion into daily life of mainstream discourses that greatly restrict the possibility for real debate, exchange, and diversity of opinions. These electronic media, largely driven by corporate conglomerates, have no precedent in American life in terms of their power both to disseminate information and to shape how national identity is configured, comprehended, and experienced as part of everyday life.[20] Second, popular culture has become a powerful site for defining nationalism and national identity against diversity and cultural differences, the latter rendered synonymous with disruption, disunity, and separatism. In this populist discourse, there is a theoretical slippage that equates national identity with a common identity and the assertion of cultural pluralism with an assault on the very character of what it means to be an American. At issue here is a politics of forgetting that erases how disparate social identities have been produced, legitimated, and marginalized within different relations of power. But there is more at stake than the erasure of social memory; there is also the emergence of a racially saturated discourse that mobilizes national identity as the defining principle for a national community that is under siege. Similarly, the new nationalism in foreign policy employs the chauvinistic bravado of the market place with its call for the United States to be number one in the world. Such nationalistic bravado operates by both stigmatizing social criticism as unpatriotic and a threat to American unity and arrogantly proclaiming that Western versions of liberal democracy as practiced in the United States signal the "end of history."[21]

MEDIA CULTURE AND THE POPULIST CONSTRUCTION OF NATIONALIST IDENTITY

I want to examine briefly some populist examples of the new nationalism that emerge from different places in the cultural apparatuses that shape public opinion. In different ways, these populist voices advocate a pedagogy and politics of national identity that serve to reproduce some reactionary elements of the new nationalism. For example, expressions of the new nationalism can be found in several sites: in the backlash against multiculturalism in the public schools and universities; in the rise of the English Only movement; in the notion of the state as a stern parent willing to inflict harsh measures on welfare mothers; and in educational reforms demanding a national curriculum. Ideological signposts pointing to the new nationalism can be found in analogies invoking imagery of battle, invasion, and war, which increasingly shape the debates over immigration in the United States, as in the passing of anti-immigration legislation such as California's Proposition 187 and Proposition 209. Crime is represented in the dominant, white media as a black issue, implying that race can only be understood through a reductionist correlation of culture and identity. Representations of black men appear ad nauseam on the covers of magazines such as *Newsweek,* the *New York Times Sunday Magazine,* and *Time* whenever a significer is needed to mobilize and draw upon the general public's fear of crime and urban decay. Recent Hollywood films abound with racist representations that link criminality to skin color. Some of the most popular examples include *Pulp Fiction* (1994), *Just Cause* (1995), and *187* (1997).[22] All of these examples underscore how nationalism is currently being shaped to defend a beleaguered notion of national identity read as white, heterosexual, middle class, and allegedly threatened by contamination from cultural, linguistic, racial, and sexual differences.

The power of the new nationalism and its centrality to American political life is also evident in its growth and popularity in a number of popular and public spaces. One example can be found in the written and television commentaries of conservative ideologues such as Patrick Buchanan, William Buckley, and George Will on nationally syndicated television programs such as CNN's "Crossfire" and "Firing Line." For example, Buchanan represents a new version of the public intellectual speaking from such critical public sites as the news media, especially the growing number of news programs found on cable television, which are largely dominated by right-wing commentary. For Buchanan, the new nationalism is defined through a bellicose nativism that views cultural differences as a threat to national unity. Buchanan argues that the reality of cultural difference, with its plurality of languages, experiences, and histories, poses a serious threat to both national unity and what he defends as Judeo-Christian values. According to Buchanan, calls for expanding the existing potential of political representation and self-determination are fine insofar as they enable white Americans to take back their country. In this reactionary discourse, difference becomes a signifier for racial exclusivity, segregation, or, in Buchanan's language, "self-determination." For Buchanan, public life in the United States has deteriorated since 1965, because a flood tide of immigration has rolled in from the Third World, legal and illegal, as our institutions of assimilation disintegrated. Ushering in the discourse of nativism, Buchanan asks: "Who speaks for the Euro-Americans? Is it not time to take America back?"[23]

Similarly, populist right-wing conservative Rush Limbaugh, who describes himself as the Doctor of Democracy, rails against the poor and disadvantaged minorities because they do not act like real Americans who rely upon their own resources, skills, talents, and hard work.[24] Limbaugh has become the populist equivalent of Beavis and Butt-Head. Combining humor, unrestrained narcissism, and outright buffoonery with a virulent and mean-spirited attack on progressive causes, Limbaugh accentuates the current appeal of the talk show that is part of a broader reactionary, conservative offensive through popular media. Perhaps the only thing interesting about Limbaugh is that he exemplifies the way in which right-wing conservatives no longer limit their political agenda to the traditional channels of policy, news, and information; they have now extended their influence to the more populist cultural realms of radio, national mainstream print, television talk shows, the world of stand-up comics, and other texts of media culture.

Rush Limbaugh, Linda Chavez, Cal Thomas, Andrew Dice Clay, and other popular media figures represent a marriage of media culture and the lure of extremist attacks in what appears as a legitimation of a new form of public pathology dressed up as entertainment.[25] Limbaugh echoes the increasingly popular assumption that an "ethnic upsurge" threatens both the American model of assimilation and the unity of America as a single culture. Extending rather than challenging the ideological assumptions that buttress the old racism and Social Darwinism, Limbaugh and others echo a call for cultural unity less as an overt marker for racial superiority than as a discourse for privileging a white minority. Within this populist discourse, racism is couched in the critique of the welfare state but serves primarily as a signifier for cultural containment, homogeneity, and social and structural inequality. Just as Charles Murray and Richard Herrnstein warn in *The Bell Curve* against the effects of immigration on the gene pool of white, middle-class Americans, and the religious right calls for a holy war to be waged in the schools to preserve the identity of the United States as a Christian nation, right-wing populist commentators add a twist to the new nationalism and its racial coding by appealing to a nostalgic, romanticized view of history as the good old days in which white men ruled, Blacks knew their place in the social and political hierarchy, and women attended to domestic work. The appeal is no longer simply to racial supremacy but also to cultural uniformity parading as the politics of nationalism, national identity, and patriotism. These antimulticultural attacks organize themselves around a view of nationalism that stigmatizes any disagreement by simply labeling critics as America-bashers. Given these circumstances, it should come as no surprise that Robert Bork, a former Supreme Court nominee and currently the John M. Olin scholar in legal studies at the conservative American Enterprise Institute, can argue in a recent book that multiculturalism is bringing us to a barbarous epoch.[26]

In the world of TV spectacles and mass entertainment, the Buchanans, Buckleys, and Limbaughs represent the shock troops of the new nationalism. On the academic front, a more refined version of the new nationalism has been advanced. Two examples will suffice, though they are hardly inclusive. In the first instance, public intellectuals writing in conservative periodicals such as *The New Republic, The New Criterion,* and *The American Spectator* have increasingly argued for the new nationalism in terms that both dismiss multiculturalism and reproduce the discourse of assimilation and common culture. Rather than analyzing multiculturalism as a complex, legitimate, and necessary ongoing negotiation among minorities against assimilation,[27] the new nationalists see in the engagements of cultural difference less a productive tension than a debilitating divisiveness. John B. Judis and Michael Lind echo this sentiment in their own call for a new nationalism:

> [T]here is a constructive and inclusive current of American nationalism that runs from Alexander Hamilton through Abraham Lincoln and Theodore Roosevelt. It emphasizes not the exclusion of foreigners, but rather the unification of Americans of different regions, races and ethnic groups around a common national identity. It stands opposed not only to nativism, but also to today's multiculturalism and economic or strategic globalism.[28]

Nationalism in this discourse becomes the marker of certainty; it both affirms monoculturalism and restores the racially coded image of Americans as a beleaguered national identity.[29] The new nationalism also pits national identity against the possibility of different groups to articulate and affirm their histories, languages, cultural identities, and traditions through the shifting and complex relations in which people imagine and construct national and postnational social formations. This is evident in the attack being waged by the right and the Republican Congress on affirmative action, quotas, immigration, bilingualism, and multiculturalism in the public schools. But the new nationalism is not confined to right-wing conservatives and evangelical Christians.

A more moderate version of the new nationalism can be found in the writings of liberals such as Richard Rorty, a prominent liberal philosopher from the University of Virginia. Whereas Buchanan, Limbaugh, and their followers might be dismissed as simply populist demagogues, public intellectuals such as Rorty command enormous respect from the academic community and the established press. Moreover, such intellectuals travel between academic and popular public spheres with enough influence to bring professional legitimacy to the new nationalism as it is taken up in television and talk-radio programs, the electronic media, and in the major newspapers and magazines in the United States. Hence, it is all the more important that arguments that reinforce the logic of the new nationalism and parade under the banner of a "tough" or "patriotic" liberalism be critically engaged, especially by individuals who find in such arguments a semblance of reason and restraint.

RICHARD RORTY, LIBERALISM, AND THE PROBLEM OF NATIONAL IDENTITY

Writing in the Op-Ed section of the *New York Times,* Richard Rorty has argued, under the headline "The Unpatriotic Academy," that left-wing academics who support multiculturalism are unpatriotic. For Rorty, the litmus test for patriotism is not to be found in social criticism that holds a country up to its professed ideals, but in a refusal on the part of this left . . . to rejoice in the country it inhabits. It repudiates the idea of a national identity and the emotion of national pride. Speaking for an unspecified group of "patriotic" Americans, Rorty, in this instance, insists that "We take pride in being citizens of a self-invented, self-reforming, enduring constitutional democracy."[30] One wonders: For whom do intellectuals such as Rorty speak? Have they appointed themselves as spokespersons for all Americans who disassociate themselves from the left? And does this generalization further suggest that one gives up respect and love of one's country if one engages in criticism that can be conveniently labeled as left wing? Does a public assertion of patriotism, as ritualistically invoked by all manner of demagogues, suggest that such rhetoric provides a certified stamp of legitimacy regarding one's own politics? Of course, Rush Limbaugh and Patrick Buchanan consistently engage in the rhetoric of love for their country while simultaneously baiting gays, Blacks, feminists, and others. Moreover, one must consider the implications of Rorty's attack on the left social critics in view of the ways in which the government engaged in red-baiting during the 1920s and the McCarthy witch hunts of the 1950s. Is he suggesting that left-wing theorists (as if they were a homogeneous group) should be policed and punished for their lack of patriotism? There is a recklessness in Rorty's charges that places him squarely in the camp of those who would punish dissenters rather than support free speech, especially if it is speech with which one disagrees. Maybe Rorty was simply being rambunctious in his use of the term *unpatriotic,* but given the way in which the term has been used historically in this country to squelch social criticism, such a lapse of historical memory seems unlikely. So what is the point?

Rorty seems to be caught between liberal guilt and the appeal of a rabid conservatism that equates cultural differences with a threat to national unity, a threat that has to be overcome. Having posited such an equation, Rorty then takes the extraordinary step of identifying all those academics who support some version of multiculturalism as posing a threat to the social order. For Rorty, there is no contradiction in feeling one's heart swell with patriotism and national hope and feeling shame at the greed, the intolerance, and the indifference to suffering that is widespread in the United States.[31] In this theoretical sweep, multiculturalism is not addressed in its complexity as a range of theoretical positions that run the ideological gamut extending from calls for separatism to new forms of cultural democracy. Multiculturalism for Rorty is simply a position that exists under some absolute sign. In this reductionistic perspective, there are no theoretical differences between multicultural positions espoused by academic leftists such as Hazel Carby, Guillermo Gomez-Pena, June Jordan, and bell hooks, on the one hand, and liberals such as James Banks, Gregory Jay, or Stanley Fish on the other.[32] But there is more at stake here than Rorty's suspect appeal to patriotism. Social criticism is not the enemy of patriotism, it is the bedrock of a shared national tradition that allows for many voices to engage in a dialogue about the dynamics of cultural and political power. In fact, national identity must be understood within a broader concern for the expansion and deepening of democratic public life itself.

I believe that Rorty's notion of national identity closes down, rather than expands, the principles that inform a multicultural and multiracial democracy. However, Rorty is important in terms of exemplifying the limits of the reigning political philosophy of liberalism. Rorty's gesture towards tolerance "presupposes that its object is morally repugnant, that it really needs to be reformed, that is, altered."[33] As David Theo Goldberg points out:

> Liberals are moved to overcome the racial differences they tolerate and have been so instrumental in fabricating by deluding them, by bleaching them out through assimilation or integration. The liberal would assume away the difference in otherness maintaining thereby the dominant of a presumed sameness, the universally imposed similarity in identity.[34]

National identity cannot be constructed around the suppression of dissent. Nor should it be used in the service of a new fundamentalism by appealing to a notion of patriotism that equates left-wing social criticism with treason, and less critical forms of discourse with a love of retrograde forms of nationalism and national identity. It is precisely this type of binarism that has been used, all too frequently, throughout the twentieth century, to develop national communities that make a virtue of intolerance and exclusion. Moreover, this kind of logic prevents individuals and social groups from understanding and critically engaging national identity not as a cultural monument but as a living set of relations that must be constantly engaged and struggled over.

Rorty's facile equating of national identity with the love of one's country, on the one hand, and the dismissal of forms of left social criticism that advocate multiculturalism, on the other, is simply an expression of the new nationalism, one that views cultural differences and the emergence of multiple cultures as a sign of fragmentation and a departure from, rather than an advance toward, democracy. Rorty's mistake is that he assumes that national identity is to be founded on a single culture, language, and history when, in fact, it cannot. National identity is always a shifting, unsettled complex of historical struggles and experiences that are cross-fertilized, produced, and translated through a variety of cultures. As such, it is always open to interpretation and struggle. As Stuart Hall points out, "national identity is a matter of 'becoming' as well as of 'being'. . . . [It] is never complete, always in process. . . . [It] is not eternally fixed in some essentialized past [but] subject to the continuous 'play' of history, culture, and power."[35]

The discourse of multiculturalism represents, in part, the emergence of new voices that have generally been excluded from the histories that have defined our national identity. Far from being a threat to social order, multiculturalism in its various forms has challenged notions of national identity that equate cultural differences with deviance and disruption. Refusing a notion of national identity constructed on the suppression of cultural differences and social dissent, multiculturalism, especially its more critical and insurgent versions, explores how dominant views of national identity have been developed around cultural differences constructed within hierarchical relations of power that authorize who can or cannot speak legitimately as an American. Maybe it is the insertion of politics and power back into the discourse on difference that threatens Rorty so much that he responds to it by labeling it as unpatriotic.

Pitting national identity against cultural difference not only appeals to an oppressive politics of common culture, but reinforces a political moralism that polices the boundaries of identity, encouraging uniformity and ensuring intellectual inertia.[36] National identity based on a unified cultural community suggests a dangerous relationship between the ideas of race, intolerance, and the cultural membership of nationhood. Not only does such a position downplay the politics of culture at work in nationalism, but it erases an oppressive history forged in an appeal to a common culture and a reactionary notion of national identity. As Will Kymlicka points out, liberals and conservatives often overlook the fact that the American government,

> forcibly incorporated Indian tribes, native Hawaiians, and Puerto Ricans into the American state, and then attempted to coercively assimilate each group into the common American culture. It banned the speaking of Indian languages in school and forced Puerto Rican and Hawaiian schools to use English rather than Spanish or Hawaiian.[37]

What is problematic about Rorty's position is not simply that he views multiculturalism as a threat to a totalizing notion of national identity; more important is his theoretical indifference to counternarratives of difference, diaspora, and cultural identity that explore how diverse groups are constructed within an insurgent multiculturalism that engage the issue both of what holds us together as a nation and of what constitutes our differences from each other. Viewing cultural differences only as a problem, Rorty reveals a disturbing lacuna in his notion of national identity; it is a view that offers little defense against the forces of ethnic absolutism and cultural racism that are so quick to seize upon national identity as a legitimating discourse for racial violence. There is an alarming defensiveness in Rorty's view of national identity, one that reinforces rather than challenges a discourse of national community rooted in claims to cultural and racist supremacy.

PEDAGOGY, NATIONAL IDENTITY, AND THE POLITICS OF DIFFERENCE

Critical educators need a notion of national identity that addresses its political, cultural, and pedagogical components. In the first instance, national identity must be addressed as part of a broader consideration linking nationalism and postnational social formations to a theory of democracy. That is, the relationship between nationalism and democracy must address not only the crucial issue of whether legal rights are provided for all groups irrespective of their cultural identity, but also how structures of power work to ensure that diverse cultural communities have the economic, political, and social resources to exercise both the capacity for collective voice and the possibility of differentiated, directly interpersonal relations.[38] Rather than waging war against the pluralization of cultural identities and the crucial spheres in which they are nurtured and engaged, educators must address critically how national identity is constructed in the media, through the politics of state apparatuses and through the mobilization of material resources and power outside of the reach of the state.[39] As part of a broader politics of representation and distributive justice, this suggests the need for progressive cultural workers to provide the pedagogical conditions and sites "open to competing conceptualizations, diverse identities, and a rich public discourse" necessary to expand the conditions for democracy to flourish on both a national and global level.[40]

Second, national identity must be inclusive and informed by a democratic, pluralization of cultural identities. If the tendency towards a universalizing, assimilative impulse is to be resisted, educators must ensure that students engage varied notions of an imagined community by critically addressing rather than excluding cultural differences. Although the approach toward such a pedagogy is culturally inclusive and suggests expanding the varied texts that define what counts as knowledge in public schools and institutions of higher education in the United States, there is also a need to create institutionalized spaces obligated to transdisciplinarity and multicultural studies. But such pedagogical spaces must be firmly committed to more than a politics of inclusive representation or simply aimed at helping students to understand and celebrate cultural difference (e.g., Martin Luther King, Jr., Day). The politics of cultural difference must be a politics of more than texts; it must also understand, negotiate, and challenge differences as they are defined and sustained within oppressive and systemic networks of power.[41] Critically negotiating the relationship between national identity and cultural differences, as Homi Bhabha has pointed out, is a negating activity that should be valued for making a difference in the world rather than merely to reflect it.[42]

What educators need is a pedagogy that redefines national identity not through a primordial notion of ethnicity or a monolithic conception of culture but as part of a postmodern politics of cultural difference in which identities are constantly being negotiated and reinvented within complex and contradictory notions of national belonging. A collective dialogue over nationalism, national identity, and cultural differences is not going to be established by simply labeling certain forms of social criticism as unpatriotic, or national identity as a shared tradition that exists outside of the struggles over representation, democracy, and social justice. If American society is to move away from its increasing defensiveness about cultural differences, it will have to advocate a view of national identity that regards bigotry and intolerance as the enemy of democracy, and cultural differences as one of its strengths. However, even where such differences are acknowledged and affirmed, it is important to recognize that they cannot be understood exclusively within the language of culture and identity, but rather as a part of an ethical discourse that contributes to a viable notion of democratic public life. Among other things, this suggests a need for a pedagogy and language through which values and social responsibility can be discussed not simply as a matter of individual choice or reduced to complacent relativism but as a social discourse and pedagogical practice grounded in public struggles. David Theo Goldberg is right in arguing that educators need "a robustly nuanced conception of relativism underpinning the multicultural project [one that] will enable distinctions to be drawn between more or less accurate truth claims and more or less justifiable values (in contrast to absolute claims to the truth or the good)."[43] The issue here is not merely the importance of moral pragmatism in developing a pedagogy that addresses national identity as a site of resistance and reinvention. Equally important is the political and pedagogical imperative of developing a postmodern notion of democracy in which students and others will be attentive to negotiating and constructing the social, political, and cultural conditions for diverse cultural identities to flourish within an increasingly multicentric, international, and transnational world.

In short, if national identity is not to be used in the service of dema-gogues, it must be addressed pedagogically and politically in order to un-ravel how cultural differences have been constructed within the unequal distribution of resources, how such differences need to be understood around issues of power and struggle, and how national identity must be taken up in ways that challenge economic and cultural inequality both domestically and on a global scale.

NOTES

[1] This paper represents a revised version of Chapter 7, which appeared in Henry A. Giroux, *Fugitive Cultures* (New York: Routledge, 1996).

[2] For an analysis of such economic and social changes that have marked the global landscape, along with the emerging theoretical and political discourses that have marked such changes, see various articles in Avery Gordon and Christopher Newfield, eds., *Mapping Multiculturalism* (Minneapolis: University of Minnesota Press, 1996), and David Goldberg, ed., *Multiculturalism: A Critical Reader* (Cambridge: Basil Blackwell, 1994).

[3] Judith Squires, Editorial, *New Formations,* No. 24 (Winter 1994), p. v.

[4] Some major critiques that center on the lack of specificity in some of the writing on diaspora, immigration, and postcolonialism can be found in: Inderpal Grewal and Caren Kaplan, "Introduction: Transnational Feminist Practices and Questions of Postmodernity," in Inderpal Grewal and Caren Kaplan, eds., *Scattered Hegemonies* (Minneapolis: University of Minnesota Press, 1994), pp. 1–33; Ien Ang, "On Not Speaking Chinese: Postmodern Ethnicity and the Politics of Diaspora," *Social Formations,* No. 24 (March 1995), pp. 1–18; Craig Calhoun, "Nationalism and Civil Society: Democracy, Diversity, and Self-Deter-mination," in Craig Calhoun, ed. *Social Theory and the Politics of Identity* (Cambridge, MA: Basil Blackwell, 1994), pp. 304–335; Benita Parry, "Signs of Our Times: A Discussion of Homi Bhabha's *The Location of Culture,"* third text Nos., 28/29 (Autumn/Winter 1994), pp. 5–24. Benita Parry, in particular, offers a brilliant analysis regarding the theoretical pitfalls in a politics of representation in which notions of diaspora, hybridity, and difference serve to subsume "the so-cial to textual representation [and represent] colonialism as transactional rather than conflictual." Parry, ibid., p. 12.

[5] For an excellent analysis of this issue, see Katya Gibel Azoulay, "Experi-ence, Empathy and Strategic Essentialism," *Cultural Studies* 11:1 (1997), pp. 89–110.

[6] Arjun Appadurai. "Patriotism and Its Futures," *Public Cultures,* 5:3 (1993), p. 417.

[7] Arjun Appadurai. "Patriotism and Its Futures," *Public Cultures*, 5:3 (1993), p. 418.

[8] Gayatri Chakrauorty Spivak and David Plotke. "A Dialogue on Democracy," in David Trend, ed., *Radical Democracy: Identity, Citizenship, and the State* (New York: Routledge, 1996), p. 210.

[9] Both of these quotes are taken from Judith Squires, Editorial, *New Formations*, No. 24 (Winter 1994), p. vi.

[10] Stuart Hall. "Culture, Community, Nation," *Cultural Studies*, 7:3 (October 1993), pp. 353.

[11] Christopher Newfield and Avery F. Gordon, "Multiculturalism's Unfinished Business," in Avery F. Gordon and Christopher Newfield, eds., *Mapping Multiculturalism* (Minneapolis: University of Minnesota Press, 1996), p. 105.

[12] This issue is discussed in Will Kymlicka, "Misunderstanding Nationalism," *Dissent* (Winter 1995), pp. 130–137.

[13] The literature on nationalism and national identity is much too voluminous to cite here, but excellent examples can be found in Benedict Anderson, *Imagined Communities* (London: Verso Press, 1991); Partha Chatterjee, *The Nation and Its Fragments* (Princeton: Princeton University Press, 1993); Homi Bhabha, ed., *Nation and Narration* (New York: Routledge, 1990); Edward Said, *Culture and Imperialism* (New York: Alfred K. Knopf, 1993); Andrew Parker, Mary Russo, Doris Sommer, and Patricia Yaeger, eds., *Nationalisms and Sexualities* (New York: Routledge, 1992); Etienne Balibar and Immanuel Wallerstein, *Race, Nation, Class: Ambiguous Identities* (London: Verso Press, 1991). Some excellent recent sources can be found in Craig Calhoun, ed., *Social Theory and the Politics of Identity* (New York: Blackwell, 1994).

[14] Paul Gilroy. *The Black Atlantic: Modernity and Double Consciousness* (Cambridge: Harvard University Press, 1993), p. 3.

[15] Benedict Anderson. *Imagined Communities*, 2nd ed. (London: Verso Press, 1991), p. 6.

[16] Homi K. Bhabha. "A Good Judge of Character: Men, Metaphors, and the Common Culture," in Toni Morrison, ed., *Race-ing Justice, Engendering Power: Essays on Anita Hill, Clarence Thomas, and the Construction of Social Reality* (New York: Pantheon, 1992), p. 233.

[17] Gerald Graff and Bruce Robbins. "Cultural Criticism," in Stephen Greenblat and Giles Gunn, eds., *Redrawing the Lines* (New York: MLA, 1992), p. 434.

[18] For a critique of both of these positions, see Ien Ang, "On Not Speaking Chinese: Postmodern Ethnicity and the Politics of Diaspora," *New Formations*, No. 24 (Winter 1994), pp. 1–18; Ghassan Hage, "Locating Multiculturalism's Other: A Critique of Practical Tolerance," *New Formations*, No. 24 (Winter 1994), pp. 19–34.

[19] See, for example, Joe R. Feagin and Hernan Vera. *White Racism* (New York: Routledge, 1995).

[20] Of course, the work of Herbert Schiller and Noam Chomsky are seminal reading on this issue. For example, see Noam Chomsky, "The Manufacture of Consent," in Noam Chomsky, *The Chomsky Reader,* edited by James Peck (New York: Pantheon, 1987), pp. 121–136.

[21] I am referring to Francis Fukuyama, *The End of History and the Last Man* (New York: The Free Press, 1992).

[22] I take up the issue of Hollywood's portrayal of racism and violence in Henry A. Giroux, *Channel Surfing: Race Talk and the Destruction of Today's Youth* (New York: St. Martin's Press, 1997).

[23] Pat Buchanan quoted in Charles Krauthammer, "The Real Buchanan Is Surfacing," *The Cincinnati Enquirer,* March 3, 1990, A4.

[24] Rush H. Limbaugh, III. *See, I Told You So* (New York: Pocket Books, 1993), p. 26.

[25] For a brilliant analysis of this phenomenon, especially the marketing of Beavis and Butt-Head, see Douglas Kellner, *Media Culture: Cultural Studies, Identity, and Politics—Between the Modern and the Postmodern* (New York: Routledge, forthcoming).

[26] Robert H. Bork. *Slouching Towards Gomorrah* (New York: Reagan Books, 1996), p. 23.

[27] Homi K. Bhabha. "Beyond the Pale: Art in the Age of Multicultural Translation," *Kunst and Museum Journal,* 5:4 (1994), p. 15.

[28] John B. Judis and Michael Lind. "For a New Nationalism," *The New Republic* (March 27, 1995), p. 21.

[29] This is paraphrased from Stuart Hall, "Culture, Community, Nation," *Cultural Studies,* 7:3 (October 1993), p. 357.

[30] Richard Rorty. "The Unpatriotic Academy," *New York Times* Op-Ed, Sunday (February 13, 1994), E15.

[31] Rorty, ibid.

[32] For an excellent critique of positions that fail to make a distinction between the mix of multicultural positions, see Avery Gordon and Christopher Newfield, "Introduction," in Gordon and Newfield, eds., *Mapping Multiculturalism* (Minneapolis: University of Minnesota Press, 1996), pp. 1–39.

[33] David Theo Goldberg. *Racist Culture* (Cambridge, MA: Basil Blackwell, 1993), p. 7.

[34] David Theo Goldberg, ibid. p. 7.

[35] Stuart Hall. "Cultural Identity and Diaspora," in Jonathan Rutherford, ed., *Identity, Community, Culture, Difference* (London: Lawrence & Wishart, 1990), p. 225.

[36] Jonathan Rutherford, "A Place Called Home: Identity and the Cultural Politics of Difference," in Jonathan Rutherford, ed., *Identity, Community, Culture, Difference* (London: Lawrence & Wishart, 1990), p. 17.

[37] Will Kymlicka, "Misunderstanding Nationalism," *Dissent* (Winter 1995), p. 132.

[38] Craig Calhoun. "Nationalism and Civil Society: Democracy, Diversity, and Self-Determination," in Craig Calhoun, ed., *Social Theory and the Politics of Identity* (New York: Blackwell, 1994), p. 311.

[39] David Goldberg. "Introduction: Multiculturalism Conditions," in David Theo Goldberg, ed., *Multiculturalism: A Reader* (Cambridge, MA: Basil Blackwell, 1994).

[40] Craig Calhoun. "Nationalism and Civil Society: Democracy, Diversity, and Self-Determination," in Craig Calhoun, ed., *Social Theory and the Politics of Identity* (New York: Basil Blackwell, 1994), p. 327.

[41] On this issue, see Nancy Fraser, *Justice Interruptus: Critical Reflections on the "Postsocialist" Condition* (New York: Routledge, 1997).

[42] Homi Bhabha. "Beyond the Pale: Art in the Age of Multicultural Translation," *Kunst and Museum Journal,* 5:4 (1994), p. 22.

[43] David Theo Goldberg. "Introduction: Multicultural Conditions," in David Theo Goldberg, ed., *Multiculturalism: A Critical Reader* (Cambridge, MA: Basil Blackwell, 1994), p. 15.

CHAPTER 6

On "Having Differences" and "Being Different"

From a Dialogue of Difference to the Private Language of Indifference

GEORGE DAVID MILLER AND
MARK ROELOF ELEVELD

1. EGOCENTRISM, ETHNOCENTRISM, AND SEPARACENTRISM

Egocentrism states that a person views the world only from her or his particular perspective. Ethnocentrism states that a group only views the world from the group's particular perspective. Egocentrism and ethnocentrism are looking at the world from a single frame of reference. But this does not entail that "different" people outside this frame of reference cannot look at the world from this frame of reference. The presumption is that others can and should understand. This is not the case with respect to separacentrism. Separacentrism states that a group only sees the world from a single point of reference and that "different" groups can never fathom this same frame of reference. Experiences of the group are invisible to or untranslatable to other groups. Whereas untranslatability of experience is characteristic of separacentrism, it is not characteristic of egocentrism or ethnocentrism.

Our investigation allows for an understanding of the essential conditions in a world that works within classifications, divisions, and categories—a world seen through centrisms. Created by humans, classifications are used for the purpose of manipulation and the subjugation of others. An obvious example is racism. Racism is the view that race division—races created by humans on the basis of banal, predetermined, biologically inherent conditions such as skin color—is a classification to split human beings apart. This classification, that one's racial group is superior to another, is the view that members of other races are ultimately objects—because they are seen as "being different"—over which to exercise one's will without expecting, or claiming to expect, moral responsibility for actions considered reprehensible against human beings. As Adolph Hitler once admitted:

> I know perfectly well, just as well as those tremendously clever intellectuals, that in the scientific sense there is no such thing as race. . . . [But] I as a politician need a conception which enables the order which has hitherto existed on historic bases to be abolished and an entirely new and anti-historic order enforced and given an intellectual base.

The idea conveyed by Hitler is that humans are the creators of classification and, in this case, race. Hitler's example shows that all centrisms are products combined under the roof of one common factor greater than any of its separate parts, that which is the core of humanity itself: being human.

As liberatory pedagogues in a pluralistic society in which many different groups are oppressed in many different ways, we are especially concerned when separacentrism occurs between groups oppressed by the same oppressor. Under the current presentation of the so-called "American dream," the division between many oppressed groups is a means of enabling the current powers that be, the oppressors, to remain intact. For example, the current swing of the right within government has used the platform of welfare reform as a wedge to divide groups and to create even greater political conservativism in America. This view has argued that white middle-class tax dollars are being drained by nonworking minorities and women. This notion is a tactic used by the current powers, once again the white male leaders, to instill fear and animosity between oppressed groups. A good example of this is the L.A. riots of 1991 in which Korean owners, an oppressed minority group, were out in the streets shooting other oppressed groups, specifically Blacks, in order to save their homes and businesses from being robbed. The government has created the concept that all minorities are lazy and unethical beings who rob taxpayers of their money through welfare. This image taken literally during the riots, actually a rebellion against the current political system by oppressed peoples such as Blacks and Koreans, pitted the two oppressed groups against each other and, thus, created separacentrism. The point being that both oppressed groups were blind to each other's conditions of oppression despite its being, in many ways, the same. On the one hand, Blacks fought against the oppressive nature of the system by burning and looting symbols of consumerism, and the Koreans, on the other hand, fought against Blacks to protect their products. Again, the point is that through the manipulation of the government (the oppressor), both groups were separated from one another and instead of fighting the forces that oppressed them directly, they fought against one another. The oppressor pitted the two oppressed groups against each other through separacentrism.

Separacentrism prevents dialogue from occurring between such groups. Separacentrism is a divide-and-rule technique that transforms "having differences" into "being different." "Having differences" connotes the continuation of dialogue, even in the friction of difference. "Being different" assumes all groups have essential differences that prevent communication and cooperation. Being different is the essence of separacentrism. By focusing on being different, separacentrism is indifferent to other oppressed groups. No communication, no dialogue, no understanding, no cooperation takes place between oppressed groups. If the focus is on being different instead of having differences, then divide and rule has been highly successful.

As liberatory pedagogues, our goal should be to prevent dialogue on having differences from becoming a dialogue on being different. This does not mean to endorse the naive sentiment of the oppressor: "We are all human or we are all Americans; you oppressed can be just like us." Such an invitation to join "us" is less an invitation for the oppressed group to join than it is for a few individuals of the group to be co-opted and used to maintain the status quo. This is nothing more than a false invitation of inclusion, another enticement like the Horatio Alger myth. Such invitations from the white phallic America to oppressed groups are, at best, tepid. When the oppressor says to the oppressed "You are human like us, you are not different," this is less affirmation of the humanity of the oppressed and more a denial of culpability in the dehumanization of the oppressed. Such a statement masks the concrete historical and social differences between the oppressor and the oppressed. Such a statement claims value inherent in the already existing system. The system relies on separacentrism through the claims that all should be like me, for example, just like all good Black boys should want to be like Michael (Jordan). The paradox is that accessibility to these ideals is inherently impossible for most to attain within the created system. The reason all should want to be like Michael is specifically because all cannot be like him. Oppressors scream for sameness in order to mask difference. The obliteration of difference in this case prevents the disclosure of degrees of oppression.

The United States is steering toward a pluralism of being different rather than a pluralism of having differences. If this continues, then alliances between oppressed groups will be less likely and the status quo will go unchallenged. Accordingly, liberatory schooling in the United States must deemphasize being different and emphasize having differences. The former is antidialogical, the latter dialogical.

Our paper will discuss the formation of difference, the relationship between being different and indifference, and, finally, "difference" as divide and rule. Liberatory schooling, we argue, must do all it can to prevent having differences from devolving into being different.

2. THE FORMATION OF DIFFERENCE

We begin by examining the lexical definitions of *differ, difference,* and *different.* The verb *differ* means to make unlike, dissimilar, or distinct; to have contrary or diverse bearings, tendencies, or qualities; to be unlike, diverse, or various in nature, form, or qualities, or in some specified respect; to have differences; to quarrel. The noun *difference* means the condition, quality, or fact of being different, or not the same in quality or in essence. The adjective *different* means having characters or qualities that diverge from one another; of another, nature, form, or quality; in a weaker sense, used as a synonym for *other,* as denying identity, but without any implication of dissimilarity. *Difference* can mean not having the same quality in essence, or it can also mean the denial of identity without implying dissimilarity. Difference can connote having a different essence or nature from the other (being different); or it can connote nonidentity without implying dissimilarity (having differences). Our subsequent chain of arguments shall suggest that being different lays the groundwork for indifference.

In the *Introduction to the Phenomenology of Spirit,* Hegel explains the experience of the alien or unfamiliar:

> A reception of this kind is usually the first reaction on the part of knowing something unfamiliar; it resists it in order to save its own freedom and its own insight, its own authority, from the alien authority (for this is the guise in which what is newly encountered first appears), and to get rid of the appearance that something has been learned and of the sort of shame that is supposed to involve. (Hegel, 1977, p. 35)

When we first confront the unfamiliar, the alien, we resist it to save our freedom, insight, authority from an alien authority. We don't want anyone to know we learned from an alien authority, for that would involve the shame of acknowledging that our perspective is not supreme. In the famous section on "Master and Slave," Hegel describes how two consciousnesses come into conflict with one another and how one must conquer the other in order to gain the other's acknowledgment. The single consciousness is fearful after recognizing that the egocentric world around it is false and intrinsically based on intersubjectivity. Consciousness engages in a duel of death with the other to maintain its identity. In this conflict, one consciousness becomes the master, the other the slave. Unfortunately, this immediate interaction is an alienating factor not promoting understanding but instead "being different."

Sartre defines the conflict in another way. Like Hegel, Sartre contends that our understanding of the world comes in the form of consciousness. Adopting a phenomenological framework, Sartre sees intentionality as essential to consciousness, and this means that consciousness is transcendent. It is directed toward the outside for content. Through its free choices, consciousness creates itself via intersubjectivity. The fundamental point is that the other is the other precisely because it is related to the "I." But what occurs when the other is seen as what is not the "I?" What if the relationship exposes that "I" is different for the other, specifically in the mode of being different? The "I" becomes alienated by the facticity of its egocentrism from the other. A Black person, for instance, can become separated from a world that is dominated by white people because Black people can never be white. Upon recognition of the other being white and themselves Black, an automatic fear and frustration can occur. So Sartre's conflict with difference is a conflict of anguish and fear.

Difference need not be seen as coming into conflict with the other, in the Hegelian or Sartrean sense. In *Lesbian Ethics,* Sarah Hoagland offers a viable alternative to the Hegelian model. In the experience of difference, people can see to what degree each is being oppressed. In contrast to merging, the experience of difference points out boundaries between people, helping them to see that their agendas are not identical. Fear of difference prevents us from attending to one another. We can only connect with difference when we give up control, when we allow ourselves to be enhanced by the unfamiliar instead of being destroyed by it. Being open to being enhanced by difference stands in stark contrast to the Hegelian or Sartrean model of difference as something alien and something that must be overcome.

Hegel, Hoagland, and Sartre's accounts of difference can be incorporated into an analysis of difference from the perspectives of both the oppressor and the oppressed. Oppressors and oppressed see difference in a much different manner. Oppressors do not see difference as a threat to their very being. Difference does not endanger them. Difference can be enjoyed precisely because it is not a threat. Difference can be viewed at a distance. Difference can be avoided. Difference can be co-opted, controlled, diffused. Difference can be chosen. Difference does not force itself on the oppressors. Difference does not invade oppressors. Oppressors can see difference as enhancing their being.

The oppressed, however, see difference as a threat to their very being. They have been made, first of all, to feel different. As Freire says in *Pedagogy of the Oppressed,* cultural invasion denigrates the oppressed, putting labels like "inferior," "ingrates," "shiftless," "diseased," and "mixed blood" on them. Oppressors dehumanize the oppressed with these differences, emphasizing the oppressed's being different. This difference serves to alienate the oppressed. This difference is put upon them by their oppressors. The oppressed keenly feel their difference. Difference to them is an opprobrium, a badge of dishonor and disgrace. This is certainly not a difference that they have chosen. This is a difference of degradation. In Sartre's and Hegel's philosophies, difference is experienced initially as alienating. The oppressed undergo great psychological pain and development in order to free themselves of this fear of or conflict with difference. However, if that time period of development is manipulated and disfigured, as is the case in the oppressor/oppressed relationship, then *difference* becomes *being different* instead of *having differences.* Oppressors can confidently dwell within difference because they possess the power and ability to control what difference means. Oppressors are not under subjugation to justify their existence—their very being—in the same manner the oppressed are.

The oppressed are made to feel this difference in every aspect of their lives: economically, aesthetically, politically, and socially. Having internalized these differences, some of the oppressed want to belong to the oppressor class. Many simply wallow in a terrible self-image. Their being different is a negative thing. Difference is a threat to their very being. Difference cannot be controlled. Difference cannot be avoided. Difference cannot be chosen. Difference is not distant; difference is embedded in the oppressed. As more ipecac is provided and how the oppressor operates becomes evident to the oppressed, a new kind of difference occurs. This is a difference that wants no intercourse with other differences. It is so sick of being invaded by difference, it no longer wants difference. It is unrelated difference. It is indifference. The exhaustion and trauma arising from the destruction of the oppressor's poison leave the weakened body to focus only on itself and its recuperation. It then affirms its own being different, making itself unique and the center of the universe. In the process, it may turn the tables and depreciate its oppressors, in a Nietzschean inversion of values. Or it may rest in unrelatedness (or so it believes). We can again turn to Hegel and the *Phenomenology of Spirit* to describe this unrelatedness. Hegel refers to it as the "Law of the Heart." Persons of the heart will find their hearts divided and will only be able to maintain their own standards by denigrating as the perverse the public standards that they, with others, covertly acknowledge.

> Therefore heart-throb for the good of humanity, therefore, passes over into the ravings of insane self-conceit, into the rage of consciousness to save itself from destruction by casting forth from itself the perversion that itself really is, and by making every effort to see it, and to speak of it, as being elsewhere. (Hegel, 1977, pp. 289–90)

For Hegel, this leads to a war against all, including self. All values, created and fostered by an oppressive society that classifies having differences as being different, are seen as perverse and foreign to groups separated from one another. These same ideas of indifference, alienation, and nihilism lead toward what Hegel called the "Law of the Heart" and are echoed in Bret Easton Ellis's book *American Psycho:*

> That is how I lived my life, what I constructed my movement around, how I dealt with the tangible. This was the geography around which my reality revolved; it did not occur to me, ever, that people were good and that a man was capable of change or that the world could be a better place through one's taking pleasure in a feeling or a look or a gesture, of receiving another person's love or kindness. Nothing was affirmative, the term "generosity of spirit" applied to nothing, was a cliche, was some kind of bad joke. Sex is mathematics. Individuality no longer an issue. What does intelligence signify? Define reason. Desire meaningless. Intellect is not a cure. Justice is dead. Fear, recrimination, innocence, sympathy, guilt, waste, failure, grief, were things, emotions, that no one really felt any more. Reflection is useless, the world is senseless. Evil is its own permanence. God is not alive. Love cannot be trusted. Surface, surface, was all that anyone found meaning in . . . this was civilization as I saw it, colossal and jagged. (Ellis, 1991, p. 278)

In its being different, the oppressed class, like the people in the "Law of the Heart" or Ellis's book, denies itself the opportunity to have differences with other oppressed groups. This is because it is not ready to be enhanced by those differences. The differences of other groups are still seen as invading instead of as enhancing. Separacentrism emerges from this experience of difference. The oppressed group's being different is a reaction to cultural invasion and the constant battle to exorcise the image of the oppressor.

3. DIVIDE AND CONQUER: SEPARACENTRISM AND INDIFFERENCE

In this next section, we shall examine the relationship between separacentrism, separatism, and indifference. Whereas separatism is often justified, separatism that becomes separacentric is dangerous to the separated group.

W. E. B. DuBois argues for separatism on the following grounds:

> Where separation of mankind into races, groups, and classes is compulsory, either by law or custom, and whether that compulsion is temporary or permanent, the only effective defense that the segregated and despised group has against complete spiritual and physical disaster, is internal self-organization for their self-respect and self-defense. (DuBois, 1995, p. 555)

To use Freire's language, the oppressed must do everything possible to expel the image of the oppressor. The presence of the oppressor—physically, psychologically, and spiritually—must be exorcised. Education becomes, then, a kind of ipecac, helping us to expel the poison before it spreads throughout the system and finally kills us. Much of this poison is self-hatred, the cure for which is self-affirmation.

Let us look at justification for separatism from a lesbian point of view. In Sarah Hoagland's *Lesbian Ethics,* which we have heard described as a survival handbook for lesbians, we find the following basis for separatism. Many lesbians do not want their feelings and judgments challenged; they need space for their feelings. Being challenged by the oppressor will stifle their development. We see this rationale adopted with respect to all-female or all-Black schools. According to Hoagland, separation is necessary to avoid demoralization. Without separation, lesbians (1) cannot be moral agents outside the dominant/subordinate framework of heterosexuality; (2) lose focus of their anger and desire to depoliticize these emotions, which are redirected into scapegoating; (3) cease to believe that something is wrong; and (4) lose belief that they can make a difference. Hoagland sees separatism as positive only if it is not simply a separatism for survival, but is a separation for diversity and growth. Hoagland, like Freire, recognizes that reform is simply another form of co-optation. She criticizes feminist reforms because their focus is on men and the fact that such reforms address men's conceptions of women, not women's values. She also contends that feminist reforms depend on men to bring about change. Finally, the focus is on the value change in men rather than the value change in women (Hoagland, 1992, pp. 54–59, 191, 214–215, 228–230). Hoagland's fundamental point throughout is that lesbian self-definition cannot be accomplished in the heterosexual community and that co-optation is equally pernicious to that aim. Lesbians must withdraw from the existing ground of meaning to refocus on a lesbian framework. Community must not be formed because of outside threats or traditions, but in the belief that we can enact our values. Separatism is a refusal to act according to the oppressor's system. In withdrawing from the system, separatists refuse to energize it. This withdrawal is a form of engagement that can topple a system. However, oppressed groups cannot achieve power without coalition. As Martin Luther King, Jr., once said:

> In a multiracial society no group can make it alone. It is a myth to believe that the Irish, the Italians, and the Jews—the ethnic groups that Black Power advocates cite as justification for their views—rose to power through separatism. It is true they stuck together. But their group unity was always enlarged by joining in alliances with other groups such as political machines and trade unions. To succeed in a pluralistic society, and an often hostile one at that, the Negro obviously needs organized strength, but that strength will only be effective when it is consolidated through constructive alliances with majority groups. (King, 1986, p. 586)

If, as Hoagland says, the couriers refuse to deliver the messages of the king, then the king is rendered powerless. But this analogy needs to be restructured in order to be congruent with reality in a pluralistic society. We see that many different couriers exist in a pluralistic society (besides the postal service, UPS, Federal Express, and other smaller couriers, the phone companies, Internet, etc.). If one of the couriers resists, then what does it matter to the king? The king can always use the other couriers. If some of the couriers resist, but not cohesively, then that, too, won't bring about the demise of the king. Only through a coalition of couriers through a planned withdrawal of services will the king be rendered impotent. Where did the Million Man March lead? Where did the March on Washington lead? Separatism may lead to short-term self-affirmation, but by its very definition it is insignificant in the revolution against the forces that are oppressing the affirmation.

Separatism is often necessary for the survival of a group. The group must put up walls to defend itself from alien forces. But the dominant powers want separatism, for this ensures divisiveness. As explained earlier, the ultimate goal of oppressors is separatism among the oppressed. At the very extreme, oppressed groups whose very survival depends upon separation are justified in separating. This separation is justified in the same way an abused wife is justified in separating from an abusive husband. If self-survival depends upon separation, separation is justified. This does not condone separacentrism. It does, however, play into the hands of the divide-and-conquer strategy of the oppressors. We might even want to refer to this as the "Babel strategy." When God wanted to prevent the building of the Tower of Babel, the Lord made all the workers speak in different languages. Unable to communicate with one another, all work stopped, and the workers quarreled among themselves. Cooperative ventures become difficult in a climate of separatism. In some sense, we have to know how to speak different languages and not simply our own. We can have cooperation among those groups who are justified in their separation. We can speak in a "different voice," to borrow from the title of Carol Gilligan's famous book, but not so different that we cannot hear each other. If each separate group speaks in a different voice that is untranslatable to others, then dialogue is impossible. If we cannot hear one another, then we cannot discern differences.

Separacentrism lays the foundations for indifference. We shall develop this point by adopting and reformulating Hegel's view on indifference. When people have differences, they differ in opinion. Having differences does not mean the same thing as being different. Having differences suggests the dialogue continues even though parties disagree. I can have differences with you, but that does not mean that we cannot dialogue. Having differences still connotes a process, although perhaps an antagonistic one. Having differences is an act directed toward others, including others. Being different does not connote process. Being different connotes essential differences. Such differences can never be reconciled.

Being different takes the oppressed group into isolation, without any relatedness to other groups. Having differences suggests antagonism, but also relatedness. Being different means an essence not related to other essences. This represents, as we said before, indifference. Having differences is the basis for continued dialogue; being different is the basis for no such interaction. Being different is separation from a shared humanity. Being different is an alienation from other groups of human beings. Being different prevents groups from having differences. Being different is the essence of indifference. For being different identifies my essence as separate from yours. This can be explained by examining what Hegel means by indifference in the *Phenomenology of Spirit* (Hegel, 1977, pp. 68–69). In the section titled "Perception" (this is but one place Hegel refers to "indifference" in the text), Hegel describes a "simple togetherness of plurality" in which properties are "indifferent to another, each is on its own and free from the others," each being "a simple relating of self to self" leaving "the others alone . . . connected with them only by the indifferent Also." The universal holding them together is thinghood. Looking at the properties of salt in this way, we see its properties (white, tart, cubical) are in the same place (the simple Here), but "they do not affect each other in this interpenetration. . . . The whiteness does not affect the cubical shape, and neither affects the tart taste, etc.," Hegel explains.

If we relate this idea to separatism, we have the following scenario: Blacks, Jews, lesbians, and so forth, relating only themselves to themselves, held together by an abstraction (thinghood). While existing in the same Here (the United States), they are indifferent to one another. In this vision of the United States, different groups are bound together by an indifferent Also. Hegel says that "the Thing is the Also, or the universal medium in which the many properties subsist from another, without touching or canceling one another." This represents an isolationism within the same country, an internal isolationism. In the same way, white, tart, and cubical are indifferent to one another in the salt, so Blacks, Jews, and lesbians are indifferent to one another in the United States. This is sham indifference, however. Hegel will show that the qualities of the salt must exist in relation to one another in order to exist at all, so Blacks, Jews, and lesbians must also exist in relation to one another. The essence of salt, what it means to be salt, consists of its color, shape, and taste. Salt is less than salt without any of its essential features. The same can be said for human relationships and human communities. The makeup of the society of the United States consists of many different groups. In similar fashion, the makeup of the individual groups is also dependent upon outside groups for its creation. What it means to be Black is in part what it means for Blacks to associate with whites. The same can be said for lesbians or any other group within the United States. This is why separatism, which leads to separacentrism, fails. We cannot avoid relationships. Indifferent pluralism promotes an ideology of being different. Interactive pluralism promotes an ideology of having differences. The ideology of being different is: "We only care about how we look at the world; the way you look at it is your business, but we don't really care all that much how you look at it." Separacentrism lays the groundwork for absolutism that can only be known by or revealed to the separated group.

Another problem inherent with separacentrism is intellectual incest and knowledge xenophobia. The more pronounced the separation, the less intercourse with "different" points of view, then the more knowledge xenophobia. This is exemplified by the plight of Jews of the sixteenth, seventeenth, and eighteenth centuries. As Jews became ghettoized, so did their intellects. As Cecil Roth contends:

> Keen intelligences were wasted by dealing with trivial themes. That which was meant for mankind was confined to a simple bleak street. The intellectual fecundity which can result only from constant fertilization and cross-fertilization of human intercourse became impossible. (Roth, 1935)

Separacentrism is the basis for intellectual incest and xenophobia. Had Martin Luther King, Jr., been separacentric, then would he have found the works of Gandhi, or even cared whether such a person existed and what strategies this person proposed to challenge an oppressive regime? Had Paulo Freire been separacentric, would *Pedagogy of the Oppressed* be a medley of "different" perspectives?

According to Freire, well-meaning professionals unwittingly employ "a divide-and-rule" strategy by having the oppressed take "a focalized view of problems rather than seeing them as a dimension of a totality" (Freire, 1973, pp. 122–123). Freire offers the example of community development being broken into local communities without studying the communities as totalities and as part of a larger totality (area, region, continent, world). Similarly, educators who focalize differences prevent an oppressed group from recognizing their relationship to other oppressed groups and their differences. The micromanagement of difference, perhaps brought about by the fragmentation and compartmentalization of much schooling, culminates in divide and rule. The micromanagement of difference creates difference that is not difference; it also creates false differences between oppressed groups and prevents a holistic perspective on the issue of oppression.

4. CONCLUSION

In the same way that capitalism blurs the distinction between needs and whims and collapses the latter into the former, so the pedagogy of the oppressors blurs the distinction between being different and having differences and, likewise, collapses the latter into the former. Let us look at the tendencies in this country, one of which is different groups falling away from each other at seemingly great speeds. It might as well be that these different groups dwell in different countries or on different planets for that matter. Each group wants nothing to do with other groups, has no desire to discern difference. The dominant group has successfully divided and conquered. The dominant group stays in power, while different oppressed groups fight among themselves and emphasize their differences. The affirmation of being different plays right into the divide-and-conquer strategy. It lays the groundwork of true indifference, of profound alienation. Under such circumstances, without hope, without trust, without commonality, nothing is possible.

The function of intellectuals of oppressed groups is complex. One of their chief functions is to create ways to expel the graven images of the oppressor from the souls of their people. This is essential for self-determination. Yet this is not the only duty. Intellectuals must be more farsighted than believing that expulsion of the oppressor's image is their sole goal. To prevent intellectual inertia and intellectual incest from becoming rampant, intellectuals of oppressed groups must seek other ways of knowing. This can greatly benefit the oppressed group. Intellectuals who are strictly "centric" do a disservice to their group.

Being different is not a basis for dialogue. As Freire says, dialogue is the movement toward the continued humanization of others. It would be a wonderful trick indeed to humanize others by ignoring them. The continued personalization or humanization of others depends on the premise that others are human or persons as I am. Being different stifles dialogue, creating more and more distance between oppressed groups in such a way that they cannot hear one another and view themselves as unrelated to one another.

The pervasive nihilism of our era is not the result of the "death of

God," as existentialists are fond of saying. We can endure the death of God. What we cannot endure is the death of dialogue. Dialogue is based on love, hope, trust, and faith in other people. The death of dialogue means the "death of other people." Our lack of love for them, our lack of faith and trust in them, and hopelessness with respect to creating common ground is to alienate one from the other to such a great extent that we cannot communicate. And without communication, then others dissolve into—to twist a verbalism of our day—virtual unreality.

REFERENCES

DuBois, W. E. B. (1995). *W. E. B. DuBois: A Reader.* New York: Henry Holt and Company.

Ellis, Bret Easton. (1991). *American Psycho.* New York: Vintage Books.

Freire, Paulo. (1970). *Pedagogy of the Oppressed.* Trans. Myra Bergman Ramos. New York: Continuum.

Hegel, G. W. F. (1977). *Phenomenology of Spirit.* Trans. A.V. Miller. Analysis of Text and Foreword by J. N. Findlay. Oxford University Press.

Hoagland, Sarah Lucia. (1992). *Lesbian Ethics: Toward a New Value.* Palo Alto, CA: Institute of Lesbian Studies.

King, Martin Luther, Jr. (1986). "Where Do We Go From Here? From Chaos to Community." In *Testament of Hope,* ed. James M. Washington. San Francisco: Harper.

Roth, Cecil. (1935). *A Short History of the Jewish People.* Oxford: East and West. Quoted in Edward H. Flannery (1985), *The Anguish of the Jews: Twenty-Three Centuries of Antisemitism.* Revised and updated edition. New York and Mahwah: Paulist Press.

CHAPTER 7

Politics of Explanation
Ethical Questions in the Production of Knowledge

THOMAS HEANEY

> *Intellectuals are no longer needed by the*
> *masses to gain knowledge: the masses know*
> *perfectly well, without illusion; they know far*
> *better than the intellectual and they are cer-*
> *tainly capable of expressing themselves. But*
> *there exists a system of power which blocks,*
> *prohibits, and invalidates this discourse and*
> *this knowledge, a power not only found in mani-*
> *fest authority of censorship, but one that pro-*
> *foundly and subtly penetrates an entire societal*
> *network. Intellectuals are themselves agents of*
> *this system of power: the idea of their responsi-*
> *bility for "consciousness" and discourse forms*
> *part of the system.*
>
> —MICHEL FOUCAULT, 1977, P. 207

In "The Brave Little Tailor," the Brothers Grimm told of a mild-mannered man of unassuming build and intellect. It seems that one day his shop was beset with flies, and in his frenzied attack on the situation, as chance would have it, he destroyed several of the insidious insects with one blow. As anyone who has attempted to maim or kill the pesky beast knows, it is difficult to overcome one, much less seven flies. And so it was inevitable that later, as the tailor reflected on the significance of the day's events, he came to realize that this was a rather extraordinary accomplishment, one that stood out in sharp contrast to his humdrum existence and one that certainly ought to be recorded. So he wrote a sign, which he proudly displayed, first in his shop, and finally on a cord hung from his neck. The sign simply stated, "seven with one blow." Henceforth, all that saw the sign trembled in fear; villains, giants, no one could help but be intimidated by the knowledge that this otherwise dwarf of a man was capable of leveling seven with one blow.

This story serves to introduce several important themes in any discussion of the politics of research and explanation. First, it exemplifies a relationship between knowledge and power. Knowledge, formally documented in the proposition "seven with one blow," promoted and sustained the illusion that the tailor was formidable and someone to be feared. Second, it exemplified the role of power in creating explanations and meaning. The significance of the slaughter of seven flies with one stroke of the morning's newspaper was interpreted in a manner most likely to enhance the social status and prestige of the signifier, namely, the perpetrator of the slaughter. This was accomplished, as we will later see, in a manner not unusual in the social sciences: not by falsifying the data, but by ignoring, albeit unwittingly, critical and determining questions that might yield information about the nature of the seven upon whom the fatal blow was inflicted. In fairness to the tailor, he made no attempt to hide the information when asked. Quite simply, and fortunately for the tailor's adventure, he did not encounter any critical questions during his journey. For his "seven with one blow" was an adequate and true proposition, expressing the empowerment he had found within his own modest experience.

The two themes emerging from this story need elaboration: first, the relationship between knowledge and power; and second, the influence exerted by the wielders of power over processes that produce knowledge.

POWER AND KNOWLEDGE

Power and knowledge are "essentially contested concepts" (Sallie, 1955). Such concepts are not only the source of endless debate, but they derive their meaning from assumptions of value and policy. They rest ultimately on what Gouldner (1970) calls "background assumptions," which are composed of sentiments, the conception of reality accented by personal experience. Such assumptions constitute the individual and social grounding of an essentially contested concept. One cannot define concepts such as *power* or *knowledge* without reference to the political position of the person employing them. Political points of view are embedded in definitions and can be revealed through careful conceptual analysis.

Power

Power can be, and frequently is, understood as simply the capacity for action. Many adult educators have taken to using the term *empowerment* in this way, suggesting that their successful clients of schooling have developed the "power" to read or to operate complex machinery. Such powers are better termed *capacities* (or the grating neologism, *competencies*). However, a definition that equates power with ability inadequately explains the social dimensions of power. In the social order, power is an ability to act, which is often exercised by affecting the behavior of others (Craig and Craig, 1979). But even this understanding of power falls short, failing to provide guidelines for distinguishing between the exercise of power and other forms of influence; for example, overwhelming evidence or love that equally affects the behavior of others.

Lukes (1974) has argued that, in the world of social relationships, power is exercised in conflict over goals, decisions, strategies, and position. Power is more than mere capacity, which, when exercised, affects the behavior of others; it is also a capacity exercised at the cost of the other's capacity to act. Our tailor exercised power over his neighbors when he affected them in a manner contrary to their own inclinations to otherwise belittle, rob, or even maim such an obvious mark. Knowledge, represented in the proposition "seven with one blow," became a protective shield for the tailor, thwarting the assaults of brigands and giants. For the tailor, as for us, power was attained when he was victorious over competing interests.

There are three dimensions in this latter view of power. The first emphasizes open and explicit conflict in decision making, wherein power is established by the outcome. Power inheres in the one who, by reason of superior strength, mental acuity, or both, prevails over the opposition. Competitors lock horns; power is to the victor.

But certainly not all power is characterized by force. The exercise of power is like the skill of the surgeon, the knife being best inserted in a person whose mind and senses have been dulled. Power is most effective and most secure when it becomes so much a part of the background that it is unobserved and internalized. In the second dimension of power, its wielders systematically exclude potential competitors from the process of decision making. The public agenda is controlled in order to eliminate from discussion those issues that are potentially threatening to the interests of the powerful. This dimension of power is characterized by "a mobilization of bias" (Bachrach and Baratz, 1970) that causes decisions to appear inevitable and irreversible. Thus, the existence of conflict is obscured. Power is maintained by nondecisions, defined as:

A means by which demands for change in the existing allocation of benefits and privileges in the community can be suffocated before they are voiced, or kept covert; or killed before they gain access to the relevant decision-making arena; or, failing all of these things, maimed or destroyed in the decision implementing stage of the policy process. (Bachrach and Baratz, 1970, p. 44)

The capacity to enforce nondecisions by keeping an issue from ever being raised is a profound, if largely invisible, form of power. In this regard, the role of educators in maintaining and stabilizing dominant forms of power is best described in terms of what is not contained in the curriculum, namely, critical questions excluded frequently in the name of maintaining a neutral posture. Nonknowledge and limited access to critical questions are a prior condition of nondecisions. The control and manipulation of knowledge, as well as the resulting mobilization of bias, represents a more economical and far-reaching exercise of power than reliance on overt force or the direct imposition of will.

While the second dimension of power weakens opposition by withholding critical knowledge, the third and ultimate dimension of power eliminates opposition by the imposition of a false consciousness. Here the wielder of power "influences, shapes, and determines conceptions of the necessities, possibilities, and strategies of challenge in situations of latent conflict" (Gaventa, 1980). Such mind control need not conjure up images of *1984* and *Walden Two*. The mechanisms of this dimension of power simply involve the inverse of information control. Images propagated by mass media and education not only exclude understandings and meanings that have a high risk of unmasking conflict (as in the second dimension of power), but also include explanations that negatively affect self-concepts and expectations regarding "realistic" modes of behavior.

Those over whom power is exercised in power's first dimension are losers in a game, the rules of which, although frequently unfair, are nonetheless openly proclaimed. In the second dimension of power, the rules are hidden from view so that the losers frequently are unaware they have been victims in a rigged competition. Paulo Freire, in his analysis of the dynamics of power, reserves the term *oppressed* for those who are silenced by power's third dimension. The oppressed speak with a voice that is not their own (Freire, 1970, p. 34). Their very consciousness is the product of constant conditioning and a well-integrated fantasy created in the interests and images of the powerful. The oppressed are not only powerless but reconciled to their powerlessness, perceiving it fatalistically, as a consequence of personal inadequacy or failure.

This reconciliation to powerlessness inhibits self-determining action and fosters increased dependency. Dependency further precludes the development of a positive and self-affirming consciousness and thus lends to the dominant order an air of legitimacy. The ultimate product of highly unequal power relationships is a class unable to articulate its own interests or perceive the existence of social conflict. Speaking of such a class, Mueller notes, "they have been socialized into compliance, so to speak, they accept the definitions of political reality as offered by dominant groups, classes or government institutions" (1973, p. 9).

Knowledge

In all of this, the principal instrument for the establishment and protection of power in its second and third dimensions is the control of knowledge. Thus is knowledge linked to power. Although knowledge is naively thought to encompass direct and practical reflections of the world, nonetheless it comprises interpretations and explanations of experience that are shaped by social institutions, the media, and formal education by instruments of hegemony controlled directly or indirectly by the interests of power. Knowledge is understood here as more than the mere comprehension of reality-reducing experience to an unrelated sequence of "facts," but rather as the ordering of our experiences into a significant and meaningful whole. Such knowledge is about the world, not of the world. Knowledge about the world is constituted by the attempt to explain the logic of experience and is not reducible to experience itself. Knowledge of the world, on the other hand, is unreflective, immediate, and often unarticulated.

It is not primarily in its ordering of experience that knowledge about the world derives its importance for power, but in the significance it attributes to that ordering. The detective is empowered, not by establishing possible motives for the butler and that the butler was alone with the victim only minutes before the murder occurred, but by an interpretation of those elements based on an assumption that the murderer had both reason and occasion for committing the deed. Experience is essential to knowledge, but it is the interpretation and manipulation of experience that constitutes knowledge about the world. To know is to make sense of experience.

The discipline of "making sense" has, since Heidegger, been known as *hermeneutics,* an interpretive method based on processes employed in everyday life. All understanding is guided by hermeneutics, determined in part by our finite existence in time, history, and culture (Reason and Rowan, 1981). It is one of the canons of this activity that all interpretations are created to show the meaning of phenomena for the interpreter's own situation. "No one is really interested in understanding something that is totally irrelevant for himself [sic] and for the society in which he lives" (Kockelmans, 1975). We are interested in those things that excite us because of our political commitments, because of our personal history, because of our vested interest in status, love, and security. Knowledge, infused as it is with our quiet and not so quiet passions and commitments, offers one of our best hopes for a humane social reconstruction. But, as Gouldner points out, its strength is also its weakness. Knowledge is also historically shaped by forces that embody limits and pathologies (1979, p. 5).

RESEARCH: WHERE KNOWLEDGE MEETS POWER

While researchers have traditionally aspired to disinterestedness in their quest for knowledge, knowledge in which no one is interested is unlikely to be remembered, much less published. Interests are frequently hidden and difficult to determine. Economic, political, and social systems ascribe "interests" to participants in those systems in ways that are subtle and, at times, clandestine. Interests of a group are, for example, easily confused with the interests of those who hold power within the group (Davidson, 1995). Workers, for example, are assumed to need skills and knowledge that, in actuality, represent the corporate interests of management.

Major industries have grown for the specific purpose of creating and defining "wants," advertising and educational systems among them. Such interests and "needs," to the extent they are destructive to self or environment, can hardly be held to represent genuine interests. They represent rather the corporate and institutional interests of big business and the growing professional classes. The "disinterestedness" of traditional research represents such a systemic interest nurtured and sustained by academics in order to maintain a position of privilege and to protect their monopoly over the production and legitimation of knowledge.

Reason and Rowan have concluded that "what people put forward as the truth is always related in some very powerful way to what they want to be true" (1981, p. 136). The challenge is to determine how "what we want to be true" and the ideals and values upon which that "want" is based are socially determined. What instruments of power mold and shape our desires, our expectations, and our vision? Since it is by virtue of these wants that we grant the attribute of "true" to certain propositions and "false" to others, how is it that these criteria for the validation of knowledge come to be shared? How are "judges of truth" selected, and what are the mechanisms for the social determination of legitimate knowledge? Michel Foucault addresses these questions. For him, "truth" is a system of ordered procedures for the production, regulation, and distribution of statements or "discourses." In his 1970 lecture on "The Order of Discourse," he shows how rules for the formation of knowledge are linked to the operation of power. Discourses not only exhibit internal principles of logic and order, but are bound by regulations enforced through social practices, which include employment and tenure, juried selection of articles and papers, and invitations to join panels of late-night talk shows.

> Truth isn't outside power, or lacking in power: contrary to a myth whose history and functions would repay further study, truth isn't the reward of free spirits, the child of protracted solitude, nor the privilege of those who have succeeded in liberating themselves. Truth is a thing of this world: it is produced only by virtue of multiple forms of constraint. And it induces regular effects of power. Each society has its régime of truth, its "general politics" of truth: that is, the types of discourse which it accepts and makes function as true: the mechanisms and instances which enable one to distinguish true and false statements, the means by which each is sanctioned, the techniques and procedures accorded value in the acquisition of truth, the status of those who are charged with saying what counts as true. (Foucault, 1980, p. 131)

Thus, truth is linked in circular fashion with the system of power that sustains it and to the effects of power that it induces. It is this reciprocal causal interaction that Foucault calls a "régime of truth." Knowledge is constituted by power either by exclusion or by inclusion. On the one hand, exclusion occurs through invalidation in which the conceptual framework of a dominant ideology is used to attack and exclude deviant forms of discourse. On the other hand, exclusion also occurs by inattention when counterdiscourses are simply not seen or are beyond the purview of "mainstream" thought.

Inclusion, however, is a far more complex phenomenon. It occurs whenever political assumptions—that is, assumptions about social relations of power—are embedded in the very fabric of discourse. As embedded concepts, these assumptions appear to be neutral, but they nonetheless function to buttress and support dominant forms of power.

Exclusion

The exclusion of discourse that deviates from institutional interests is the point and counterpoint by which knowledge is produced. An example from the field of adult education is found in the "deschooling" controversy that grew out of discussions at the Center for International Documentation. Illich (1970) challenged prevalent thinking concerning the foundations of modern educational systems and the history of schooling. His discourse was built on a framework that combined a personalist psychology with critical theory and analysis. Despite the fact that this discourse was built on concepts central to the theoretical and practical posture of adult educators, the voluntary nature of learning and self-direction, the discourse itself was almost totally neglected in the body of knowledge included in the curriculum of graduate study in adult education. Although the conflict has been acknowledged occasionally in foundations studies (Elias and Merriam, 1980), it is the implied purpose of foundations to give emphasis to those frames of reference and modes of discourse upon which dominant forms of practice have been constructed. The structural dominance of schooling models in adult education demands the exclusion (or minimization) of discourse that contravenes this practice.

But how could it be otherwise? How could candidates for advanced degrees that will qualify them for privileges within an adult education bureaucracy be expected to seriously consider a critique of the very foundations upon which their future security is premised? And how could professors of adult education (or professors in any field of study, for that matter) retain their psychic equilibrium while struggling to establish their peership with university faculties and simultaneously entertain forms of discourse that demystify and devalue the structures and purpose of the university?

Inclusion

More difficult to perceive is the inclusion of concepts and forms of discourse that positively reinforce and even constitute relations of power. What is needed is methodical clarification of levels of meaning that surround key concepts in a mode of discourse, deriving clues from both the context in which the concepts are expressed and the operational applications of the concepts in day-to-day life. Both Foucault (1965) and Thomas Szasz (1970) provided early examples of this form of analysis in their studies of the concept of "madness," *Madness and Civilization* and *Ideology and Insanity,* respectively. The central theme of these independent studies is that madness does not signify a "reality," but rather posits an interpretation of social deviance. It has proven economically and politically advantageous to incarcerate those who resist patterns of behavior imposed by the state and reinforced by "common sense" under the guise of treatment, rather than to subject them to more overt forms of punishment. Thus, a new theoretical discourse in the form of the "science" of mental health enters the university's curriculum as guardian of social and political practices, a discourse that legitimizes followers of the social order as "sane" and denounces deviants as "mad."

In another example, more specifically related to adult education, considerable attention has been given to the concept of "need." Of special note is the work of Marie Rolland-Barker (1982), whose analysis of Lindeman, Bergevin, and Knowles enabled her to elaborate a conceptual framework in which usually embedded political and ethical questions were brought to the surface. Who determines need? How are needs influenced or induced as "felt need"? To what extent is "need" a historical construct used to legitimize the imposition of bureaucratic services? Is it not true that adult educators need illiterates, in whose service they find gainful employment, more than illiterates need them? More recently, Collins (1991) has taken up this theme:

> Even though true needs cannot be identified by merely asking people what they want, it is not the role of adult educators to make the actual distinctions on behalf of others. Rather, their task is to organize pedagogical situations where it becomes possible to understand more clearly how needs are constituted, whose interests are served, and in what ways they emerge in the context of everyday lives. (p. 68)

A second example from the field of adult education is found in Kenneth Levine's analysis of functional literacy (1982). "Functional literacy," currently used to justify a variety of workplace and job-related programs, is insidiously ambiguous, while at the same time promoting a comfortable but illusory consensus about the effects of literacy both for learners and society. Levine notes that the value ascribed to literacy is historically and culturally conditioned. In a hierarchy based on merit, the "competencies" included in the notion of functional literacy are constantly in flux. Wide possession of a particular literacy will devalue it. The concept of functional literacy is thus placed beyond the reach of any strictly empirical operationalizing procedure.

The theory of functional literacy ignores what Hirsch calls the "positional economy" (1977), that is, goods, services, or social relationships whose high value is based on scarcity. Once some people stand on tiptoe in order to get a better view, others will be forced to do the same, each person ending up in his or her original relative position. Functional literacy trades on the prior existence of concealed assumptions about the nature and functions of literacy in society, which, in turn, are related to prevalent notions of citizen rights and the good life, both of which are politically structured to maintain both the privileged position of the already literate and the relatively "underprivileged" position of the newly literate.

These examples provide an observable set of political and historical relations between concepts, madness, need, functional literacy, on the one hand, and social institutions and the relations of power, on the other. The effectiveness and stability of power rests on the installation of a commonly agreed upon font of "truth," a "common sense," that supports the status quo. Knowledge, primarily a product of universities and other state-sanctioned institutions, becomes an expression of pervasive and dominant relations of power in society.

EXPLAINING EXPERIENCE IN THE FACE OF POWER

The crisis facing world economic and political systems demands an almost constant rethinking of explanations of experience. The old ways of making sense no longer work, and we are increasingly challenged to devise new ones. A liberal promise of full employment now yields to enthusiasm for a hoped for, single-digit margin of joblessness. Immigrant labor, once essential to the high profits of agribusiness, now is used to explain reductions in real income and to support new restrictions on immigration and the demand for "English only." Workers now learn to blame themselves for being "less productive" than their counterparts in Japan and Germany, thus justifying union "give backs" and massive reductions in the workforce.

All of this requires the collective energies of persons and institutions responsible for the production and dissemination of knowledge. Foucault has written, "A wide range of professionals (teachers, psychiatrists, educators of all kinds, etc.) will be called upon to exercise functions that have traditionally belonged to the police" (1977, p. 212). Political ideology has assumed greater importance in reviewing political rhetoric, whether in the stump speeches of presidential candidates or in Newt Gingrich's "Contract with America." Controls on learning resources, access to information, travel to disfavored countries, and so forth forestall the development of explanations that counter dominant discourse.

As soft repression becomes harder, it is useful to look to the not-so-distant historical lessons of countries where the interests of power are unscrupulously enforced. In El Salvador, the university was simply closed so that only the rich, who could afford to send their children out of the country, could provide for a college education. In Guatemala, progressive faculty members were commonly shot in the streets, to be replaced in their classrooms with military personnel. In Bolivia, close to three hundred professors were executed, representing a monumental loss of resources to so small a country. It is, perhaps, surprising in the context of U.S. campuses in the 1990s to find academics taken so seriously.

Outside of dictatorships and military juntas, the role of academics is less overt, less the object of constant surveillance. On the third level of power, the politics of officially sanctioned knowledge is always a matter of compromise. Michael Apple (1993), speaking of compromise, notes:

> These, of course, are not compromises between or among equals. Those in dominance almost always have more power to define what counts as a need or a problem and what an appropriate response to it should be. But these compromises are never stable. They almost always leave or create space for more democratic action. (p. 10)

Given this situation, what are we as researchers and teachers to do? Having seen the relationship between knowledge and power, we cannot naively assume to free ourselves and the knowledge we produce from political influence or consequences. Power is always a contextual element in our efforts to explain the world; the subtle, lifelong influence of our privilege as academics is easy to ignore and enters into our explanations through the reciprocal spiral of exclusion and inclusion. So where do we begin?

Research is grounded in autobiography, even if unacknowledged. Research, the systematic and rigorous examination of experience, begins with the systematic and rigorous examination of the political and social commitments of the researcher. For whom do we work? Whose interests are best served by our explanations of the world? What questions do we include, and what questions do we exclude, in order to focus on those interests? These are complex questions, as we have seen, requiring many layers of analysis as we move from the superficial to the infrastructural, the subtheoretical level of domain assumptions and sentiments, both of which liberate and constrain our thought. Without autobiographical self-reflection, the knowledge we produce is likely to be shaped and manipulated by interests we neither comprehend nor control.

But to know ourselves is not to change our behavior. Our reflections might leave us conscious, as well as conscientious servants of a world order that provides us with sufficient income, privilege, and security. Professors and students alike might continue to ignore the political implications of their research, no longer because of adherence to academic "neutrality" or a homogenistic notion of "truth," but rather because of the decision to avoid conflict with those who provide salaries, grades, or status. At issue is an ethical question that each researcher must address: not whether to serve political interests, but which political, economic, and class interests to serve. The question brings to consciousness a possible choice between narrow self-interest and the interests of those without position, reputation, status, or privilege. Freire calls this possible fragmentation of self "class suicide" (1978).

But for those of us who are not suicidal, but nonetheless see our solipsistic preoccupation with greater and greater clarity about less and less, as nothing more than the insulation of existing practices from the onslaught of critical questions, what then are we to do? Given the pervasive interlocking of power and explanation, we do not ask how do we free knowledge from the influence of power, but rather how do we, in collaboration with others, democratically participate in the creation of informed, reflective, and knowledgeable power. In addressing such a question, the task of research would be to engage in shared discourse through the exercise of shared power. This has been the underlying dynamism of Freire's pedagogy in developing nations: inquiry linked to political struggle and immediate gains through social reconstruction is highly productive of shared discourse, new knowledge, and literacy, seen not as technical mastery over words, but as attaining a voice.

There are at least three tasks to which time and energy might be directed. First, further development of meta-research, on research, is essential as a means of subjecting methodologies and the politics embedded within them to greater scrutiny. Second, researchers should expand their understanding (and occupation) of "open spaces" in which the alienating interests of power are not viewed as dominant spaces that contradict one another within institutions and systems supporting the production of knowledge. Finally, divesting themselves of professional pretensions, researchers should encourage the further development of participatory forms of research that involve those without power who have usually been merely the objects of inquiry.

Research on Research

Research on research brings us into contact with the processes by which we explain our experiences and create meaning. Just as objects that are too small or too far distant require instruments to be seen, so do complex questions require tools in order to be addressed. Tools not only sharpen focus, they also distort, give false emphasis to insignificant detail, and force interpretations. Tools are limiting as well as empowering. At times, the sharp focus itself might block our vision. Clarity, as Gouldner points out, sometimes depends on poor rather than good vision, blurring complex details in order to better see the main structure (1979, p. 8).

Tools are also limiting in another way. It has been noted that we shape our tools and, thereafter, our tools shape us. The framework within which we operationalize our research limits the questions that we can reasonably ask. As the psychologist Abraham Maslow noted, "If our only tool is a hammer, every problem looks like nails." If our only tool for research is mathematical manipulation, then our "meaningful" experiences will be reduced to those that can be measured. The results might be statistically significant, but politically (and humanly) insignificant; the choice as to whether to be deeply interesting or accurately boring be comes a function of our tools.

The task of meta-research should ultimately be about expanding the tools at our disposal, knowing the limits and biases of each, drawing on multiple paradigms and disciplines, to achieve binocular vision and thus to gain perspective. The bureaucratic organization of knowledge by discipline separates research according to specialized and discrete tools that are possessively clung to by scholars. Exclusive ownership of these tools brings privileges that scholars seek to protect, much as carpenters and electricians seek to protect their privileges through closed union shops.

Disciplines are frequently defined according to the methods employed in their attempt to explain the world. Crossing the barrier of a discipline can result in cynical rejection by peers on both sides of the barrier. A strategic compromise is the establishment of interdisciplinary alliances that bring together researchers from many fields to pursue common inquiries.

Occupying Open Spaces

The potential for such an alliance derives from contradictions within the social organization of the university. Academic departments of education, grounded in a psychological paradigm, have fine-tuned research tools for the detailed measurement of educational systems and learning within those systems, but within the limits of that paradigm have failed to produce compelling theories of learning outside the guided mediation of schooling. Even Alan Tough (1971), in his study of "independent" adult learning projects, was forced to operationalize his definition of learning as a form of do-it-yourself schooling. This is not to say that there is not readily at hand tools to deal with more transcendent and critical questions about learning and society. An increasing number of adult education researchers have dealt with these questions, and in doing so have moved outside the narrower confines of educational discourse and found open spaces sustained by alternative paradigms for the production of knowledge.

Open spaces for educational research have been created by critical theory (Hart, 1992; Apple, 1993; Mezirow, 1994; Welton, 1995), revisionist history (Schied, 1993), phenomenology (Collins, 1991; Stanage, 1987), ethnography (Thomas, 1993), and other cross-disciplinary approaches, each providing a frame of reference that places the researcher, her commitments and allegiances, in full view. Such frames, legitimized within academic disciplines, nonetheless provide open space for the juxtaposition and combination of disciplines, which allows for diverse and, at times, divergent points of view. This binocular (or multiocular) vision leads to shared discourse across barriers and outside the limits of our respective fields.

Participatory Research

Shared discourse is the result of a shared process of inquiry. Explanation of human phenomena, the assumed focus of educational research, needs to be grounded in the experiences of those it purports to explain, to involve a collaboration if not a blurring of the distinction between the researcher and the subject of research. The "truth" of our discourse is less a function of the relationship between our propositions and the world than it is a function of the relationship between and among knowers. That is, our constructs find their validity intersubjectively, when they transcend the knowledge of a single knower.

Fact, empirically grounded in experience, measurable, and replicable by many researchers, is not the goal of research. The fundamental and ultimate concern of research is explanatory knowledge about the world, which makes sense of experience and is never simply reducible to statements of "fact." Influences of power and political context are always present, even when not objects of attention. The significance of new knowledge, the meaningfulness of our research, rests on the thoroughness with which we have understood the intersubjective and political context of our discourse. The art of explaining is dialogical. It moves in propositional form through one frame of reference to another, from knower to knower, being modified, amended, revised, abridged, contradicted, focused, and broadened in cross-disciplinary reinterpretation. It is heterogenistic, yielding many "truths."

The professional vested interest of academic researchers counters: some participants in this dialogue are better qualified to determine the truth of the matter, have mastery of more sophisticated tools of analysis, and bring to bear a far greater wealth of background resources. Clearly, making sense of the world is too important a task to be left in the hands of amateurs.

Judgments about better qualifications, more sophisticated tools, and greater resources are judgments of value, which are, in part, assertions of power and privilege. To the extent that tools and resources have value, they are valued by all, perhaps even more by those who do not possess them. To the extent they are the accoutrements of political position and privilege, they will require institutions and sanctions to preserve their alleged value. Community activists might not ask researchers for an original copy of their credentials, but they respect any person's ability to comprehend and explain complex matters relating to the issues of power and human rights with which they struggle.

Antonio Gramsci (1971) observed that intellectuality has been traditionally identified with an academic elite whose political attachments to their historic class are barely concealed. Nonetheless, intellectuality is an attribute of all. The fact that it is identified with an elite is merely an expression of powerful class interests that limit access to the university and the means by which intellectuality is legitimized. There is another manifestation of intellectuality that emerges among the thinking and organizing elements of every social class that Gramsci calls the "organic intellectual," whose work it is to develop knowledge specifically related to the exercise of power within that class (pp. 5–7). Such intellectuals play an essential role in social movements for democratic change.

Adult education in the United States has in its historic origins an inexorable link with movements for social change. From the exhortations of Edward Lindeman (1989) at the birth of adult education as a field of study to the remarkable achievements of the Highlander Center in Tennessee (Horton and Freire, 1990), adult education has as a central theme the building of democracy through ongoing reflection and action. Consistent with this theme has been the development of "participatory research" as a concept that embraced the role of common people, whom Myles Horton called the "uncommon common people," in the production of knowledge. This approach to research identifies adult learning not as assimilation of the explanations of others, an emphasis found within school-based education, but rather as the production of meaning and knowledge. Adult education is research (Hall, 1977; Parks et al., 1993).

Adult education contains within its own pedagogical forms and social purposes the framework for redefining research in the face of power. To the extent that issues of power are articulated in situations wherein power holds dominion and by those who are held in its grasp, to that extent can explanations and meanings be developed that inform strategies for change. The aim of adult education for Lindeman (or of participatory research for Hall) is not to inform minds, but to transform society. It is this vision of researcher as educator that allows us to move beyond knowledge of the world to an informed reconstruction of the social order.

REFERENCES

Apple, M. W. (1993). *Official Knowledge: Democratic Education in a Conservative Age.* New York: Routledge.

Bachrach, P., and Baratz, M. S. (1970). *Power and Poverty: Theory and Practice.* New York: Oxford University Press.

Collins, M. (1991). *Adult Education as Vocation: A Critical Role for the Adult Educator.* New York: Routledge.

Craig, J. H., and Craig, M. (1979). *Synergic Power.* Berkeley, CA: Proactive Press.

Davidson, H. (1995). "Making Needs: Toward a Historical Sociology of Needs in Adult and Continuing Education," in *Adult Education Quarterly,* 45:4, 183–196.

Elias, J. L., and Merriam, S. (1980). *Philosophical Foundations of Adult Education.* Huntington, NY: Robert K. Krieger Publishing.

Foucault, M. (1965). *Madness and Civilization: A History of Insanity in the Age of Reason.* New York: Vintage Books.

Foucault, M. (1977). *Language, Counter-Memory, Practice.* Ithaca, NY: Cornell University Press.

Foucault, M. (1980). *Power/Knowledge.* New York: Pantheon Books.

Freire, P. (1970). *Pedagogy of the Oppressed.* New York: Seabury Press.

Freire, P. (1978). *Pedagogy in Process: The Letters to Guinea-Bissau.* New York: Seabury Press.

Gaventa, J. (1980). *Power and Powerlessness: Quiescence and Rebellion in an Appalachian Valley.* Urbana: University of Illinois Press.

Gouldner, A. W. (1970). *The Coming Crisis of Western Sociology.* New York: Basic Books.

Gouldner, A. W. (1979). *The Future of Intellectuals and the Rise of the New Class.* New York: Seabury Press.

Gramsci, A. (1971). *Selections from the Prison Notebooks.* London: Lawrence and Wishart.

Hall, B. L. (1977). "Creating Knowledge: Breaking the Monopoly," Working Paper No. 1. Toronto: International Council for Adult Education.

Hart, M. (1992). *Working and Educating for Life: Feminist and International Perspectives on Adult Education.* New York: Routledge.

Horton, M., and Freire, P. (1990). *We Make the Road by Walking: Conversations on Education and Social Change.* Philadelphia: Temple University Press.

Illich, I. (1970). *Deschooling Society.* New York: Harper & Row.

Kockelmans, J. (1975). "Toward an Interpretation or Hermeneutic Social Science," in *Graduate Faculty Philosophy Journal,* 5:1.

Lindeman, E. (1989). *The Meaning of Adult Education.* Norman: University of Oklahoma.

Lukes, S. (1974). *Power: A Radical View.* London: Macmillan Press.

Mezirow, J. (1994). "Understanding Transformation Theory," in *Adult Education Quarterly,* 44:4, 222–244.

Mueller, C. (1973). *The Politics of Communication: A Study in the Political Sociology of Language, Socialization and Legitimation.* New York: Oxford University Press.

Parks, P., Brydon-Miller, M., Hall, B., and Jackson, T. (eds.). (1993). *Voices of Change: Participatory Research in the United States and Canada.* Westport, CT: Bergin & Garvey.

Reason, P., and Rowan, J. (eds.). (1981). *Human Inquiry: A Sourcebook of New Paradigm Research.* New York: Wiley.

Rolland-Baker, M. (1982). "A Conceptual Analysis of the Notion of Need in Adult Education." *Proceedings of the Twenty-third Adult Education Research Conference.* Lincoln: University of Nebraska Press.

Sallie, W. B. (1955–1956). "Essentially Contested Concepts," in *Proceedings of the Aristotelian Society, 56,* 167–198.

Schied, F. M. (1993). *Learning in Social Context: Workers and Adult Education in Nineteenth-Century Chicago.* DeKalb, IL: LEPS Press.

Stanage, S. (1987). *Adult Education and Phenomenological Research.* Malabar, FL: Kreiger Publishing.

Szasz, T. (1970). *Ideology and Insanity: Essays on the Psychiatric Dehumanization of Man.* New York: Doubleday.

Thomas, J. (1993). *Doing Critical Ethnography.* Newbury Park, CA: Sage Publications.

Tough, A. (1971). *The Adult's Learning Projects.* Toronto: Ontario Institute for Studies in Education.

Welton, M. (ed.). (1995). *In Defense of the Lifeworld: Critical Perspectives on Adult Education.* New York: SUNY Press.

CHAPTER 8

Upstream in the Mainstream
Pedagogy Against the Current

ROBERT E. BAHRUTH AND STANLEY F. STEINER

I must recognize that students cannot under-
stand their own rights because they are so ide-
ologized into rejecting their own freedom, their
own critical development, thanks to the tradi-
tional curriculum. Then, I have to learn with
them how to go beyond these limits, beyond
their own learned rejection of their rights.
—PAULO FREIRE (SHOR & FREIRE, 1987, P. 107)

INTRODUCTION

"Just tell me what I need to know to get an A," a familiar phrase often
heard from incoming college students resultant from years of schooling
in our public school system. As critical pedagogues, we often inherit
such students who have been conditioned into a teacher-centered model
of discourse. Students have learned to respond to the expectations of the
teacher: parroting, memorizing, and regurgitating from a series of facts
and official bodies of knowledge promoted by the mainstream canon.
The resulting "stupidification" (Macedo, 1994) demands a counterhegemonic pedagogy.

In this chapter, we will problematize student nonengagement in response to counterhegemonic pedagogical praxis. According to Leistyna
(1996), praxis is "the relationship between theoretical understanding and
critique of society . . . and action that seeks to transform individuals and
their environment" (p. 342). In order to problematize nonengagement,

This chapter was originally published in Rudolfo Chávez Chávez and James
O'Donnell (Eds.), *Speaking the Unpleasant: The Politics of (non)Engagement in
the Multicultural Education Terrain* (SUNY Press, 1998). Permission obtained.

119

we also provide our understanding of nonengagement in relation to resistance, a description of our praxis, and organic examples to contextualize the evolving willingness to engage on the part of our students in response to our efforts. Over the years it has become more and more apparent to us that learning requires engagement on the part of the learners (Smith, 1981). Gadotti further states:

> All pedagogy refers to practice and intends to be put into practice. It makes no sense without practice, as it is the science of education. To act pedagogically is to put theory into practice *par excellence*. It is to discover and elaborate instruments of social action. In doing so, one becomes aware of the essential unity between theory and practice. Pedagogy, as the theory of education, cannot abstract itself from the intended practice. Pedagogy is, above all, a theory of praxis. In pedagogy, the practice is the horizon, the aim of the theory. Therefore, the educationalist lives the instigating dialect between his or her daily life—the *lived school* and the *projected school*—which attempts to inspire a new school. (p. 7)

To engender student engagement, in which students are involving their very beings and human conditions in the meaning-making of academic subjects, one must recognize that learner backgrounds and life experiences, including their academic experiences, are the only tools they have in order to engage in current learning. Prepackaged lectures and curriculum or test-driven instruction tend to be oblivious to student-based meaning-making and propelled by an applied scientific notion that learners are "identical empty vessels which, if filled with the same substance, would yield the same, replicable results" (Ada, 1990, p. ix). The basic assumption here, that students are identical empty vessels, is not only erroneous, but punitive to students who have nonmainstream experiences and backgrounds. Even the metaphors or stories teachers use to present lessons are clearly biased toward learners from dominant cultural backgrounds. For us, this inspired an effort to provide our students with a university experience that would prepare them for the pluralistic classrooms that they would be encountering as teachers.

As teacher educators, we began by recognizing the shortcomings of our efforts within more traditional approaches to pre-service and in-service preparation in which school reform efforts have been consistently superficial and cosmetic at best, without the deep structural changes necessary to produce true restructuring. Although the pedestrian perception exists of college as a place where professors are concerned with and students are challenged to explore new ideas, dialogue of a high intellectual ante is rare in most classrooms, and the transmission model of passivity among students prevails (Boyer, 1987; Fox, 1993; Steiner & Bahruth, 1994). Technicist approaches have led to the deskilling of teachers (Beyer & Apple, 1988), and the call for the intellectualization of the profession (Giroux, 1988, 1996) requires that we stop insulting the intelligence of teachers while we begin to forge a pedagogy based on their organic experiences with education. The need to deconstruct monolithic educational practices must be accompanied by pedagogical recommendations anchored in the experiences of educators who have been willing to experiment with research-based pedagogical shifts, in which engagement becomes the critical focus (Giroux & McLaren, 1986; Giroux, 1996).

Alternatives need to be made clear for present and future educators, along with respective ramifications. As teachers we can flow with the mainstream and subsequently reproduce hegemony, or we can question the status quo and problematize the system that has continually failed in its stated intentions of promoting a democratic society, and thereby take steps toward transforming society through teachers as cultural workers. Taking the path of critical pedagogy requires a philosophical shift. The teacher is no longer the only knowledge base. Nor is the current knowledge base sufficient for teaching. Teacher-scholars would have to explore and understand social, political, and historical contexts of hegemony (Chomsky, 1995) to be effective in counterhegemonic pedagogy (Giroux, 1983). Teachers are no longer the dominant voice in the classroom. Students are asked to become active learners, critical thinkers, nonpassive, and their voices are respected as constructive contributors. We collectively work to become a community of learners.

In an effort to build such a community, Shor (1990) purports that the initial challenge of the critical educator is to deconstruct authoritarian modes of discourse in traditional classrooms and to establish a democratic "culture circle" (Brown, 1978) in which students' lived experiences are invited and encouraged in the construction of meaning. "A progressive position requires democratic practice where authority never becomes authoritarianism, and where authority is never so reduced that it disappears in a climate of irresponsibility and license" (Freire, 1987, p. 212). Although there is no simplistic formula for generating a pedagogical space that turns on a culture circle, it is clear that understanding

Freire's praxis, coupled with experience and reflection, has provided us with evolving criticity as practioners.

AN EVOLVING SENSE OF CULTURE CIRCLES

Robert first read about culture circles in a 1978 publication by Cynthia Brown entitled, *Literacy in 30 Hours: Paulo Freire's Process in North East Brazil.* Freire's work was unknown to him at the time; it was the notion of teaching literacy in thirty hours that captured his attention. The process described in the book seemed incredibly natural, and the eloquence and humility of the pedagogy was astounding. It has since taken more than ten years of scholarship to comprehend the subtleties of reading the word *world* (an effort deemed worthwhile and driven by a gnawing discontent with traditional approaches to literacy and learning). Of course, our transformation as educators is ongoing *(Caminante no hay camino, el camino se hace al andar . . .)*. Two major pieces that consolidated Freire's pedagogy for Robert came in the dialogues between Ira Shor and Freire (1987) and between Freire and Macedo (1987). Most empowering was the way in which Freire expanded the notion of literacy to include reading the world and writing the world as cultural agents and subjects rather than as objects of history, thus becoming a basis for establishing a culture circle as a pedagogical space.

Orchestrating a culture circle is intellectually demanding and requires constant reflection and criticity of one's own pedagogy. The physical space is rearranged in an attempt to provide pedagogical spaces in which students can develop their voices in a human environment of respect and affirmation. Arranging students in a circle is a pedagogical move whereby the physical environment of the classroom is transformed from the straight row, front-facing arrangements found in traditional classrooms. The change in physical arrangements provides the opportunity for a change in the human environment in the classroom as well; however, other changes must accompany this rearrangement if a culture circle is to evolve. The eye contact among the learners is important, and just the shift can capture the curiosity and imagination of students. To complete the shift the teacher must also consider a change in discourse patterns and views of authority, knowledge, curriculum, and learning. What is apparent is that a culture circle does not evolve simply by having students sit in a circle.

Our challenge is to provide a focus without dismissing the voices of participants in the dialogue. Teachers must recognize both conscious and unconscious attempts to derail the discourse. The focus is often maintained by asking follow-up questions. We are not attempting to lead all students to a singular destination other than the evolution of their own criticity. Knowing absolutely where a circle is headed would be antithetical to critical pedagogy and would exclude the teacher as a participant-learner in the circle. It would also be acritical in that it would reify the teacher as authoritative representative of an immutable, static body of knowledge (hooks, 1994), so we may as well have remained seated at the desk in the front of the rows! Further, we would be presenting ourselves as though we have arrived, when we wish to demonstrate the importance of maintaining a disposition toward lifelong learning.

The teacher's charge is to oversee the evolution of a human environment in which all participants, including the teacher, share their wrestlings to make meaning of their development based upon the experiences they bring to the classroom (Freire & Macedo, 1995). Rather than dismissing their life experiences, the teacher recognizes that students can only make new meanings based upon prior understandings anchored in the organic nature of their knowing. The teacher must provide a space in which all views can be voiced freely and safely. Only when all views are heard can we claim that the heterogeneous nature of our culture is most widely represented in the circle. We begin by deconstructing prior school experiences in the mainstream.

To provide this contrast, we reflect upon Hermán García's (1995) account as a Mexican American growing up and receiving a mainstream education as a sobering testimony of having student culture ignored in school. He was consistently asked to give up his "ethnic survival kit" (Trueba, 1991); a disregard of first language and cultural diversity, placement in a more technical track because of generalized intellectual abilities of minorities, low expectations that diminished any hope of higher education, too few minority teachers, and an absence of formally educated role models among the impoverished are all acts of academic oppression (Chávez-Chávez, Belkin, Hornback, & Adams, 1991).

Rudolfo Anaya (1995), another victim of mainstream education, conceptualized the effects on any students with the slightest bit of diversity: "As a lifelong educator, I have argued for years that education must take into account the culture of the individual child. No one can develop his full potential in an uncomfortable environment; one only learns to escape from an uncomfortable environment as quickly as possible" (p. 400). Critical pedagogues realize the importance of student voice and consciously work to provide the pedagogical spaces for mutual appreciation and understanding to develop. In contrast to male-dominated, teacher-filtered discourse, the majority of students require time and guidance to find their voices and grow into a community of learners. The transition toward building such a democratic classroom presents challenges for the critical pedagogue. Students accustomed to the "flattering pedagogy" (Morton, 1992) of mainstream education may initially respond through nonengagement to critical pedagogy. They may get frustrated in their search for the "right answer." Students have been disabled by traditional, teacher-curriculum-centered pedagogy that has misled them into believing in the myth of "authoritative right answers." Marie Montessori's (1964) notion of flexibility of thought is a feature of the dialogue that often transpires in culture circles when all voices are heard and considered. Students eventually discover that there are no simplistic, monolithic solutions to the struggle for a democratic society and that democracy lies within the ongoing dialogue, the struggle itself, ever in progress. Democracy is not achieved by *naming* itself so, any more than all rhetorically labeled educational programs are *valid* and *pedagogically sound.* To clarify, we find it necessary to delineate our current understanding of the ways students respond to differing pedagogical settings.

RESISTANCE, NONENGAGEMENT, AND ENGAGEMENT

It seems that the terms *resistance* and *nonengagement* can be used to describe two different populations of students and their ways of responding to two different pedagogical paradigms. They seem to be in complementary distribution. Nonengagement differs from resistance in the sense that students who resist traditional schooling are responding to pedagogical practices that are politically biased against them for the very ways in which they are different. *Resistance,* then, becomes the critical term that replaces discipline in that it forces the interrogation of pedagogical practices rather than placing the blame on the victim while leaving the pedagogy unchallenged, as the term *discipline* does.

Nonengagement differs from resistance in that it refers to student response to critical pedagogy and cultural studies in which the pedagogy is not giving them cause to resist but inviting them to discover their own voices. Student nonengagement is most often the conscious or unconscious rejection by learners from the dominant culture to discovering their own voices, to critical thinking, and to the subjectification of their learning experience. It is easy to appear successful in a system that emphasizes memorization and test-taking abilities and a hidden curriculum that rewards students for their mainstreamness of neatness, punctuality, and deference to authority. However, these students often discover that they have weak voices or no voice at all because they have been living in a materially privileged human condition. Further, they feel threatened when the silenced voices of the dominated minority students come forth loud and clear once the pedagogical space is provided, and often those voices are intoned with anger and accusation against the very system that has rewarded students from the dominant culture.

We believe that the main source of nonengagement in critical pedagogy often comes from dominant culture students, who are distressed when the pedagogy is no longer flattering or the known delivery system that has privileged them throughout their prior educational experiences no longer exists. Suddenly, they are required to think, to analyze, synthesize, and wrestle with making meanings for themselves instead of just memorizing and parroting back disjointed or irrelevant facts from a fragmented curriculum. In culture circles they must discover their own voices, a cognitively demanding responsibility that is often a novel academic experience. However, students who have been oppressed by traditional educational experiences tend to thrive in culture circles precisely because the pedagogy addresses their frustrations and provides them with pedagogical spaces to use voices that have been silenced, ignored, or misunderstood too often in their educational experiences. Becoming critically aware of differing students' experiences provided us with the need to critique our own ways of approaching student learning, which has led over time to a dramatic shift in praxis.

DISCOVERING THE WATER IN WHICH WE SWIM

Through our readings, years of classroom experimentation, and wrestling with meaningful learning we have come to realize that the shift in pedagogy starts within. Dykstra (1996) speaks to this act as "throwing tradition to the wind and do[ing] what made more sense," which has brought us to teach and learn in an environment that promotes disequilibrium, to question, to experience firsthand, to view through a new lens, and to "discover the water in which students swim."

In our discourse we question the myth of a prescribed curriculum as the mechanism leading to a learned individual. We question and view the "teacher-proof package" as a mechanism to devalue critical thought in order to perpetuate oppression. We lament this "deskilling of teachers" (Beyer & Apple, 1988).

The oppressive curriculum is for teachers similar to the function of recipes for women in Guatemala. In a conversation with anthropologists Margarita Estrada and Professor Brenda Penados at San Carlos University, Guatemala City in 1991, they related the lengthy preparation and painstaking cooking procedures of Guatemalan traditional dishes as an activity that oppresses and undermines a woman's status in Guatemalan culture. Estrada and Penados argue that the ritual of Guatemalan cooking as a prescribed curriculum perpetuates oppression of women and supports the male privileged status quo; both need to be questioned. When cultures of college students, teachers, or Guatemalan women are occupied with fragmented details and time-consuming busy work, these mechanisms must be recognized as tools of oppression or repression. Critical pedagogy, a pedagogy of liberation, becomes our rebirth into a world of critical consciousness and agency. Teachers become the midwives of critical consciousness.

Culture circles hold the potential to provide the pedagogical spaces necessary for the democratization and humanization of the classroom. Through problematization of the status quo, a space is provided for counterhegemonic transformation, since it is clear that the current hegemony has created a stacked deck against all but the privileged ruling class. Power becomes the focus of analysis in our quest as citizen-learners to comprehend our collective human conditions. Often the teacher's role is to pose questions that provide an intellectual space for problematizing culture itself (Freire, 1970, 1973). Dialogues evolve along generative themes involving all of the participants and connected to their realities. Some participants in a circle may be reproducing and benefiting from undemocratic cultural and social practices. Others in the circle may be victims of such practices. Yet, since this is the water in which they swim, they may not even be aware of the extent of their participation. Victims may not be aware of the roles they play as accomplices in their own victimization. The consciousness-raising dimension of Freire's pedagogy of the oppressed becomes the vehicle for empowerment of all participants to transform social and cultural practices and to challenge the myths and basic assumptions of the hegemony they have inherited through social reproduction and colonization. Only when students critically discover the water in which they swim can we expect them to view teaching in new ways. According to Giroux (1996):

> Youth signifies in all of its diversity the possibilities and the fears adults
> must face when they reimagine the future while shaping the present.

The degree to which large segments of youth are excluded from the language, rights, and obligations of democracy indicates the degree to which many adults have abandoned the language, practice, and responsibilities of critical citizenship and civic responsibility. (p. 140)

In Farsi there is the saying, "A wolf does not give birth to a lamb." As public intellectuals responsible for the next generation of teachers, we must evolve in our own criticity if we are to provide a space for our students to do the same.

COMING TO KNOW WHO WE ARE

We both came to a realization of a need to critically look at mainstream education early in our lives and have consciously made efforts along the way to restore a democratic community to which every student has an inherent right. For Stan, the feeling of nonengagement started with his formal schooling in grade school, where the notion of questioning was perceived as a personal attack toward authority and never problematized with the students in an attempt to promote critical thinking. Coming from a working-class family, he and others of the same cut in society were demoralized through lower tracked classes and nonencouragement toward higher education, and robbed of intellectual challenge unless it was sought outside school parameters. "Think about becoming a carpenter like your father" or "You'll never amount to anything anyway, why should I waste my time trying to teach you?" were echoed through the years. One day, several years after Stan had been teaching elementary school, he encountered a former high school teacher whom he informed of his current job. The teacher, in jaw-dropping shock, uttered, "I can't believe you even went to college." Thanks to his eighth-grade-educated parents, who instilled a strong work ethic and a will to dream, Stan became the first-generation college graduate on either side of the family and opened the doors for subsequent siblings and their offspring to obtain a college degree.

Robert, a member of working-class culture, was also discouraged from going to college by his high school guidance counselor and only attended at the urging of his mother. Early efforts as an educator were informed by his negative experiences in that he refused to prejudge the innate potential of any student. His transformation and empowerment, however, did not fully occur until his teaching became theoretically and philosophically charged. He began a quest as a transformational intellectual through scholarship and reflective practice, and the effectiveness of his teaching has been documented in the literature (Hayes & Bahruth, 1985; Hayes, Bahruth, & Kessler, 1991).

Both Stan and Robert share Giroux's clear perception of himself as "an historical accident" when referring to his university education. According to McLaren (1988): "Had it not been for the basketball scholarship that helped transport him from the street corners of Smith Hill to the lecture halls of the university, his life would have undoubtedly taken a different and less advantageous turn. It is both the lived sense of class difference which marked Giroux's early years and his subsequent struggle to understand the ways in which schooling empowers those with an early social advantage that bring to his writings the passion for justice and equality for which they have become known" (p. xii). In a similar vein, Macedo (1994) relates his own horror story of victimization at the hands of his high school guidance counselor, who attempted to steer him away from college and into TV-repair training on the basis of his proficiency in English. He facetiously comments, "Perhaps my guidance counselor was not really operating from a deficit-orientation model but was, instead, responding to a need for bilingual TV repairmen" (p. 1). Many times, we have found that challenging such educational practices requires us to speak the unpleasant.

As collaborating colleagues we came together through job proximity and the opportunity to work in an experimental teacher education program that was being supported through a three-year grant secured from Funding for the Improvement of Post Secondary Education (FIPSE). It was clear from our first encounter that we both were disgruntled with the present practice of teacher training and welcomed the opportunity to try something different. Our mission was to bridge content courses, methods classes, and application in an elementary classroom setting over two semesters. Normally, content/core courses and teacher education methods courses are taken in isolation, and the application of course work comes with the culminating practice of student teaching. Connections between the content in courses and the elementary classroom are left up to the college students. As the education professors of this experimental program we were given the charge of ensuring the connections. We first asked to change the entire structure of scheduling university courses. Critical of the fragmentation model of courses, eighteen hours of college credit were purposely blocked into meeting five days a week for four hours each day. Fridays were reserved for an elementary classroom experience, with a two-hour debriefing in the afternoon with students, professors, and practitioners.

Four college professors, two from the humanities area and two from teacher education, came together to team-teach this block of courses. (In a subsequent semester, two professors from math and science teamed with another teacher education professor). The composition of pre-service elementary teachers reflected the largest percentage of diversity among all education courses. We were 25 percent Hispanic, 1 percent African-American, 1 percent Native American, 1 percent Basque, 50 percent nontraditional and traditional students, and 20 percent were males, who constituted the majority in our entire college. Students initially were self-selected into this alternative teacher education preparatory program. Our challenges, insights, and applications of critical pedagogy to the mainstream are outlined in this chapter.

TAKING THEORY INTO ACTION

In our first team effort, working with a cohort group of pre-service elementary teachers, initial attempts at democratic discourse were not without glitches. During the first week of class, a fifty-year-old Anglo male dominated the discourse early on to the point of frustrating and alienating his peers. At this crossroad we had two challenges. First we had to raise the consciousness of the group and the student by problematizing the issue of someone dominating the discourse. The other challenge was bringing the problem into the culture circle in a nonconfrontive manner to continue the deconstruction of traditional pedagogy with an organic example from the group's dynamics. Had the praxis been confrontational, we would have reaffirmed authoritarianism, which was precisely what we did not want to do. Had we not problematized or addressed issues of democratic discourse, a student could have frustrated the pedagogy and caused nonengagement of the entire group.

If we do not postpone the syllabus and utilize the organic teachable moments of the evolving culture circle, we merely "cover" the curriculum. The curriculum becomes the antagonist of nonengagement while contributing to the development of false concepts about teaching and learning. "Students, I believe, learn as much from the process of a course, its hidden curriculum, as from the explicit content" (Schniedewind, 1987, p. 170). Critical pedagogues are aware of the "hidden" curriculum and are politically motivated to be counterhegemonic.

In order to effectively democratize the classroom we must first develop our own criticity. For example, "How do we do this without dehumanizing or demonizing the male student or taking away his needed voice?" Rather than relying on direct teacher confrontation of the male student we chose to pose questions within the culture circle. We asked the students, "Who haven't we heard from?" and "What voices are missing?" Further, "How are the missing voices essential to the democratization of the classroom?" The essence of critical pedagogy is that it is a pedagogy of question rather than a pedagogy of answer (Freire, 1991). Questions are contextual rather than rhetorical. We were asking the students to engage in the discussion in a nonthreatening manner, unlike a praxis that relies on students responding to questions in which the answers have been predetermined by teachers and curriculum guides in a mainstream program.

According to Shor (1990), "When we behave in experimental ways in a classroom, we are learning on the job how to become democratic change agents and critical teachers and participatory problem-posers. We are taking responsibility for our own redevelopment as educators" (p. 350). Shor states that this process of recreating our profession can take years. We believe working in collaboration with creative colleagues can enhance the pedagogy and lower the risk by providing sounding boards. In our case we had daily access to discuss and develop the pedagogy as it emerged. We found ourselves calling each other in the evenings and mornings before class, going for walks between classes, continually wrestling with the emergent content and brainstorming new possibilities, to the point where our spouses became frustrated with the amount of time we spent together. We had a "din in the head," a constant subconscious rumbling of thoughts and ideas, due to our intense investment in the creative and intrinsically motivating pedagogy (Krashen, 1983).

From our perspective it seems clear that students who have experienced oppressive pedagogical practices become engaged learners in critical classrooms, and, as more privileged learners have opportunities to understand the human conditions of their frustrated peers through problematization and dialogue, the formerly nonengaging students begin to transform their perspectives on schooling practices previously so normal, natural, and unproblematic to them. The process evolves into engagement on the part of all students, perhaps for the first time in any of their educational experiences, regardless of which profile they represent—privileged or oppressed. In fact, the decolonizing aspect of mainstream students through critical pedagogy often raises their consciousness to the extent that they realize no one was truly privileged in schools with so political an agenda as reproduction rather than democratization and transformation. They come to realize their own education was impoverished, not by the voices they heard in schools, but by the ab-

sence of voices that went uninvited or were silenced. The counterhegemonic experience in our culture circles, in which voice became an element of the evolving community of learners, provided our students with
a deeper appreciation for what was missing in prior educational contexts.
Part of the dialogue involved attempts to foster a meta-awareness of
community as it was evolving.

BUILDING A COMMUNITY OF LEARNERS

The intensity of our collaborative efforts generated critical questions that
we used to provoke discussions with our students. Along with the circles,
part of the counterhegemony required longer blocks of time—in contrast
with the traditional fragmentation of 50-minute class periods—for these
discussions to blossom. Rather than asking students to participate in
learning while playing cognitive hopscotch, we integrated courses and
field experiences into meeting five days a week from 8:30 A.M. to noon.
The longer time periods, the organic nature of the interaction built upon
life experiences of all the participants and the immediate needs of the
group, the appreciation of individual voices, and the democratization of
the classroom through the relinquishing of authority provided the pedagogical space necessary for developing criticity and a passion for lifelong learning.

This passion for learning must be kindled and nurtured in subtle
ways so as not to drive students further from the intended purposes of education. To begin with we must spend time getting to know the people
within our classroom community. An exercise we have engaged in begins with perceptions. Students enter a classroom and immediately begin
to size up the participants from top to bottom. Our physical appearance,
clothes we wear, hairstyle, facial expressions, the way we use our arms,
all emanate a perception in the eyes of the beholder, the classroom participants. In a limited way they are "reading the world" (Freire &
Macedo, 1987). We must extend this vision of the world into looking for
what they do not see through the eyes.

So we begin with what we know. A good place to start is by humanizing the instructor (hooks, 1994) by raising questions about ourselves.
Students are asked to predict our personality through their initial perceptions and the questions we ask. What might my hobbies be? What words
could you attach to my personality? Do I have family? What is my idea
of a good time? What is the genre of literature that I might enjoy reading? What foods do I enjoy? After the questioning we ask students to

share their perceptions of us in the group setting. Until all perceptions are shared we do not confirm or negate any of their predictions. Once the predictions have been aired, we talk about ourselves through their predictions, confirming and negating when necessary. We also allow the students to ask additional questions to clarify initial impressions. They begin to see that a person is more than initial perceptions. The real confirmations for the students' initial perceptions happen throughout the semester, as they see us as other players, other humans in the classroom community.

A continued stream of questions is used to stimulate their thinking, not necessarily expecting responses, but wanting to enhance how they think about people and about all humans. Can we know everything about a person from perceptions? How does knowing something about a person's background affect your perceptions? Would a visit to a person's home help? Our first meeting for the class was in one of our homes. We prepared a meal together. What do we really know about the way a person thinks, feels, dreams based on our perceptions? How do we really get to know someone? What does the Native American saying, "never judge a man/woman until you have walked two moons in their moccasins" mean? What does it take for people/teachers to move away from initial perceptions? By modeling the issue of initial perceptions we make connections to our role as teacher.

We talk about how initial perceptions made on the first day of school can become subliminally implanted through preceding reputation, media, fear, and lack of knowledge. Often, this limited view has a negative effect on our relationship with a child. Someone who comes to school disheveled or of a different skin color may be perceived as having a poor home life, being a slow learner, being illiterate, having a poor additude, being a trouble maker, or being a resistant learner. This negative imbalance is what we call the *Herdman effect,* a term generated from a book, *The Best Christmas Pageant Ever,* by Barbara Robinson (1972), in which all the kids of the Herdman family were socially promoted because the teachers feared the thought of having two Herdmans in the same room. Their reputations preceded them merely based on initial perceptions. The teachers never got past preconceived notions. "Those of us who presume to 'teach' must not imagine that we know how each student begins to learn" (Gussin-Paley, 1994, p. 78).

We explore the issue of perceptions and first day of school further. Excerpts from several books describing the first day of school are passed around and discussed (*Roll of Thunder, Hear My Cry,* 1976; *Savage*

Inequalities, 1991; *Bridge to Terabithia,* 1977; *When the Legends Die,* 1963; *New Boy,* 1993). We write from the perspective of a character in the story. The realities of this exercise and discussion begin to surface in the form of personal stories as our community begins to retrace past schooling experiences. Emotional outbursts of tears and suppressed hatred are unloaded into the group. We begin to deconstruct the ill effects of past schooling practices. We want to revisit critically the tradition of teachers' teaching the way they have been taught, using the same methodology for the past one hundred years (Cuban, 1984), and teachers working in isolation (Lortie, 1975). We bring these issues into the classroom community to deal with collectively, not in isolation, as tradition would dictate. The pedagogical shift becomes a community effort in the same way we might hope that our students would approach their future students. In fact, our students shared many of the pedagogical spaces we provided with their elementary students.

PROMOTING A DISPOSITION TOWARD
LIFELONG LEARNING

"When teaching and learning are seen as genuinely interactive behaviors, we discover that we cannot effectively teach *children we don't know.* Getting to know the children in a new group, say at the beginning of a year, is therefore a first priority" (Britton, 1989, p. 217).

Our pedagogy of critical educators has left its mark on these individuals. This transition in praxis from teacher-centered to a community of learners allows us to start with self, through personal story, which is the framework for lifelong learners. "I believe that the ways of telling and the ways of conceptualizing that go with them become so habitual that they finally become recipes for structuring experience itself, for laying down routes into memory, for not only guiding the life narrative up to the present, but for directing it into the future" (Bruner, 1994, p. 36). By allowing personal story into the discourse we begin to deconstruct the institutionalization of schools and education on an individual basis.

Stories from the members in the classroom community came in varied media. Some were through dialogue journals, others through reflective writing and/or group debriefings. Participants also presented their personal portfolios to the entire classroom community, and many of the more profound stories occurred at the end of the class during portfolio presentations.

Alice, an African-American, came to realize the impact the drive-by shooting of her brother when she was twelve had had on her schooling from that point on. For the first time in the twenty years since her brother's death she revisited, through a humanizing pedagogy, the significance of that event in her life. She now understood why her mother was so adamant about an education as a way out of inner-city Chicago. The environment created by the culture circle provided the safety for her to share and enrich the lives of us all.

Janet, a twenty-year-old Anglo, released the anger that had been caused from an unfair generalization about her character that a teacher had allowed to be printed in the school newspaper. It changed the way other students and teachers looked at her for the rest of her high school career, and she vowed never to let such an injustice happen again. At the time of this writing, Janet was spearheading a grassroots movement to block the closing of a recreational facility on the poor side of town. A new facility had been built for the affluent, with prohibitive membership fees for low-income people. The evolving criticity of the students was affecting the way they looked at the world around them, fulfilling an application of Freirean pedagogy, each becoming agents of history through action.

Arlene, an early college dropout, returned to the college system twenty years later. She shared her story of a system of denial to be class valedictorian because she was not from the "right" family. Her self-esteem had been so damaged that it took nearly twenty-five years to get the college degree she justifiably deserved. Through a safe atmosphere, the culture circle, Arlene found an opportunity to share her personal story, deconstruct significant events in her life, and reconstruct a future for herself.

Colleen, a single mother and first-generation college attendee, came to the first meeting in one of our homes and had isolated herself in a corner. Upon noticing this behavior we engaged her in dialogue. As we came to understand Colleen we learned there was a reason for her shriveled body posture, nonexistent eye contact, and poor self-esteem. All had been systematically stripped from her through the course of her prior schooling. In the course of getting to know her we also learned she had no family support system, and the classroom became her new family. By the end of the class, Colleen had become the group historian, had taken photos, and had organized a class publication.

Rod, married and a father of four children, had positioned himself to come to school full time. For the first time in his life he wrestled with meaningful learning in the group debriefings. This pedagogy is in contrast to his prior schooling. He completed our class and then found himself back in the traditional, dehumanizing structure of some college courses and resisted the insult to his intelligence. He nearly got booted out of the university but was determined to become a critical educator. Rod realized the battles a risk-taker must face. The entire pedagogy we had been working through the previous semester got challenged by the system. Rod did not give up. He accepted the failing grades, rethought his plan of action, and decided to play the game to prove a point of the ridiculousness of transmission model classes. He retook courses he had previously failed and got As and Bs. Through the lessons learned he has become determined not to be a colonizer of minds but to educate towards critical literacy.

Juanita, a Mexican American, first generation high school graduate and now college student, shared her struggles posed by a predominately mainstream elementary and secondary education. Despite the obstacles, Juanita was able to draw on one year in the fifth grade when she had a teacher who empowered her through an additive bilingual praxis, which reified her home language and culture (Hayes, Bahruth, & Kessler, 1991). An affirmation of the impact of good teaching was reaffirmed in our class during her portfolio presentation. Juanita told of another teacher she had in high school who gave her a failing grade: "I wrote to my fifth-grade teacher and told him I was getting A's in all my classes except science. I told him 'but that's all right Mr. B, because I know it's something wrong with my science teacher and not me.'" She knew in her heart that it was not her, but the biased teaching that was responsible. The impact of that fifth-grade teacher did not end there. Juanita felt an obligation to pass on the legacy of empowering pedagogy by becoming a teacher herself.

Another extension of generating a posture toward lifelong learning that has a lingering effect on the students' minds is through literature shared in group or directed toward an individual based on a personal story or shared experience. "Your story reminds me of a book I read. You might find that story interesting to read." Each story connects us to another story/book/article. We model the benefits of lifelong learning by suggesting a book, by further reading or making copies for the group, or by reading aloud during class time. This action becomes reciprocal between teacher and student. Students' voices are valued and not just a parroting of the teacher. At the end of the course we had one student, Sarita, comment that she had read more books for this class, not required reading, because the format had stimulated her curiosity enough to go to the library and check them out on her own. Another student, Mark, surprised us all during his portfolio presentation when he handed out copies that listed the books mentioned or discussed over the course of one semester. The list included four pages of single spaced titles. Discovering the utility of literature, a lifelong reading posture starts with modeling.

One example of students' reflecting personal empowerment occurred while discussing children's reading faddish literature. Out of curiosity, a student had read one of the books in *The Babysitters' Club* series and reported to the group that the one she had read featured a male babysitter in the title and on the cover, yet in actuality that character never babysits throughout the entire book. In her opinion the title was misleading and left her disgruntled, which in turn led her to problematize this misrepresentation with elementary students. Another student in our group connected that story to his reading of *The Empire's Old Clothes,* by Arial Dorfman, who chastises the subliminal messages portrayed through Disneyized distortions of folklore, which led to Neil Postman's *Amusing Ourselves to Death* and the mind programming that occurs by television taking us away from narrative story and from reading good literature. We ended the discussion with the importance of not discouraging children's reading by taking away such limited children's literature or not allowing them to discuss this literature, but problematizing the limitations with children and redirecting them toward quality literature. These college students were empowered beyond a useless textbook and regurgitation of meaningless content.

Through modeling the teaching and learning within a community of learners we believe our students will become the change agents in their schools. We recognize that this restructuring of classroom protocol will be met with resistance in most school settings, but we have problematized this several times in our classes. Like any new situation, we talk about them reading the world they have entered first and then to begin planting the seeds among believers, people who are sincere about teaching children to become lifelong learners. In some cases, there may only be one other person with whom to collaborate. Most importantly, students, parents, and colleagues will follow if you practice what you preach, if you walk your talk. Anybody who has been empowered to be a critical pedagogue, a member of the community, a reader of the world, a lifelong learner will never consider the notion of public education under the traditional model again. Despite the challenges they face in the future, these students have the tools and dispositions now in place not to let the obstacles be walls but doors to walk through. We know and they know the experience they received from a liberating pedagogy has changed them for life. In the highest expression of literacy, they have become writers of the world (Freire & Macedo, 1987).

EXTENDING THE PEDAGOGICAL SHIFT

Student empowerment within the university presents a set of challenges that must be dealt with too. Over the years, we have become more overt in the politics of our pedagogy and more aggressive in our deconstruction of the status quo. Ironically, as we have become more adept at the pedagogy of question and the orchestration of culture circles, we have met with less and less nonengagement. Several factors seem to be at play here. First, we often have students requesting and attending our other courses, providing a critical mass (pun intended) of engaged students early in the course. As these students dialogue and interact with "newcomers" to our courses, we find them generating their own acute critical questions. Second, the general widespread attacks on education from a complete spectrum of ideologies are becoming too loud to ignore. Our early focus on the deconstruction of the myths of neutrality and homogeneity in mainstream schooling helps students to discover sooner the water in which they swim. According to Freire (as translated in Gadotti, 1994), "The defenders of neutrality of literacy programs do not lie when they say that the clarification of reality at the same time as learning to read and write is a political act. They are wrong, however, when they deny that the way in which they deny reality has no political meaning" (p. 59). The general reaction of students after just a few classes is anger when they realize *what has been missing* in their education. We challenge them to view the political nature of education and to determine early in their careers whether they are going to be "teachers as intellectuals" (Giroux, 1988) or "intellectual dupes" (Crichton, 1993). The following anecdotes reflect more recent experiences with nonengagement and how we have been able to defuse it.

Recently, our teacher education program added a course on diversity to the catalogue requirements. A few students expressed concern about the addition of one more course to their program. In our first class meeting, a group of eleven Anglo students sat waiting to begin. They were welcomed to the class, asked to arrange their desks in a circle, and given a skeletal syllabus listing the text, literature to be used, and a rough outline of the semester, along with requirements, evaluation procedures, and other details usually found in a syllabus. After a brief introduction of the course, students were asked to introduce themselves and to explain what they hoped to get out of the class.

One student complained outright and asked for a justification of the new requirement. He explained that he had no intention of ever teaching in a culturally diverse classroom. When asked if it would matter more to him if he realized that he was presently sitting in a culturally diverse classroom, he surveyed the room, apparently looking for ethnically/racially diverse (unfortunately, diverse based upon a mainstream yardstick) classmates. Suspicions were verified when he said this class was a "normal" classroom. So, we began with mapping the many ways we were diverse as a group as our first activity in making the familiar unfamiliar or discovering the water in which we swim.

A female student offered gender as one example of diversity. We formed small groups and began discussing other ways diversity can exist in a classroom beyond the obvious, superficial distinctions we have become so conditioned to notice and respond to, often in negative ways. By the end of the period, as the groups reported their findings, we had a wide range of categories of diversity represented; from obvious factors, including rural/urban backgrounds, religion, socioeconomic status, political affiliations, age, and quality of educational experiences, to more subtle distinctions, including handedness, hobbies and interests, family structures, ideological orientations, strengths and weaknesses, fears and phobias, and those who loved or hated Rush Limbaugh. As Giroux (1996) states:

> Educators must rework the discourse(s) of cultural studies to provide
> some common ground in which traditional modernist offerings of dif-
> ference and politics around the binaries capital/labor, self/other, sub-
> ject/object, colonizer/colonized, white/black, man/woman, majority/
> minority, and heterosexual/homosexual can be reconstituted through
> more complex representations of identification, belonging, and com-
> munity. (p. 135)

In the process, we deconstructed two myths: that of homogeneity, and, more importantly, the myth of the mainstream yardstick itself. After the first session, the students were open for engagement and receptive to a series of activities and discussions that would allow us to mark the twain of the mainstream. At the end of the course one student wrote:

> Dear Roberto,
>   I'm not sure I want this reproduced because it deals mostly with the
> members of the class. Before class even began, I had a pretty good idea
> where you stood. The articles and discussions helped solidify in my
> mind the how and why.

The most significant experience for me has been watching the class members change their attitudes. I guess I experienced the transformation myself last semester, but watching it was great fun. It really works!

At the beginning of this semester, some members of the class had doubts about the way you ran the class. Terms like "waste of time," "irresponsible," and "unprofessional" were used to describe their frustration at "trying to live with ambiguity." I first noticed the change begin when one student said they wished they didn't have to do all the busy work for their other classes, so they could spend more time on the "real stuff" for this class. Later, during a discussion on which instructors they would recommend, one of the (formerly) most vocal critics said, "Bahruth, for one." Of course these discussions took place before your arrival, but I can't help wondering if you would really be surprised at the level of animosity or the depth of the complete turnabout of thinking. You must have seen it before, often. Is that why the pre-FIPSE* warning about living with ambiguity was necessary? One thing I noticed about FIPSE was that it worked well as long as we felt safe. When we felt threatened (grades, etc.) we wanted *answers*. Maybe that accounts for the hostility at the beginning of the class—safety is a rare thing in most classes.

I was fortunate to have a booster shot of Bahruth to back up the first immunization, and glad I have more in my hands now that I can refer to.

Of course the content was great, but seeing the actual change in class members was most impressive!

Shelly

FIGHTING THE RAPIDS OF TRADITION

We would be hiding some truths if we did not talk about the resistance we and our students received from other faculty. After a semester or two of taking classes with us, students actively resist traditional teacher-centered classrooms, which previously went uninterrogated. The backlash from our colleagues comes in the form of comments such as, "You are ruining our students," and "You incited the students to gang up on me," and "The students are not as respectful . . . They question my assignments and my tests," or "They question my authority." We have also

* FIPSE = Funding for the Improvement of Post Secondary Education, an experimental integrated methods project from which many of our anecdotes are de-

been requested: "Could you put the chairs back in rows?" by colleagues sharing classrooms with us. The idea of teaching through critical questions to make the familiar unfamiliar has produced our response, "Should I ask the person using the room before me to put the chairs in a circle when he or she is finished?"

On the other hand, we more often receive praise from colleagues who recognize the important contributions these same students make in their classrooms. Comments like, "The FIPSE students stand out," or "These students are more articulate than many of my graduate students," "The quality of the students' work stands out among their classmates," and "They ask questions that reflect deep thought." Once the criticity is awakened they are no longer docile and passive learners. They no longer simply absorb official bodies of knowledge but question and filter course content. In their evolving philosophical and theoretical understandings, based upon direct experience with critical pedagogy, the act of reflective practice becomes second nature. Students carry this criticity further by actively voicing their frustrations on faculty evaluations.

These same students know they still may be obligated to take course work from traditional-type faculty, but they now enter these classes knowing they have the choice in what they want to take away, and for the first time they are playing "the game" by their own rules. They have acquired coping strategies in order to get the diploma, but the impact of becoming a critical thinker is set in motion for life. Student resistance to pedagogical structures representative of much of their educational experience prior to our classes demonstrates that we have been successful in making the familiar unfamiliar and helping our students to discover the water in which they swim.

The additudes and dispositions toward traditional forms of grading shifted from teacher-centered to one that reflected two levels: (1) requiring responsibility from the individual student and (2) reciprocal responsibility among the community of learners. Students engaged in dialogue journals with one other member of the class. Journals were used to engage participants in a means to formalize some of their thinking and often to offer a beginning point for the day's discussion. A multitude of activities that blended theory, content, and practical applications with elementary students were interjected throughout the semester. In smaller groups, students collaborated with practitioners to develop and implement these activities. Results, from celebrations to reconsiderations, were brought to culture circle debriefings with students, faculty, and practitioners, again, providing a voice for all. We approached grading through a pedagogy of question rather than a hierarchical performance standard. From the beginning, students knew the ongoing and culminating exercise would be to create portfolios reflecting questions that evolved from the group as a whole. What do teachers need to know? What actions do teachers take to guarantee learning for all? What is important for others to know about you? What might your classroom look like in the future? In the process of the collective experience and the qualitative measures used, our goal was to charge their professional development intellectually; therefore the activities required analysis, synthesis, and application of what they were learning. Portfolios oblige students to take control of, and reflect upon, their learning. In a few cases, students self-selected out of teacher education when faced with the challenge of controlling their own destiny and the demands of a deeper sense of teaching. As a community we dealt with this change in group dynamics and career redirection with these students. The community of learners was sensitized to a world beyond "just becoming a teacher."

Students participating in the environment of a culture circle discover their voices, in most cases, for the first time in their career, and now have a posture to look at life through new lenses. They regain a sense of reading the world that has been stripped through their formal schooling. In the classroom setting of the culture circle, students become interdependent, not dependent on the teacher. We break down the status quo, the damaging legacy of "teachers teaching in isolation" (Lortie, 1975). We become a community of learners, and students take that belief and practice into their professional world. Teachers "render themselves obsolete" (Calkins & Harwayne, 1987), and students become empowered to carry the pedagogy forward.

CONCLUSION

In order for this pedagogical practice to happen in our lives within the university system, we looked for and initiated a language of possibility. Macedo (1994, p. 152) raises three extremely provocative questions about colleges of education and their ability to provide the pedagogical spaces necessary to educate for transformation rather than social reproduction. Often the rigid structures of bureaucracies impede the very change their leadership would claim they are attempting to provide. Change must be recognizable, understandable, and evaluated by status quo standards. However, certain specific recommendations would be helpful to those who wish to practice critical pedagogy.

First, physical structures such as time and space must be taken into consideration. We have gravitated toward longer time slots for our courses and away from the 50-minute Monday, Wednesday, and Friday fragmented structure. The critical mass of discourse necessary to allow a culture circle to evolve must be at least 90 uninterrupted minutes. We have often had three-hour-long classes in which students have commented that the discussion was so rich that the class seemed shorter than many of their 50-minute lecture-format classes.

Second, we request rooms where the furniture is movable, with enough space for us to form a circle, and where we can set up cooperative groups as well. The way the university constructs buildings is still based on lecture-format models. Space is managed to determine class capacity based on straight rows facing forward. Administrators need to know and come to appreciate alternative models for education so that they can accommodate various needs.

Third, current evaluation procedures are shallow and actually deter professors from using anything but flattering pedagogy that does not disrupt student comfort zones. "In essence, measurement against common standards creates strong pressures to conform to implicit, unexamined standards. Regardless of initial statements of purpose of the student surveys or of denials about their present use, it is the case that student surveys and *selected* testimonials are the sole data in the category of teaching upon which tenure, promotion, and salary decisions are made. As a result there is no real innovation in teaching at the university, and professors are not really encouraged to even consider such innovation" (Dykstra, 1995).

Since part of nonengagement may manifest itself when a disgruntled student (often one who is used to "getting the A" without having to do much thinking) is suddenly challenged by the pedagogy, we run the risk of receiving a harsh evaluation rather than the mediocre, almost neutral, evaluations of professors who do not stray from tradition. Traditional evaluation instruments are flawed and are a poor measure of critical pedagogues; however, administrators can provide leadership that would protect professors who are taking the risk to depart from a transmission model of discourse in their classrooms (Morton, 1992). Certainly, for nontenured faculty, support from administrators must be sought and guaranteed.

Finally, in relation to administrative dispositions, encouragement, patience, interest, and understanding would be signs of true leadership and support of attempts to provide a richer educational experience for students, one they would not want to leave on the counter. As Eiseley

(1987) observed: "A university is a place where people pay high prices for goods which they then proceed to leave on the counter when they go out of the store" (p. 117). Critical pedagogy is the pedagogy of other, and deans and department chairs must not jump to demonize or marginalize efforts simply because they are not recognizable (Gabbard, 1993). We must find our voice. "I say this because I need to suggest what it was like to learn to pay heed to the silences. I say it because I realize how it made me attentive to multiplicity, to perspectivism, to the importance of having enough courage to look through my own eyes—and, yes, speak in my own faulty voice" (Greene, 1994, p. 16). Similarly, Villanueva (1993) problematizes the plight of minority voices in the hegemony of academia. We must engage our administrators in dialogue to educate them about critical pedagogy, and a disposition of true leadership would he to consider a praxis that departs from and even challenges the status quo.

As we see things, in our profession we have two choices. We can succumb to the mainstream and become programmed toward deskilling our intellect, or we can become critical pedagogues and liberate ourselves and those who choose to join in the dialogue. In the words of James Moffett (1989), we leave you with this critical question: "One generation sometime has to fish or cut bait, has to *mean* it when it posts its noble goals, has to face the fear of actually achieving what it says it wants for its young. Are we that generation, or will we just provide more instances in the pattern of history. . . ?" (p. 24)

REFERENCES

Ada, A. F. (1990). *A Magical Encounter: Spanish Language Children's Literature in the Classroom.* Compton, CA: Santillana.

Anaya, R. (1995). *The Anaya Reader.* New York: Warner Books.

Beyer, L. E., & Apple, M. W. (1988). "Values and Politics in the Curriculum," in Landon E. Beyer and Michael W. Apple (Eds.), *The Curriculum: Problems, Politics and Possibilities* (pp. 3–16). Albany, NY: SUNY.

Borland, H. (1963). *When the Legends Die.* Philadelphia: J. B. Lippencott.

Boyer, E. (1987). *College: The Undergraduate Experience in America.* New York: Harper & Row.

Britton, J. (1989). "Writing-and-Reading in the Classroom," in Anne Haas Dyson (Ed.), *Collaboration through Writing and Reading: Exploring Possibilities* (pp. 217–246). Urbana, IL: NCTE.

Brown, C. (1978). *Literacy in 30 Hours: Paulo Freire's Process in Northeast Brazil.* Chicago: Alternate Schools Network.

Bruner, J. (1994). "Life as Narrative," in A. Haas Dyson & C. Genishi (Eds.), *The Need for Story: Cultural Diversity in Classroom and Community* (pp. 28–37). Urbana, IL: NCTE.

Calkins, L. M., & Harwayne, S. (1987). *The Writing Workshop: A World of Difference.* Portsmouth, NH: Heinemann.

Chávez-Chávez, R., Belkin, L. D., Hornback, J. G., Adams, K. (1991). "Dropping Out of School: Issues Affecting Culturally, Ethnically, and Linguistically Distinct Student Groups." *The Journal of Educational Issues of Language Minority Students, 8,* 1–21.

Chomsky, N. (1995). "A Dialogue with Noam Chomsky." *Harvard Educational Review, 65*(2), 127–144.

Crichton, M. (1993). *Acceptance Speech from the National Press Club.* New York: National Public Radio.

Cuban, L. (1984). *How Teachers Taught: Constancy and Change in American Classrooms, 1890–1980.* New York: Longman.

Dorfman, A. (1983). *The Empire's Old Clothes: What the Lone Ranger, Babar, and Other Innocent Heroes Do to Our Minds.* New York: Pantheon Books.

Dykstra, D. I . (1996). "Teaching Introductory Physics to College Students," in Catherine Fosnot (Ed.), *Constructivism: Theory, Perspectives, and Practice,* (pp. 182–204). New York: Teachers College Press.

Dykstra, D. I. (1995). *Toward a Scholarship of Teaching: Against the Dichotomy Between Research and Teaching.* Unpublished manuscript.

Eiseley, L. (1987). "The Sorcerer in the Wood, 1947–1966," in Kenneth Heuer (Ed.), *The Lost Notebooks of Loren Eiseley.* Boston: Little, Brown.

Fox, M. (1993). *Radical Reflections: Passionate Opinions on Teaching Learning and Living.* New York: Harcourt Brace.

Freire, P. (1970). *Pedagogy of the Oppressed.* New York: Continuum.

Freire, P. (1973). *Education for Critical Consciousness.* New York: Continuum.

Freire, P. (1987). "Letter to North-American Teachers" (Carman Hunter, trans.), in Ira Shor (Ed.), *Freire for the Classroom: A Source Book for Liberatory Teaching* (pp. 211–214). Portsmouth, NH: Heinemann.

Freire, P. (1991). "Forward," in Eleanor Kutz & Hephzibah Roskelly, *An Unquiet Pedagogy: Transforming Practice in the English Classroom.* Portsmouth, NH: Boynton/Cook & Heinemann.

Freire, P., & Macedo, D. (1987). *Literacy: Reading the Word and the World.* New York: Bergin and Garvey Publishers, Inc.

Freire, P., & Macedo, D. (1995). "A Dialogue: Culture, Language, and Race." *Harvard Educational Review, 65* (3), 377–402.

Gabbard, D. A. (1993). *Silencing Ivan Illich: A Foucauldian Analysis of Intellectual Exclusion.* San Francisco: Austin & Winfield.

Gadotti, M. (1994). *Reading Paulo Freire: His Life and Work.* Albany, NY: SUNY.

Gadotti, M. (1996). *Pedagogy of Praxis: A Dialectical Philosophy of Education.* Albany, NY: SUNY.

García, E. H. (1995). "The Mexican Americans," in Carl Grant (Ed.), *Educating for Diversity: An Anthology of Multicultural Voices* (pp. 159–168). Needham Heights, MA: Allyn & Bacon.

Giroux, H. (1983). *Theory and Resistance in Education: A Pedagogy for the Opposition.* South Hadley, MA: Bergin and Garvey.

Giroux, H. (1988). *Teachers as Intellectuals.* New York: Bergin & Garvey.

Giroux, H., & McLaren, P. (1986). "Teacher Education and the Politics of Engagement: The Case for Democratic Schooling." *Harvard Educational Review, 56*(3), 213–238.

Greene, M. (1994). "Multiculturism, Community, and the Arts," in A. Haas Dyson & C. Genishi (Eds.), *The Need for Story: Cultural Diversity in Classroom and Community* (pp. 11–27). Urbana, IL: NCTE.

Gussin Paley, V. (1990). *The Boy Who Would Be a Helicopter: The Use of Storytelling in the Classroom.* Cambridge, MA: Harvard University Press.

Hayes, C. W., & Bahruth, R. (1985). "Querer es poder," in Jane Hansen, Tom Newkirk, and Donald Graves (Eds.). *Breaking Ground: Teachers Relate Reading and Writing in the Elementary School* (pp. 97–108). Portsmouth, NH: Heinemann.

Hayes, C. W., Bahruth, R., & Kessler, C. (1991). *Literacy Con Carino.* Portsmouth, NH: Heinemann.

hooks, b. (1994). *Teaching to Transgress: Education as the Practice of Freedom.* London: Routledge.

Kozol, J. (1990). *The Night Is Dark and I Am Far From Home* (2nd. ed.). New York: Touchstone.

Kozol, J. (1991). *Savage Inequalities.* New York: Crown Publishers.

Krashen, S. (1983). "The Din in the Head, Input, and the Language Acquisition Device," in John Oller & Patricia Richard-Amato (Eds.), *Methods that Work.* (pp. 295–301). Rowley, MA: Newbury House.

Lortie, D. C. (1975). *Schoolteacher: A Sociological Study.* Chicago: University of Chicago Press.

Macedo, D. (1994). *Literacies of Power: What Americans Are Not Allowed to Know.* Boulder: Westview Press.

McLaren, P. (1988). "Forward: Critical Theory and the Meaning of Hope," in Henry Giroux, *Teachers as Intellectuals.* New York: Bergin & Garvey.

Moffett, J. (1989). "Introduction," in Anne Haas Dyson (Ed.), *Collaboration through Writing and Reading: Exploring Possibilities* (pp. 21–24). Urbana, IL: NCTE.

Montessori, M. (1964). *The Montessori Method.* Cambridge, MA: Robert Bently.

Morton, D. (1992). "On 'Hostile Pedagogy,' 'Supportive' Pedagogy, and 'Political Correctness': Letter to a Student Complaining of His Grade." *Journal of Urban and Cultural Studies, 2* (2), 79–94.

Paterson, K. (1977). *Bridge to Terabithia.* New York: Crowell.

Postman, N. (1985). *Amusing Ourselves to Death: Public Discourse in the Age of Show Business.* New York: Viking.

Robinson, B. (1972). *The Best Christmas Pageant Ever.* New York: Harper-Collins.

Schniedewind, N. (1987). "Feminist Values: Guidelines for Teaching Methodology in Women's Studies," in Ira Shor (Ed.), *Freire for the Classroom: A Source Book for Liberatory Teaching* (pp. 170–179). Portsmouth, NH: Heinemann.

Shor, I. (1990). "Liberation Education: An Interview with Ira Shor." *Language Arts, 67* (4), 342–353.

Shor, I., & Freire, P. (1987). *A Pedagogy for Liberation: Dialogues on Transforming Education.* New York: Bergin & Garvey.

Smith, F. (1981). "Demonstrations, Engagement and Sensitivity." *Language Arts 58* (1), 103–112.

Steiner, S., & Bahruth, R. (1994). *In the Spirit of Collaboration: Experimental Elementary Teacher Preparation* [film]. Boise, ID: Simplot-Micron Instructional Technology Center.

Storey, D. (1993). *Newboy.* Reprint from *Rethinking Our Classrooms Workshops.* Washington, DC: Network of Educators on the Americas.

Taylor, M. (1976). *Roll of Thunder, Hear My Cry.* New York: Dial Books.

Trueba, H. (1991). "Dreams Come in All Languages." Keynote address at the Wisconsin State Conference on Bilingual ESL/Multicultural Education, Peewaukee, WI.

Villanueva, V. (1993). *Bootstraps: From an American Academic of Color.* Urbana, IL: NCTE.

CHAPTER 9

The Prairie Is Wide
Conrack Comes to "The Rez"

DAVID A. GABBARD

My former department chair in the School of Education and Human Services at Eastern Montana College took great pride in the fact that Martin Ritt's film *Conrack* had become such an immutable component of his sections of the freshman-level educational foundations course. Had I been interested in winning his political patronage, I might have taken his frequent recommendations to view the film more seriously. For better or worse, I never held such an interest. Therefore, I never saw the film until just recently, when I was doing research for a chapter on the Gullah for Anna Marie Evans's collection: *Teaching the Diaspora.*[1]

Hindsight, in this instance, only confirms the intuitive distrust that I held toward my chair's taste in films. Any feedback that I would have given him on *Conrack* would have heightened our ideological tensions and weakened my already precarious political status within the School of Education.

On the other hand, watching *Conrack* would have clarified the expectations that my chair and the dean held toward my activities as a member of a "professional development school" (PDS) initiative at the

I would like to thank Dr. Karen Adams for assisting me with information, and Dr. Sandra Lent and Virginia Dittrich for their comments and laughter on earlier drafts of this paper.

This article is dedicated to Sandra, in memoriam, whose friendship and support live on between its lines, and to all educators, who continue the struggle for

St. Charles Mission School on the Crow Reservation. Having seen *Conrack* and having read the book from which it was adapted (*The Water Is Wide*, by Pat Conroy [a.k.a. "Conrack"]),[2] I now know why my efforts in that initiative failed to meet their expectations. I am also better able to understand why the School of Education bestowed its most prestigious teaching award upon one of my chair's former graduate students for implementing E. D. Hirsch's ideas on "cultural literacy" into the middle-grades curriculum at St. Charles.

The model of pedagogy presented in *Conrack* parallels what my chair's former student (I'll call him "Peter Jefferson") sought to create at the mission school. Given my colleague's obvious enthusiasm for both, I'm not surprised that my efforts at St. Charles elicited such strong ambivalence from him. We were clearly working at cross-purposes.

DOING "SOMETHING"

I came to Montana straight out of my doctoral program, during which I focused much of my attention on the writings of Ivan Illich. Even today, I believe that Illich ranks among the most important intellectual figures of our era. Illich taught me to recognize the violence of state-mandated schooling. In conferring upon itself the authority to determine the needs of others, the state denies people the right to self-determination. Even though we typically think of the public subsidy that the state organizes in support of this enterprise as a means of "helping" people improve their lives, Marianne Gronemeyer echoes Illich's sentiments in pointing out how the sort of "help" offered in the name of educational opportunity conceals an implicit threat to those who might consider rejecting the offer.[3] The state threatens to meet any attempt to "Just Say 'No' to School" with economic as well as social reprisals. Apart from living with the stigma of being labeled "uneducated," a refusal to attend school or, at least, to partake of state-regulated home schooling, condemns a person to a life of modern immiseration. Because the state perceives the economy to be the primary object of its governance, it has gradually sought to strip people of the right to exist independently from the market. To accomplish this, the state has taken up the task of undermining individuals' abilities to determine their own needs as well as their ability to determine how to meet them. The logic of statecraft dictates that the economy should determine people's needs and that the market represents the only possible means by which those needs can be met. Thus, the state reduces the idea of "work" to a commodity located in what is now called a "job market." People can only find the means for meeting their market-induced needs through the job market, where they rent their energies to those who have already determined the direction in which those energies should be channeled.

The art of government now regulates people's opportunities to meet whatever needs the economy imputes to them by imposing on them the need to attend school. One must attend school in order to get a job. Over the past thirty years, however, the population has continued to grow while the number of jobs offering wages capable of supporting a family has decreased. Job displacement created by automation and off-shore production has frustrated the steady decrease in real wages. Though labor economists such as President Clinton's former Secretary of Labor, Robert Reich, inform us that most of the jobs presently available in the labor market, and even those of the future, require very little skill, the art of government must tend to people's insecurities by continuing to preach the secular gospel of schooling. Should you lose your job to a machine or to an even more poorly paid employee in some other nation where the cost of doing business is kept in check by U.S.-sponsored, neocolonial terrorism, you should not define your plight in terms of corporate greed and government complicity with corporate greed. Rather, you should understand that your outmoded job skills resulted in your unemployment; you simply failed to ensure your value to the company that rented you. To redeem your value, you must update your job skills. To make yourself once again valuable to those who would control your destiny, you must consume more school.

By the time that I began visiting the St. Charles Mission School, the secular gospel of compulsory schooling had already penetrated the consciousness of the Crow children. When I asked a class of ten sixth-grade students to write a paragraph describing what they perceived to be the purpose of education, nine of them dutifully reproduced the party line: education will help me get a job.

Cynicism would have forced me to repress the pain and moral outrage that I felt as I read their responses. After all, why should I have been so shocked? Although it doesn't gratify us to admit it, we all know that the only reason we tolerate school is because we're afraid of the economic consequences of not submitting to its inane rituals. As Illich says in the opening of *Deschooling Society,* "Many students, especially those who are poor, intuitively know what schools do for them. They school them to confuse process and substance."[4] Real learning becomes incidental to the treatments that people endure in school. We learn to go through the motions, to regurgitate what is thrown at us. We tacitly agree to jump through whatever hoops we have to in order to get to the next stage in an ever-expanding process. And even though young people intuitively know that school sucks, thousands of them flock into schools and colleges of education each year, where they train to do the same things to others that they hated when those things were done to them. (On a more positive note, statistics reveal that here in North Carolina fewer and fewer teachers are willing to take part in this masochism: 50 percent of them leave the profession after five years or less.)

Instead of allowing cynicism to condition me into a passive acceptance of the secular gospel's efficacy in teaching these children to view themselves as needy persons and, thereby, its efficacy in forcing them into dependency upon the school, the state, and the job market, I began formulating a strategy to disrupt the practices responsible for generating these debilitating effects. This strategy hinges on the recognition that each of us is born into a preexisting social order, complete with its own historically unique set of cultural patterns. Language acquisition constitutes a major portion of the socialization process that initiates us into the social world. More than providing us with the sounds of language, language acquisition entails a subliminal internalization of our language's silences—the silent rhythms of culture that tacitly structure our patterns for understanding and, consequently, acting in the world. These shared patterns that we acquire as part of the language of our cultural group come to form what we typically refer to as "common sense." And these patterns remain commonsensical to us until we encounter members of some other cultural group who differ from us not only in the sounds of their language but also in its silences.

As Illich explains, "it is not so much the other man's words as his silences which we have to learn in order to understand him." To merely master the sounds of another's language limits our understanding of the other's view of the world. Hence, it impedes our ability to communicate. Learning the silences of another's language, the deep cultural meanings held within and between its sounds, requires tremendous effort. And this effort must begin with listening, in what Illich characterizes as the "silence of deep interest," for the cultural patterns within and between the words of another.[5]

Throughout the remaining weeks of that semester year, I stayed away from the mission school. In keeping with Illich's lessons on the silence of deep interest, I decided that I should keep quiet in order to cultivate my understanding of the Crow, their language, and their culture. In addition to purchasing numerous books by Crow authors, I began inquiring into opportunities for learning the Crow language. Before I could locate a teacher, however, the dean called me into his office and upbraided me for failing to live up to my contractual commitment to his PDS initiative. Threatening to recommend that I not be reappointed to my tenure-track position, he scolded: "I don't care what you do, but do something!" When I told him that what I was doing was "listening," he refused to accept the idea that, among those children, I was the one who was the most uneducated. In his mind, rectifying the deficit in my own knowledge did not fit into the logic of professional development. In order to make him and his initiative look good, I needed to make myself a visible and active reformer.

That next semester I began working with the sixth-grade teacher whose students had written on the purpose of education. She was developing a curriculum unit on Africa, and I volunteered to help her make the material more relevant to the historical context of the Crow.

The Crow children obviously identified with the cultural experiences of African-American and Latino youth. Most of them, particularly the older students, wore the same sort of clothing worn by urban youth gangs. Starter jackets, high-top sneakers, and baseball caps worn with the bill facing backwards were commonplace. Even their body language mimicked the affect of the rappers that they watched on MTV.

Using the connection that they had made with the urban youth scene as a jumping-off point, I decided to base the curriculum unit on the shared experiences of Africans and the indigenous peoples of the Americas. Using a world map, I asked them to locate Africa. Then I asked them to locate the Americas. Once they had shown me where these continents were located, I asked them to look closely at the lines drawn within the boundaries of each of the three continents.

"What do those lines tell you?" I asked.

One of the kids replied: "The lines are there to mark the borders of each of the countries."

"Very good, then," I replied. "Why did the Africans decide to draw the lines where they did?"

Silence engulfed the room. They knew how to answer that question, but they were nervous to carry on in that direction of inquiry.

"Come on," I implored them. "Why did the African people draw those lines where they did? Did the people in those different nations just agree that this is where we should divide our countries?"

"They didn't draw the lines," called out one of the girls, sitting at her desk with her eyes looking down into her hands on her lap. "They didn't?" I asked incredulously. "But it's Africa; it's their continent! What do you mean they didn't draw the lines separating their countries? If they didn't, who did?"

Thus, we began the unit on Africa by focusing on its colonization by Europeans. Soon enough, after some discussion of slavery, I turned their attention to the western hemisphere. Again, I asked them to tell me who drew the lines separating the various nations of the Americas, and they had no problems predicting the direction in which I was moving the conversation. After all, it was 1992 and the indigenous peoples of the Americas had already begun to organize a countercelebration to mark the quincentennial of Columbus's invasion of America. I was pleasantly surprised by the knowledge that these kids already possessed regarding Columbus's genocidal activities in the Caribbean. We spent the rest of the school year discussing the cultural achievements of Africans and Native Americans and comparing the manner in which colonial domination had shaped the experiences of indigneous populations on both sides of the Atlantic.

As successful as I felt these conversations were, I could tell from her body language that the teacher in this sixth-grade classroom was not comfortable with my efforts to link the unit on Africa to the historical and contemporary experiences of the Crow. Even though the dean said that he didn't care what I did as long as I did something, I knew that he would interpret any criticisms from the school administration as an indication that I was trying to subvert his PDS initiative. When I returned to campus from summer break, I was not surprised to learn that he had reassigned me to a different partnership school.

Sadly, I lost all contact with the children at St. Charles. I never saw them again except for one morning toward the end of the following academic year—my last year at Eastern Montana College. They were all bussed into Billings for a special "professional development school" awards day ceremony. It was during that ceremony, with many Crow parents and grandparents sitting in the audience, that the dean presented Jefferson with the School of Education's Award for Teaching Excellence in recognition of his noteworthy achievement in bringing Hirsch's cultural literacy program to the Crow reservation. If they only knew, I thought to myself, what they were being asked to celebrate. . . .

DECONSTRUCTING *CONRACK*

I didn't need to have seen *Conrack* nor to have read *The Water Is Wide* to feel ashamed that I was employed by an institution that would honor the importation of Hirsch's project into a reservation school. But Pat Conroy's chronicle of the year (1969–1970) that he spent teaching Gullah children on Yamacraw Island off the coast of Beaufort County, South Carolina, offers us a useful heuristic through which to interpret and grasp the violence of Jefferson's cultural literacy program.

Though somewhat popular among liberal educators such as Jefferson and my former department chair, neither the book nor the film do anything to increase our awareness of the Gullah and their history. In fact, Conroy never uses the term *Gullah* in referring to the children in his classroom. In his eyes, they are simply another group of poor black children, but whose poverty is exacerbated by their physical separation from the dominant culture on the mainland. And, since they cannot access the dominant culture and its institutions to help lift themselves out of poverty, Conroy takes it upon himself to bring that culture to them.

Yamacraw is one of many sea islands off the coast of South Carolina and Georgia that are home to the Gullah. African in their ancestry, one theory suggests that the Gullah descended from runaway slaves who established the original communities on the sea islands after fleeing from their "owners" on the mainland. Another theory asserts that a colonial experiment with rice plantations brought the Gullah to the islands. After the plantation owners decided that the physical environment on the islands was too harsh for "human" habitation, however, they left the Gullah to fend for themselves. In either case, their isolation from the dominant institutions and culture of the mainland proved to be advantageous to the Gullah. Not only did it secure their independence from slavery, it also increased their ability to retain much of their traditional culture and, hence, their African identity.

Conroy was very deliberate in his decision to teach on Yamacraw. For him, it was a highly symbolic act—a signification that he had broken with his racist and militarist past. However, in many ways, Conroy's self-described metamorphosis is analogous to a transformation in global political-economy that Wolfgang Sachs and the various contributing authors to his *Development Dictionary* attribute to President Harry S Truman's 1949 inaugural address.[6] According to Gustavo Esteva, in mutating the conceptual underpinnings of global economization, Truman's Point Four Program ushered in a new era in world history—"the era of development."[7]

The term *economization* refers to the historical process through which economic reasoning has come to dominate the manner in which all human activities, relationships, and values are lived, experienced, and conceptually formulated. Throughout its history, which Esteva traces back to late-medieval Europe, economization has declared war on traditional cultures, their autonomy, and the subsistence orientation that they bring to human activities. In proposing "development" as a postwar program for world peace, Truman succeeded in delinking economization from the violence of its colonial past, which is central to Conroy's own past as a flagrant racist and the son of a military pilot. Just as Truman pronounced during his inaugural address that "the old imperialism—exploitation for foreign profit—has no place in our plans," Conroy wants to disassociate himself from his own racist and militarist background.

To convince himself of his own transformation from "redneck Neanderthal" to "passionate do-gooder," Conroy sets out on his mission to Yamacraw. In doing so, he clearly aligns himself with Truman's call for "a bold new program for making the benefits of our scientific advances and industrial progress available for the improvement and growth of underdeveloped areas."[8] Though the intentions that it affects under the guise of "development" insinuate an essential goodness and a compassionate desire to help those afflicted by "underdevelopment," economization retains the same destructive properties that it held throughout its colonial era. With those properties now concealed beneath the benevolent cause of development, economization has increased its stealth and, thereby, its effectiveness in waging what Illich describes as its "war against subsistence."[9] It is precisely this war that Conroy has taken up arms to join when he assumes his teaching position on Yamacraw Island. Blinded by his new altruistic self-image, however, he cannot recognize the violence in his actions and, therefore, cannot grasp the underlying reasons for his frustrations and his failure.

Thus, we can interpret Conroy as a living metaphor whose conceptualization of the world shifted from a colonial model to a neocolonial development model, mirroring the changes that Truman's Point Four Program would have on the patterns of global economization. And, insofar as the development model of reality both motivated and informed his pedagogical aims on Yamacraw, we can develop a critique of Conroy's pedagogy that accounts for his frustrations and failures from the criticisms directed toward "development" by Sachs, Esteva, Illich, and others.

What Esteva finds so remarkable about Truman's inaugural address is that "by using for the first time in such context the word, *underdeveloped,* Truman changed the meaning of development and created the emblem, a euphemism, used ever since either discretely or inadvertently to the era of American hegemony."[10] This observation leads us to consider that Truman's Point Four Program merely carried the "four freedoms" of Roosevelt's Atlantic Charter forward into the postwar era—freedom of religion, freedom of speech, freedom from fear, and freedom from want. The Atlantic Charter intended to communicate the allegedly anti-imperialist commitments that guided the formation of U.S. foreign policy prior to the nation's entry into World War II. As Esteva implies, however, the internal planning record documents a far different set of commitments than those advertised in the Charter.

As early as 1939, members of the U.S. policy-planning community accurately predicted that World War II would leave the industrial infrastructures of the colonial powers of Europe in ruin. Anticipating a German victory, members of this elite, business-dominated policy network set out to determine and enunciate to the federal executive "the political, military, territorial, and economic requirements of the United States in its potential leadership of the non-German world."[11] By the middle of 1941, they had arrived at a conclusion regarding the territorial requirements for their ever-expanding economic interests. In July, the scope of those requirements, which they had designated as the "Grand Area," included "the Western hemisphere, the United Kingdom, the remainder of the British Commonwealth and Empire, the Dutch East Indies, China, and Japan."[12] By the middle of December, however, after the Japanese invasion of Pearl Harbor pushed the United States into the war, the Council on Foreign Relations and the government committed themselves to the defeat of the Axis powers and the formation of "a *new world order* [emphasis added] with international political and economic institutions . . . which would join and integrate all of the earth's nations under the leadership of the United States."[13]

U.S. entry into the war, then, expanded the territorial vision of the Grand Area as the United States positioned itself to create the world's first truly global empire—a *pax Americana*. As Council of Foreign Affairs director Isaiah Bowman wrote just a week after U.S. entry into war: "The measure of our victory will be the measure of our domination after victory."[14] Just how that domination was to be secured and legitimated had yet to be determined.

In April of 1941, the Economic and Financial Group of the Council on Foreign Relations warned that:

> If war aims are to be stated which seem to be concerned solely with Anglo-American imperialism, they will offer little to people in the rest

of the world, and will be vulnerable to Nazi counter-promises. . . . The interests of other peoples should be stressed, not only those of Europe, but also of Asia, Africa, and Latin America. This would have a better propaganda effect.[15]

In acknowledgement that the "formulation of a statement of war aims for propaganda purposes" differs "from the formulation of one defining the true national interest," these elite planners committed themselves to developing a war statement that would "cultivate a mental view toward world settlement after this war which will enable us to impose our own terms, amounting perhaps to a pax-Americana."[16] That statement arrived in the form of the Atlantic Charter and the four freedoms that it professed to advance.

Set against this backdrop taken from the internal planning record, Truman's pronouncement on January 20, 1949, that "the old imperialism—exploitation for foreign profit—has no place in our plans" appears to be as dubious as Roosevelt's advertised desire to free all of humanity from want and fear. In pressing forward with the propaganda campaign initiated under Roosevelt, however, Truman cast U.S. foreign policy in the postwar era in terms of the benevolent cause of development.

Gustavo Esteva makes a very important observation in pointing out that global economization began first in Europe.[17] Its effects there mirrored many of the effects it would have on non-European populations once economic growth necessitated economic expansion—a necessity that gave rise to global economization's colonial era that ended, technically at least, at the end of World War II. Throughout the duration of its history and across its various transmutations, economization has declared war on traditional cultures, their autonomy, and their subsistence-oriented activities. Entire cultures and peoples have disappeared in its wake. Even those that have survived are no longer recognizable.

Expanding economization's reach beyond European boarders required considerable military force and numerous variants of racism to justify the intentions and consequences of conquest. Conroy identifies both militarism and racism as central to what we shall call the colonial period in the evolution of his character. To begin with, he informs us that his father was a career pilot with the U.S. Marine Corps. He tells us that throughout his boyhood he "worshipped the Marine Corps, her planes, and her pilots."[18] Eventually, he went on to earn his college degree from The Citadel. Most significantly, for Conroy, the "Corsair became a symbol of the past."[19] Within the context of global economization, we know that the Corsair symbolizes a past in which colonial domination was achieved and maintained by the technological superiority of the colonizer's weaponry. Beginning with Columbus, the early history of global economization is a story of military conquest as the great imperial powers set about transforming peoples and their commons into resources for economic growth. It is a past very closely tied to the history of the Gullah, whose ancestors were forcibly integrated into the international labor market via the largest forced migration in history, the slave trade.

Throughout much of the colonial era, the merchants and mercenaries of global economization did not even contemplate the idea that they might be impinging upon anyone else's human rights. Initially, Christianity was used to create the pretext for ignoring other people's humanity. Since beasts did not have souls, and since Africans, Asians, and indigenous peoples of the Western hemisphere were like beasts, perhaps they didn't have souls either. Therefore, if they resisted colonization, they could be slaughtered with virtual impunity. As religious institutions lost their influence and the modern nation-states took form, theories of scientific racism began performing the time-honored task of legitimating European domination of the world. Some people, after all, are not intelligent enough to govern themselves, and so they must be governed—all for their own good, of course.

Conroy explains that these colonial traditions were also part of the "mental view" of his youth. "My early years," he says,

darkened by the shadows and regional superstitions of a bona fide cracker boy, act as a sobering agent during the execrable period of self-righteousness that I inflict on those around me. Sometimes it is good for me to reflect on the Neanderthal period of my youth, when I rode in the backseat of a '57 Chevrolet along a night blackened Carolina road hunting for blacks to hit with rotten watermelons tossed from the window of the speeding car, as they walked the shoulder of the thin backroads. We called this intrepid form of entertainment "nigger-knocking," and it was great fun during the carnival of blind hatred I participated joyfully in during my first couple of years of high school.[20]

Racism and militarist nationalism played vital roles in legitimating the patterns of conquest and domination that characterized the global economy's colonial era. But as the atrocities of Hitler's Third Reich demonstrated the fullest expression of these ideologies and their potential consequences, racism, militarism, and nationalism lost much of their propaganda appeal by the end of World War II. The proper "mental view toward world settlement after this war which will enable us to impose our own terms, amounting perhaps to a pax-Americana," would require new conceptual foundations.

Although Conroy mentions that he visited Dachau while vacationing in Germany after he had taken his first teaching job, it was not this indelible experience that he credits with having affected his transformation. Rather, it was "the 1960s and the turbulence of social change [the Civil Rights Movement in particular] and the ominous presence of the unholy Asian war [that] killed [his] dreams of flight and soldierdom. From the ashes of the Corsair," he adds, "rose the passionate do-gooder."[21]

Though Esteva casts suspicion on Truman's intentions, his real concern lies not with the deceit spread by the Point Four Program as a propaganda campaign, but with the efficacy of that campaign in successfully cultivating the desired "mental view toward world settlement." He writes:

> Never before had a word (underdevelopment) been universally accepted on the very day of its political coinage. A new perception of one's own self, and of the other, was suddenly created. . . . Underdevelopment began, then, on January 20, 1949. On that day, two billion people became underdeveloped. In a real sense, from that time on, they ceased being what they were, in all their diversity, and were transmogrified into an inverted mirror of others' reality: a mirror that belittles them and sends them off to the end of the queue, a mirror that defines their identity, which is really that of a heterogeneous and diverse majority, simply in terms of a homogenizing and narrow minority. . . . Since then, development has connoted one thing: to escape from the undignified condition called underdevelopment.[22]

Between the time of Truman's address and Conroy's decision to seek a teaching position on Yamacraw, John F. Kennedy put the principles of the Point Four Program into action through the Alliance for Progress—an international "aid" program directed toward promoting economic development in Latin America. Shortly after Kennedy's assassination, Lyndon Johnson initiated a parallel "war on poverty" at home with his "Great Society" programs, which were primarily concerned with "urban development" on behalf of the poor in America's crowded cities. Both the foreign and the domestic policies of the United States reflected a so-called benevolent concern to "help" those who had somehow missed out on their share of economic growth. Reflective of just how profoundly the benevolent spirit of the early development era influenced his "mental view," Conroy's intentions prior to seeking a teaching position on Yamacraw Island were to join the Peace Corps. Having given up on his application with the Peace Corps, he tells the district school superintendent in Beaufort Country during his interview for the position, that "Yamacraw seemed like a viable alternative." To this the superintendent responds, "Son, you can do more good at Yamacraw than you could ever do in the Peace Corps. And you would be helping Americans!"[23]

Writing in Sachs's *Development Dictionary,* Marianne Gronemeyer says that "the positive image of help that is firmly seated in people's heads originates in old stories—the Good Samaritan binding up the wounds of the man who fell victim to robbers, or the legend of St. Martin sharing his coat with a beggar." What she finds common to all of these old stories is their:

> characterization of help as unconditional—given without regard to the person in need, the situation, the probability of success, or even the possibility of injury to the person offering aid. . . . The helper is simply overwhelmed by the sight of need. The help provided in these circumstances is like the compassion itself—much more an event than a deliberate act.[24]

The offers of help presented in the name of development, however, are hardly so innocent, despite the belief of some. Help loses its innocence when the need for it is diagnosed by strangers with a strategy for economic and political control. At that point, help loses its unconditionality and becomes an instrument through which one can impose upon others the obligation of good conduct.

Though it seems to contradict our common sense, the brand of help offered under the ideology of development also threatens those to whom the help is extended. Illich detects the same paradox in Truman's Point Four Program as a program for world peace. Illich associates this type of peace with the Roman notion of *pax.* "When the Roman governor raises the ensign of his legion to ram it into the soil of Palestine, he does not look toward heaven. He faces a far-off city; he imposes its law and its order."[25] Following a line of argumentation first developed by Karl Polanyi in *The Great Transformation,* Illich identifies the peace offered under development as a *pax economica,* which amounts to little more than a formal peace between economic powers as they proceed to wage a war against the rich diversity of traditional, subsistence-oriented cultures that existed on every continent prior to global economization.

Prior to the suffering and dislocation inflicted by their forced integration into the nascent global economy's international labor market via the slave trade, the African ancestors of the Gullah enjoyed their own traditional, subsistence-oriented culture on the continent. By Illich's definition, all such traditional cultures "can be conceived as meaningful configurations that have as their principal purpose the repression of those conditions under which scarcity could become dominant in social relations."[26] To do so, these subsistence-oriented societies limit their notion of human "needs" to that which is necessary to their community's survival. A people's needs take shape in relation to what natural forms of abundance they find in the commons and in relation to the social availability of means for drawing upon that abundance. Illich adopts the notion of the "vernacular" to characterize such needs and the activities that people pursue toward satisfying them. He argues that this word best expresses the sense in which they can be viewed as concrete responses to concrete conditions. And he points out that the Indo-Germanic root for *vernacular* suggests "rootedness" and "abode," whereas, in the Latin usage, *vernaculum*, referred to that which was homebread, homespun, homegrown, or homemade. Vernacular activities, Illich claims, "are not motivated by thoughts of exchange," but rather they imply "autonomous non-market-related action through which people satisfy everyday needs—the actions that by their own true nature escape bureaucratic control, satisfying needs to which, in the very process, they give specific shape."[27]

Economization, on the other hand, insists on scarcity as the defining characteristic of the human condition and, therefore, the universal condition of social life everywhere. Under the law of scarcity, human needs are no longer limited to the necessities for collective survival. This law transmogrifies limited needs into unlimited wants. And while vernacular activities enabled members of traditional cultures to obviate scarcity by providing for their collective survival, economization places conceptual limits on them, defining such patterns of social behavior as incompatible with economic growth/development. Those conceptual limits manifest themselves most clearly in the law of scarcity, which proclaims that "[humanity's] wants are great, not to say infinite, whereas [its] means are limited though improvable."[28] Instead of limiting people's needs, economization limits their means to satisfy them.

It accomplishes this in a twofold sense. As just described, the law of scarcity places conceptual limits on people's means to provide for their own needs. But in presenting itself as the ultimate improvement in those means, economization also disvalues all other forms of social existence. They become signs of "backwardness" and "underdevelopment." In producing this twofold scarcity of means, economization simultaneously awards itself supreme status in a hierarchy of universal human needs. Access to the market economy constitutes every people's most basic need. Without such access, their means for satisfying other needs remain forever limited.

The Gullah were among the few peoples in this hemisphere to successfully escape from their involuntary integration into the global economy. Their isolation also empowered the Gullah to determine their own needs in relation to what natural forms of abundance they found on the sea islands and in relation to the social availability of means for drawing upon that abundance, thus creating their own emergent culture in response to their concrete conditions on the sea islands.

By the time that Conroy arrived, the Gullah's traditional culture on Yamacraw was threatened by encroaching development as well as the environmental damage created by the industrial wastes flowing into the water. The surrounding waters had always been an important component of the Gullah's commons, providing them with a major food source as well as a source of income. The environmental degradation created by mainland industries included the contamination of the oyster beds around Yamacraw, thereby disrupting the Gullah's cultural patterns as well as their commons. Thus, while they had escaped involuntary integration into the global economy, even their isolation on the sea islands couldn't protect the Gullah from its toxic effects forever. Conroy notes how the "tall columns of white smoke from the smokestacks on the mainland side of the river . . . rose like false gods on the horizons and from [his] boat were salacious and impure reminders of the absolute insistence on man that he defile all he touches."[29] However, Conroy was unable to see the threats of cultural degradation carried by his own good intentions.

In titling his book *The Water Is Wide*, Conroy implies that the Gullah's isolation has been their greatest disadvantage, blocking them from developing at the same pace as the rest of the nation. The development model of reality incapacitates Conroy from recognizing the people on Yamacraw as members of a unique cultural group whose isolation from the mainland granted them many advantages in creating and maintaining their own independent mode of existence. It restricts his vision to a perception of them as the victims of a shameful poverty in a nation of grotesque inequalities. Though these ancestors of African slaves are now citizens of the United States—the richest nation on earth—their standard of living closely resembles that of many "underdeveloped" countries. Hence, in viewing teaching on Yamacraw as a viable alternative to joining the Peace Corps, Conroy has internalized one of the great certainties of our cultural epoch—the belief that a people's economic development proceeds in direct proportion to their level of educational achievement.

Thus, Conroy defines the "otherness" of the people on Yamacraw in terms of a lack (of education and development) that the development model of reality conditions him to identify as their defining characteristic. It conditions him to view them not as Gullah children, but most fundamentally as "needy" Americans. For their part, the children do not identify themselves as Americans. They don't even know that they live within the borders of a country called the United States of America. They don't know the name of its president. They don't know that the body of water surrounding their island is called the Atlantic Ocean. They don't know who Willie Mays is. They don't know how to read, how to write, how to speak standard English, or how to count. And they certainly don't know that they are needy.[30]

As one proponent of global economization wrote in 1960:

> The economic development of an underdeveloped people by themselves is not compatible with the maintenance of their traditional customs and mores. A break with the latter is requisite to economic progress. What is needed is a revolution in the totality of social, cultural, and religious institutions and habits, and thus in their psychological attitude, their philosophy and way of life. What is, therefore, required amounts in reality to social disorganization. Unhappiness and discontentment in the sense of wanting more than is obtainable at any moment is to be generated. The suffering and dislocation that may be caused in the process may be objectionable, but it appears to be the price that has to be paid for economic development; the condition of economic progress.[31]

To help facilitate such a break between the children of Yamacraw and their "traditional customs and mores" and to convince them of their own neediness, Conroy relates that, in his classroom,

> Always we spoke about the world beyond the river. . . . Always we turned outward to where they would drift when they left Yamacraw, to the world of lights and easy people, to the dark cities that would devour their innocence and harden their dreams.[32] . . . The one goal I developed the first week that never changed was to prepare the kids for the day when they would leave the island for the other side.[33]

As the metaphorical embodiment of economization, Conroy disvalues the Gullah's traditional mode of social existence. Never does he address the peculiarity of their past and how it shaped their present. Their past, for Conroy, is merely a burden, indistinguishable from their present and a preview of their future unless someone intervenes—someone like himself. Although he recognizes, for example, "a direct connection between the education of [his] parents and the education of their children, the dreams of [his] parents and the dreams of their children," he acknowledges only "a link, straight and uncomplicated, between the parents of Yamacraw and their children"[34]—no education and no dreams, just a straight and uncomplicated link. The parental link signifies, for Conroy, that "everything [occurs] in cycles, fanged and implacable cycles. Somehow," he adds,

> I had to interfere with the cycle [on Yamacraw] or interrupt it, interject my own past into the present of my students. If I let my students leave me without altering the conditions of their existence substantially, I knew a concrete, sightless ghetto of some city without hope would devour them quickly, irretrievably, and hopelessly. I could hear some white voice coming from some collective unconscious deep within me saying, "They don't know any better. They're happy this way." Yet all around me, in the grinning faces of my students, I could see a crime, so ugly that it could be interpreted as a condemnation of an entire society . . . these children before me did not stand a goddam chance of sharing in the incredible wealth and affluence of the country that claimed them, a country that failed them, a country that needed but did not deserve deliverance.[35]

Conditioned as he is by "the law of scarcity" to view those who do not share the affluence provided for by "the American way of life" as needy, Conroy does not perceive the people on Yamacraw as Gullah; he sees them as "underdeveloped." And in understanding himself as "a symbolic bridge between the children of Yamacraw and the outside world," he seeks to render them dependent on his professional services for the salvation that his pedagogy, offered in the name of "helping," imposes on them.

CONCLUSION

Though anyone even remotely committed to the principles of multicultural education would shudder at the thought of using Hirsch's notion of cultural literacy as the basis for curricular renovation in a reservation school, the idea is not exactly without precedent. As David Wallace Adams explains in his excellent book on the history of Native American education, early "doves" discovered that educating Native Americans was a more cost-efficient means of exterminating them than the more conventional method of simply murdering them.[36] Nevertheless, I am convinced that Peter Jefferson was every bit as genuine in his desire to "help" the Crow children at St. Charles as Pat Conroy was in his efforts on Yamacraw. I am also convinced that he was was equally blind to the underlying violence of his good intentions. No less than Conroy refused to view the Gullah children as anything more than poor Blacks, Jefferson's decision to transport Hirsch's model of culutral literacy onto the reservation demonstrated the same contempt for the Crow children and their cultural identity.

NOTES

[1] Anna Marie Evans (Ed.), *Teaching the Diaspora* (New York: Peter Lang, in press).

[2] Pat Conroy, *The Water Is Wide* (New York: Bantam Books, 1972/1994), p. 19.

[3] Marianne Gronemeyer, "Helping," in *The Development Dictionary: A Guide to Knowledge as Power,* edited by Wolfgang Sachs (Atlantic Highlands, NJ: Zed Books, 1992), p. 54.

[4] Ivan Illich, *Deschooling Society* (New York: Harper, 1971), p. 1.

[5] Ivan Illich, *Celebration of Awareness* (Berkeley, CA: Heyday Books, 1970), pp. 41–51.

[6] Harry S Truman, Inaugural address, January 20, 1949, in *Public Papers of the Presidents of the United States: Harry S Truman: Containing the Public Messages, Speeches, and Statements of the President January 1 to December 31, 1949* (Washington: Government Printing Office, 1964), p. 19.

[7] Gustavo Esteva, "Development," in *The Development Dictionary: A Guide to Knowledge as Power,* edited by Wolfgang Sachs (Atlantic Highlands, NJ: Zed Books, 1992).

[8] Truman, Inaugural address, p. 19.

[9] Ivan Illich, *Shadow Work* (Salem, NH: Marion Boyars Publishers, 1981), and Ivan Illich, "The De-linking of Peace and Development," in *The Mirror of the Past* (New York: Marion Boyars, 1992).

[10] Esteva, p. 6.

[11] Memorandum E-A10, 19 October 1940, Council on Foreign Relations, War-Peace Studies, Baldwin Papers, Box 117, Yale University Library. Cited in

Laurence H. Shoup and William Minter, "Shaping a New World Order: The Council on Foreign Relations' Blueprint for World Hegemony," in Holly Sklar (Ed.), *Trilateralism: The Trilateral Commission and Elite Planning for World Management,* pp. 135–156, (Boston: South End Press, 1980), p. 139.

[12] Laurence H. Shoup and William Minter, "Shaping a New World Order: The Council on Foreign Relations' Blueprint for World Hegemony," in Holly Sklar (Ed.), *Trilateralism: The Trilateral Commission and Elite Planning for World Management,* pp. 135–156, (Boston: South End Press, 1980), p. 141.

[13] Ibid., p. 142.

[14] Bowman to Hamilton Fish Armstrong, 15 December 1941, *Bowman Papers, Armstrong File,* Johns Hopkins University Library, cited in Laurence H. Shoup and William Minter, "Shaping a New World Order: The Council on Foreign Relations' Blueprint for World Hegemony," in Holly Sklar (Ed.), *Trilateralism: The Trilateral Commission and Elite Planning for World Management,* pp. 135–156 (Boston: South End Press, 1980), p. 146.

[15] Memorandum E-B32, 17 April 1941, CFR, War-Peace Studies, Northwestern University Library, cited in Laurence H. Shoup and William Minter, "Shaping a New World Order: The Council on Foreign Relations' Blueprint for World Hegemony," in Holly Sklar (Ed.), *Trilateralism: The Trilateral Commission and Elite Planning for World Management,* pp. 135–156 (Boston: South End Press, 1980), p. 146.

[16] Minutes S-3 of the Security Subcommittee, Advisory Committee on Postwar Foreign Policy, May 1942, Notter File, Box 77, R.G. 59, cited in Laurence H. Shoup and William Minter, "Shaping a New World Order: The Council on Foreign Relations' Blueprint for World Hegemony," in Holly Sklar (Ed.), *Trilateralism: The Trilateral Commission and Elite Planning for World Management,* pp. 135–156 (Boston: South End Press, 1980), pp. 146–147.

[17] Esteva, p. 17.

[18] Conroy, p. 77.

[19] Ibid.

[20] Ibid., p. 5.

[21] Ibid., p. 77.

[22] Esteva, pp. 6 and 7.

[23] Conroy, p. 1.

[24] Gronemeyer, p. 53.

[25] Ibid., p. 54.

[26] Illich, "The De-linking of Peace and Development," p. 16.

[27] Ivan Illich, "The History of Homo Educandus," in the *Mirror of the Past* (New York: Marion Boyars, 1992), p. 117.

[28] Illich, *Shadow Work,* pp. 57–58.

[29] Esteva, p. 19.

[30] Conroy, p. 157.

[31] J. L. Sadie, "The Social Anthropology of Economic Underdevelopment," in *The Economic Journal,* No. 70, 1960, p. 302, in Gérald Berthoud, "Market," in *The Development Dictionary: A Guide to Knowledge as Power,* edited by Wolfgang Sachs (Atlantic Highlands, NJ: Zed Books, 1992).

[32] Conroy, pp. 210–211.

[33] Ibid., p. 138.

[34] Ibid.

[35] Ibid.

[36] David Wallace Adams. *Education for Extinction: American Indians and the Boarding School Experience 1875–1928* (Lawrence, KS: University of Kansas Press, 1995), pp. 19–20.

CHAPTER 10

Teaching in Our Underwear
The Liabilities of Whitcness in the Multiracial Classroom

MARYANN DICKAR

The title of this paper is drawn from a story a friend told me who has taught junior high school in New York City for twenty-five years. He explained that every year just before school starts he has the perennial teacher's nightmare, in which he finds himself in his classroom, teaching with no clothes on. This dream, which he claims is common among teachers, has always suggested for him the deep anxieties embedded within the activity of teaching—the fear of exposure, the sense of being seen "as I really am": unprepared, vulnerable, and perhaps even a fraud. He told me this story as I was trying to interpret the narratives I had been reading by white teachers about their experiences teaching inner-city students of color. I had wanted to use these narratives as a way of exploring the discourses surrounding inner-city youth. However, these narratives proved to be much more about the teachers writing them than about the students they were writing about. In fact, more than participating in discourses on inner-city youth, these narratives exposed the multiple discourses on race that white teachers employ to address difference in the classroom and to understand the educational, cultural, and political work they do as teachers.

My friend's story highlighted the concept of exposure that informs these narratives. Many of them are, in fact, exposés intended to reveal the brutalities of an unjust system. However, in the process they expose the anxieties around whiteness summoned up by the experience of teaching in environments in which the material conditions of racism are ever present and whiteness is no longer the norm and, therefore, no longer invisible. Herbert Kohl expresses this sense of exposure in *36 Children* (1967), as he faced his sixth-grade class in Harlem for the first time.

> The children entered at nine and filled up the seats. They were silent
> and stared at me. It was a shock to see thirty-six black faces before me.
> No preparation helped. It is one thing to be liberal and talk, another to
> face something and learn that you're afraid. (p. 13)

Kohl interpreted this fear as a realization of the great racial divide between him and his students. He admitted, "The weight of Harlem and my
whiteness and strangeness hung in the air as I droned on, lost in my righteous monologue" (p. 15). Kohl knew that teaching in Harlem would
mean that his students would be black; however, he was still unprepared
for the shock of experiencing himself as "the other." His whiteness was
strange, not his students' blackness. His subject position was uncomfort-
ably exposed, not as much to his students, who were used to seeing white
teachers, but to himself. Kohl suggests that part of the shame of being
seen as we really are—in our underwear—comes from seeing ourselves
as white in environments where whiteness signifies power and privilege.
I term this recognition of the cultural meanings of whiteness *the liabilities of whiteness* because the privileges that white teachers had hitherto
experienced as normal or typical and therefore invisible (in the time before they become teachers in multiracial schools) are exposed and create
challenges in the classroom.

Emily Sachar in her narrative, *Shut Up and Let the Lady Teach*
(1991), defines *the liabilities of whiteness* as a deep sense of anxiety that
plagues her the entire year.

> When I learned that I would be teaching in a school where half the fac-
> ulty and 90 percent of the students were black, I tried to examine my
> own racial attitudes and thoughts. Was I prejudiced? Might I say the
> wrong thing to the wrong people? How would I fit in? (p. 187)

Her concern that she will say the wrong thing to the wrong people suggests that if she were teaching in a white school she would not have felt
this anxiety, and thus the "wrong people" are people of color. White environments are safe, but those dominated by people of color are dangerous. Her anxiety about her ability to offend and her inability to know
what was the right thing to say suggests that she perceived the world of
face-to-face race relations as murky terrain, which she must navigate
without a map.

The ease with which she had hitherto sailed through her professional
life as a journalist was grounded in her whiteness, but in an environment
in which whiteness was suspect and scrutinized, it became a liability.

Faced with the realization of their own difference, white teachers have deployed discourses on race to minimize the significance of racial difference. Often these discourses serve to reestablish hegemonic norms rather than to challenge them and draw upon racial ideologies already present in American society in the latter part of the twentieth century. I am using *discourse* in a Foucauldian sense, as a framework or "regime of truth" that structures the ways the world is understood. In the essay that follows, I explore some of the prevalent discourses on race that inform the ways white teachers reproduce racial ideologies and the subordinate position of students of color. I suggest that a critical analysis of these discourses, academically, by teachers in their own reflections on their work and in the classroom, are necessary to an antiracist pedagogy. The three discourses I will explore here are: (1) race and power evasive discourses—avoiding race by simply not seeing race, (2) an individualistic discourse—which places the onus of success and failure on individuals, not on institutions and social structures, and (3) what I call a discourse of deflection—discourses that deflect racism either by clinging to other marginalized identities (I can't be racist because I'm . . .) or by blaming others and not oneself. All three discourses are employed by white teachers in their narratives and generally limit a dismantling of structural racism from within the public school system. Despite our best intentions and idealistic goals, these discourses reproduce racial hierarchies and the privileged position of whiteness by ignoring the historical experiences of people of color and by ignoring the complexity of the meanings of identity. If white teachers are to participate in antiracist pedagogy, we must recognize the limits of widely employed discourses on race and move beyond them. We must also help our students recognize these discourses so that they can enter into a world that they can both understand and change.

Before I begin a critique of the discourses employed by white teachers, I must place myself in this community. From 1989 to 1991, I taught in Brooklyn, New York, in a school whose student population was comprised completely of students of color. At that time, I believed it was important to open up discussions of racism with my students, but also believed that they should embrace the opportunities that education offered them and aim to become middle class. I thought that if my students could "make it" (i.e., become middle class) that they would somehow change the nature of American society by their positive contributions to it as members of the middle class. I was unaware at that time of the discourses on race I was employing, but was aware that they were contradictory. I wanted my students to be proud of their blackness, but I also wanted them to become more like me (white). I was also unsatisfied with my analysis of the racial dynamics that were ever present in the school, but I was unsure of how to move outside of the liberal framework into which I had sewn myself. This essay is part of my rethinking of my own work as a teacher, my efforts to connect the insights of a discursive analysis to the work of the classroom in the hopes of finding meaningful ways of disrupting racism.

Although in this essay I will address independently each of the three discourses named earlier, they do not function discretely. The authors of the narratives I examined strategically employed discourses that, though they can be contradictory, are used simultaneously. I am isolating them here in order to describe and critique them, but they are part of what Ruth Frankenberg has described as a "discursive repertoire." The teachers examined here are not individualists, evasivists, or deflectionists but rather are an eclectic bunch who draw upon all of these discourses in numerous ways and for different strategic purposes (1993, p. 140).

A passage from LouAnne Johnson's *My Posse Don't Do Homework* (1992) vividly depicts the ways discursive repertoires operate. Johnson's narrative is significant because she is, in many ways, an effective teacher who has found ways of motivating at-risk youth, particularly African-American and Mexican-American young men. However, despite many of her strengths as a teacher, an individualist discourse permeates her narrative as she goes to great lengths to avoid confronting or reflecting upon the ways race shapes her students' lives and her own. However, from time to time she is unable to avoid the issues and periodically shares with her reader her awareness that race and racism significantly shape her work. In one anecdote, she describes her frustration after breaking up numerous fights between black and Hispanic boys.

> I know you kids are angry . . . because the world isn't fair. Well, get over it, because it's never going to be fair. The white boys have all the money and all the power and that's the way it is. And they aren't going to give it up—to you or to me. (1992, p. 230)

After this explicit recognition that her male students must cope with a structural racism that systematically denies them the privileges of "the white boys," she asks them whether, if they had the money and the power, would they be willing to "share the wealth" and "make the world more equal" (p. 230). When none of them raise a hand, she continues,

"You're not selfish. . . . You're human. So stop expecting other people
not to be human. If you want some of that money, or some of that
power, you have to work for it. You can go to school, or practice until
you're the best at something, or start at the bottom and work your way
up—but beating up on other people isn't going to get you anywhere except in jail or dead." Suddenly, I heard my own voice, doing its soapbox soft shoe again. I felt foolish, as though I had been dancing around
in front of the class in my underwear, and I felt tired, very tired. (1992,
p. 231)

In this passage, Johnson, is very clear that racism exists and that
white people benefit from it. Though Johnson diminishes the significance of her observation and her anger by defining it as her "soapbox soft
shoe," she makes a crucial link between the recognition of structural
racism and sexism and exposure. Hearing her "own voice" speaking
against the racial and gender status quo makes her feel "foolish." Thus,
she is shamed both by her devaluing of the authority of her own feminine
voice and by her whiteness in light of her recognition of institutionalized
racism. However, even as she acknowledges racism as a structural phenomenon, she nonetheless employs race-evasive, individualist, and deflecting discourses to minimize the significance of that observation.
Though she acknowledges the structural functioning of racism, she also
immediately remedies it by instructing her students to pull themselves up
by their bootstraps—to get some of the power that the "white boys" have
by working for it, as individuals in a competitive society. However, in
light of the previous observation, the logic here is unclear. If the white
boys aren't going to give up power, how will hard work change anything? Here, a race-cognizant discourse and an individualist discourse
contradict one another.

At the same time, Johnson deploys discourses of deflection by blaming structural racism specifically on white men. As a white woman, she,
like her students, does not have access to money and power. She is one of
them, not one of the "white boys." By calling on her identity as a woman
to dismiss her own culpability and participation in white privilege and
racism, she deflects racism away from herself, dumping the burden of
guilt on white men. Also by insisting that if her students (the oppressed)
had the power, they would do unto others as has been done unto them,
she renders abuses of power and privilege, exploitation, and coercion as
natural—part of the essence of being human. By doing so, she constructs
racism, which is historically and materially specific, as a product of

human nature and therefore outside of history—it is not socially constructed but predetermined. This construction is a race- and power-evasive strategy. She denies the significance of oppressive hierarchies by defining them as part of the nature of things and, therefore, outside the purview of change. By rendering racism as a relatively mute point, she avoids addressing it as something she and her students can confront and attack. Thus, within one passage that makes sense on first reading, numerous contradictions occur. Racism is something that is structural, historically specific, and a legitimate source of student anger, but it is also completely natural and therefore inevitable. It is something they can do something about through hard work, but it is also beyond their control. Thus, Johnson offers here a clear example of how discursive repertoires operate and how they often cloud meaningful discussions of how race is overlooked, through contradictions, assumptions, and negations. These discourses operate to contain student anger rather than probe it, leaving racism unchallenged and offering students few options.

By calling upon them to dispense advice to students, Johnson reproduces them and the privileges they hide and protect, rather than critically attacking the structures that enrage both her and her students.

Although these discourses operate simultaneously, it is important to analyze them individually in order to critique the impact they have on pedagogy. One of the most pervasive discourses that operates in American racial ideology is what Frankenberg has defined as race-evasive and power-evasive discourses. Simply put, these discourses deny the significance of race by refusing to "see" race or difference and by denying the power relationships embedded within those differences. Emily Sachar's narrative employs race-evasive strategies in a number of circumstances. Sachar taught at a junior high school in the Flatbush section of Brooklyn, in a school whose population was overwhelmingly black and whose teaching staff was multiracial, half of them people of color. Her narrative offers insight into the difficult terrain of confronting race in the United States. White teachers must address the distrust and scrutiny of their colleagues of color, who are often critical of the discursive repertoires upon which white teachers rely (Delpit, 1993).

Unlike Johnson, Sachar does not, and perhaps could not, avoid discussing race—she was constantly embattled by colleagues who were suspicious of her, not only because she was a self-identified "white liberal," but also because she was the education writer for *New York Newsday* and writing a book about the school. Amidst this racially charged environment, Sachar employs race-evasive tactics to avoid confronting her own racism. Evasion marks the text from the beginning of the narrative. When asked by the principal, "Why do you want to teach inner-city children?" (1991, p. 42), she answered, "the school is close to my home, and I've always wanted to teach" (p. 43). Sachar ignored the thrust of the principal's question. He was not asking her why she wanted to teach or why she wanted to teach at Whitman Junior High. He asked her why she wanted to teach "inner-city" youth, a not so cryptic code word for the students of color who attended his school. In her answer she erased significant aspects of the identity of the students, avoiding entirely the much more difficult question about her political commitments to them.

Evasive strategies avoid naming race or recognizing the significance of racial identity in order to avoid naming the power relationships that shape those identities. In a chapter entitled "Uncivil War," Sachar chronicles tension between black and white teachers. Though she acknowledges racism on the part of white teachers, she emphasizes the racism of her black colleagues. In one anecdote she describes a classic example of a race-evasive discourse, and it provides a clear model to discuss how these discourses can be dangerous in the classroom.

> One spring afternoon, tending another teacher's unruly class, an exasperated black teacher shouted, "What's this? When whitey walks in the door, you sit down? But not for me?" The white teacher was, in turn, outraged to hear of this incident and accosted her colleague in the hall as kids swirled around. "I'm not the one who sees color. You are. . . . I don't care if the kids I teach are purple or covered with green polka dots. . . . If I saw color, I wouldn't be in this school." A few of the students came to the defense of their white teacher. "She ain't like that," one girl said. "She don't care if we're pink or blue. She's a great teacher." (1991, p. 185)

In this passage, the black teacher is construed as racist. By referring to the white teacher as "whitey," the black teacher used a racial slur, an overt expression of racial hostility. What is ignored here is that, despite the racial slur, the black teacher was calling the students' attention to issues of power, that they themselves might react differently to white and black teachers. It was inappropriate and unprofessional, to say the least, to use a derogatory term to describe another person. However, by focusing on the slur and not on the potential meaning of the whole comment, the black teacher was silenced, and his or her observations dismissed. Secondly, the black teacher is defined as a racist because he or she sees color. By claiming that she doesn't, the white teacher defines "color" as different and difference as bad. To see race, then, is to focus on difference, not on sameness. Such constructions of racial difference deny the historical and cultural meanings of difference and suggest that under the skin, we're all really white, as sameness is equated with whiteness, the norm. Insisting that one doesn't see color is to insist that skin color has no meaning in the United States.

The white teacher further dismisses the meaning of race by equating purple and polka-dotted with racial color. In so doing, she "camouflages socially significant differences of color in a welter of meaningless ones" (Frankenberg, 1993, p.149). Ultimately, her students are not purple, or pink, or blue; they are, in fact, black and brown, differences that have meaning. Importantly, the student echoes the white teacher's negation of racial difference, learning that denying difference is a morally preferable position to recognizing it. Sachar draws upon the students' support of their white teacher to vindicate the white teacher who was involved and, by extension, all color-blind white teachers. One of the lessons of the informal curriculum in this instance, then, was teaching students of color specific ways of understanding race in America, which erased their racial identities and any possible positive reasons to see race. This incident calls attention to the importance of scrutinizing the discourses we rely upon because we do teach them to our students and reproduce the assumptions embedded within them, that often work to preserve white privilege.

Also, when teachers honestly analyze their interactions with students they do see their color and learn to value difference. Vivian Gussin Paley began teaching integrated kindergarten classes with a color-blind policy. She thought the best way to deal with difference in the classroom was to ignore it. However, her narrative, *White Teacher* (1979), explores her own reevaluation of her understandings of racial difference. Drawing upon her own experiences of marginalization as a Jew in a predominantly gentile world, her interaction with black parents who valued racial and cultural difference, and her observations of children who were learning to make their way in a raced world, Paley developed a critique of race-evasive discourses.

She realized that she did see color and so did her students and that it was not talking about difference that defined it as negative. Paley's narrative offers a valuable critique of race-evasive discourses through her observations of children in the classroom.

In addition to race-evasive discourses, teachers cope with the liabilities of whiteness by employing deflecting discourses. Unlike race- and power-evasive discourses, deflecting ones do not deny that race and difference are significant. Rather, such discourses divert attention away from the potential racism of the speaker and place blame elsewhere. Deflecting discourses often use one identity to negate another. Earlier, Johnson used her identity as a woman to deflect her culpability in the evils of whiteness. Often, this discourse takes the form of "I can't be racist because I'm _____." It assumes that if one is a victim of societal oppression in any form, one cannot participate in the oppression of others. Thompson and Tyagi report that in an upper-level sociology class a professor, accused of inadvertently reproducing racist and homophobic stereotypes, retorted that "as a woman she understood subordination and would never participate in it" (1993, p. 87). This incident demonstrates how discourses of deflection enable people to dodge accusations of bigotry by claiming other subordinate identities, and it also suggests that these discourses are often employed defensively, in the face of a direct accusation of racism or a strongly implied one.

Such discourses privilege "victim" status—you can't be an oppressor if you are the victim of oppressive forces—and inform the recent trend of right-wing opponents of multiculturalism and affirmative action who claim that white men are now an "endangered species."

Other deployments of discourses of deflection more specifically blame someone else or another group for racism. This strategy deflects the culpability away from the speaker and places it squarely on another's shoulders but still functions to deflect the enactment of racism away from the speaker and to enable the speaker to avoid confronting his or her own attitudes, feelings, and actions. Over time, Sachar comes to blame the African-American women who openly distrust her and sometimes insult her rather than inspect her own attitudes. Upon hearing from her students that some of her black colleagues had told them she was a racist, she confesses to us that these accusations,

> played straight to my deepest fears: that my upbringing had left me insensitive, a liberal who condescended toward blacks and indeed, was a thoughtless bigot. I did not yet feel secure enough to consider that it might be the other way around. (1991, p. 189)

As incidents at school force Sachar's anxieties about racism to the surface, she prevents them from fully emerging by blaming her black colleagues for being racist towards her.

Though often deployed as a shield to protect speakers from the accusations of racism or introspection, deflecting discourses can also be used to direct attention to an "enemy" for strategic purposes. In Johnson's speech, she constructs "the white boys" as the enemy, enabling her to assert a unity with her students. In *Death at an Early Age* (1967), Jonathan Kozol accuses the white women who run his school of being the racists responsible for perpetuating the brutal and unjust treatment of black school children in Roxbury. In this narrative Kozol traces his own coming of age as a man and as an activist committed to the dismantling of racism. This rite of passage is embedded within his increasing awareness of injustice and his own role within that system as one who is white and relatively privileged. As Kozol works to separate himself from institutionalized racism, it becomes engendered female through his connection to women and power within the school system. Women run the school and make all significant decisions concerning the organization and utilization of resources, curriculum, and pedagogy and act to prevent Kozol from validating the life experiences of his students through the inclusion of African-American historical experience and literature. He resents the self-righteousness of these female teachers and their presumption that they know what is good for the children of Roxbury, even as they mock them and denigrate their culture, language, and heritage. This white female racism is the insidious, unredeemable racism that must be confronted and dismantled.

> I don't think that it is quite so vicious or malignant or even dangerous to pupils to come straight out and admit that you can't stand them as it is to go on and on in the way that the Reading Teacher did, and to pretend endlessly that you have some kind of massive and inscrutable and all-enveloping love for the very children whom you are at that moment destroying. It is one of the interesting and odd things about that year that, looking back, I feel so much more involvement with, and even hopefulness about, that outright bigot who called the Southern Negroes niggers than I do about the pious maiden ladies who will probably go on forever thinking that they love the people they are killing. (p. 66–67)

The ironic reference to the women as "pious" underscores Kozol's spiritual crisis as he struggles to find a way of attacking racism as he is thwarted in his efforts by these white women. They are the impious and impure who dishonestly abuse their power, whereas the male bigot is redeemable for no other reason than his frankness and, by implication, his maleness. Both power and racism (and dishonesty) are ascribed specifically to women here and throughout the narrative, letting white men off the hook for much of the brutality of the system.

Kozol separates himself from institutionalized racism by constructing the system as feminine. By blaming the white women who run the school (and who eventually fire him) for the perpetuation of racism, Kozol deflects guilt away from himself, and by focusing on their racism, he does not have to focus much on his own. Although he acknowledges, quite poignantly, that white people all benefit from racism, he is able to separate himself from it by blaming it on others. Thus, he attacks racism at the same time that he perpetuates sexist depictions of women with power.

Although Kozol is fired for his efforts, the experience and his subsequent decisions to live in Roxbury and participate in the struggle for civil rights enable him to claim himself to be almost one of them, African-Americans. By blaming racism on a specific subset of white people, he is able to deflect the liabilities of whiteness that might have complicated this positioning of himself and his work.

Kozol's ability to oppose one form of domination while maintaining another, points to the fact that the relationship between oppressor and oppressed is not a polarized—either one or the other—relationship, a central assumption of many deflecting discourses. Black feminists and other feminists of color have called attention to the simultaneity of identities with intersections of gender, race, class, and sexuality all mediating each other. Deflecting discourses ignore these crucial intersections and prevent any critical examination of the way power operates in contemporary society. Rather than clarifying experience, these discourses mask the exercise of power as they are employed to deflect or hide privilege behind a shield of victimization. Race-evasive discourses and discourses of deflection prevent the deep questioning of our assumptions and fears and ultimately protect white people from confronting their own racism and positions of power. Discourses of deflection enabled some of the teachers examined here to come to the precipice of realizing their own racism and turn away without reflecting upon it. These discourses operate not so much to deny the meaning of race, but to displace uncomfortable feelings and anxieties. Ultimately, though not race-evasive, deflecting discourses are power-evasive. In deflecting racism, white teachers often are protecting themselves from owning our privileges.

The final strand of the discursive repertoire that I want to explore here is the individualist discourse that permeates much of contemporary culture, from political speeches to television shows. This discourse is grounded in the deep traditions of liberalism in Western culture, which centers upon the free individual operating within a free market and open social hierarchy (i.e., no royalty with unfair privileges). Classical liberalism assumes that, first and foremost, we are all individuals and only secondly (if at all) embedded in a social and cultural matrix. Individualist discourses deemphasize the structures of social relations that set the parameters on an individual's life chances, such as racism, sexism, classism, and homophobia. At their worst, and unfortunately far too frequently, these discourses are deployed to blame the victims of structural oppression for their failure. When we refuse to recognize circumstances outside the individual, the only explanation for failure is individual inadequacy, even in the face of profound and sometimes obvious inequality.

Johnson's narrative acknowledges structural racism but promotes individual solutions. In the example I drew from earlier in this paper, Johnson named structural racism, sexism, and economic inequalities as clear obstacles that her students face; however, her solution is that they should work their way up. Changing the system, even critiquing it, are not options she encourages them to explore. In many ways, individualist discourses are appealing because social change is a slow process, and an individual discourse offers immediate, logical, and obvious solutions to concrete problems. Also, these discourses can, at their best, encourage students to imagine their futures, to strive for goals, and to take responsibility for their actions. Johnson's use of individualist discourses tends to focus on such outcomes but also denies some of the significant obstacles her students face.

The limitation of individualist discourses is that they leave those who employ them without a way of explaining structural oppression. Such limitations become obvious when students have to confront complex issues of race, class, and gender but have only an individualist vocabulary upon which to draw. The limitations of this vocabulary become clear in Johnson's narrative, when some of her articulate Mexican students are unable to explain why they did surprisingly poorly in mock job interviews with representatives from local corporations. All the boys in the "posse" (from whence the title, *My Posse Don't Do Homework*) got low ratings from the interviewers because of "no eye contact, hostile attitude, poor articulation, sloppy posture, unwilling to talk." Johnson confronted Raul, one of the Mexican American boys, who was generally articulate and outgoing, about why he did not make eye contact.

"I don't know," he mumbled. "I just couldn't talk to that guy."

"Why not?" I repeated.

"I couldn't," Raul said. "I don't know why, but I just couldn't do it, Miss J."

"Did he say something mean to you?"

"No," Raul said. "He was pretty nice."

"So why didn't you talk to him?"

"He's wearing that fancy suit," Raul said.

"That's just clothes," I said. "You know better than to judge a man by his clothes."

"Well, he kept staring at me," Raul said.

"How else is he going to see you if he doesn't look at you?"

"He probably thinks I'm ugly. That's why he was staring at me."

"Where did you ever get an idea like that?"

"From the magazines," Raul said. "And catalogs and stuff. I don't look like those white guys." (1993, pp. 234–235)

Raul calls attention to a number of significant issues here. First, he is unable to explain his personal failure at the interview and gropes for a way of expressing his feelings of intimidation and utter lack of confidence. Though he cannot clearly explain why the experience was so negative, he does focus on both the suit and the stare of the interviewer, calling attention to the fact that when he and the interviewer faced each other, Raul was confronting issues of race and class. Raul saw the men and suits as much more than men in appropriate business dress, as Johnson thought they were. Rather, the interviewers were representatives of an entire system of power relationships as they literally and figuratively represented corporations and corporate power. They were also white men who, in their business suits, represented a whole cultural way of being that Raul could not project himself into because he was Mexican. Raced and classed positions were being enacted in the mock interviews as students were supposed to be learning how to function in interviews, which was also about functioning in a white and middle-class world. Raul is unable to directly focus on these issues; rather, he insists that he just doesn't know why he couldn't look them in the eye. He perceives his failure in the interviews as a personal failure—apologizing, "I'm sorry I let you down" (p. 235). So does Johnson, and even as Raul points to things that hint at broader social relationships, she individualizes them, that is, "You know better than to judge a man by his clothes." He is left inarticulate by an individualist discourse, able only to hint at racial and class formations that are beyond his control but shape his experience, and Johnson, here, does not help him out.

Raul's perception that the interviewers were staring at him and judging him harshly highlights the powerlessness he felt trapped in the gaze of the corporate executive. His statement that "he probably thinks I'm ugly" is grounded in his reading of American culture, informed by his experience in it as poor and Mexican. The focus he places on catalogs and magazines as the source of his knowledge that he does not fit in corporate America suggests a connection between whiteness and wealth in publications that rely on depictions of "the good life" (and the white life) to create desire and to sell goods. The students experienced the interviewers as people who had incredible power—the power to judge—and read into them a system of economic, racial, and gendered power relationships. Moreover, they understood that within that economy, they simply did not fit in. Individualist discourses left them no way of expressing this interpretation of the interviews because such discourses deny that structures outside the individual make much difference.

Johnson's narrative demonstrates that not only do these discourses leave students unable to explain to themselves and to others what they experience, but also how culturally specific individualist discourses are. Although they parade themselves as being universal truths, they are also products of a white, bourgeois, and capitalist culture. Raul could not fit himself into the interviewers' world because he was Mexican and a member of the working class in California, a historically specific collective identity. He was uncomfortable with the protocols of the dominant bloc and aware that they didn't fit him. If individualist discourses had allowed him to think he was just like the guys in the suits, the actual interviews convinced him that he was not.

The cultural specificity of individualist discourse becomes clearer in another anecdote in Johnson's narrative. A local business expressed interest in hiring kids from "the east side," the geographical location of primarily black and Hispanic families. Johnson urged the boys to apply for them, but they refused, telling her they had all gotten jobs together washing dishes at a local university. They also told her that they didn't want to be rejected, which they assumed that they would have been because they were Mexican. Johnson responded to their solidarity in anger.

> "But you can't advance in a career if you handcuff yourself to somebody else.... You have to make your own way. Stand on your own."... They knew that I knew their posse's motto: forever together. "Well, if you're going to hold each other's hands ... at least you could get a job where you don't have to wash dishes like a bunch of illegal aliens." It was a mean thing to say, but I was feeling frustrated. (p. 237)

The connections between individualist discourses, white middle-class culture, and Americaness are made explicit here. Johnson attacks many of the values of the posse in her insistence that they enter a more competitive and atomized economy. She impugns their heterosexual masculinity by referring to their emotional bond as "hand holding," an explicitly romantic gesture and, in this instance, an implication of weakness or cowardice. By comparison, "making your own way" and "standing on your own" is manly, clinging to a peer group is not. Too, she denigrates the work they do, washing dishes, as the work of "illegal aliens," a racial slur aimed at their Mexican identities and that suggests that such work is lowly and undesirable, and most of all, not work done by Americans. Johnson is flabbergasted by their unwillingness to compete for better paying jobs because she assumes that making more money is more important than being with people you like and working where you feel comfortable. Her inability to recognize their commitments to each other and fear of the world that she wishes them to enter stems from her assumption that her values are "common sense." Why would anyone choose to make less money? Why would anyone choose to do unpleasant service work when office work is available? These assumptions are culturally specific—white and middle class—and necessary to successfully compete in a capitalist society. The values of the "posse," which center on racial and class solidarity over individual success, appear illogical to Johnson but may be grounded in knowledge and values drawn from their collective experiences of being poor and Mexican. Johnson's frustration with her students demonstrates how individualist discourses are grounded in culturally specific values and norms. The employment of individualist discourses may help students see themselves as active agents but also function to deny crucial aspects of their experience and cultural world views, leaving them confused and inarticulate.

In very explicit ways here, class and racial hierarchies are being reinforced through the assumption that individualist discourses are common sense and through the perceptions that the posse performed poorly because they, as individuals, "weren't ready" for the interviews.

The discourses on race that white teachers employ in the classroom often serve to protect the privileged position of whiteness even as they appear to be opposed to racism. Evasive discourses insist that if we do not dwell upon differences by insisting that we don't see them, we have somehow obliterated the meaning of difference. These assertions, however, do not obliterate our students' very real experiences of racism. By denying that our personal and collective histories inform how we "see" race and live it, these discourses deny that race is historically and socially constructed. By insisting that race is equivalent to the color of our skin—what is on our surface—these discourses flatten out race by literally rendering it as something that is only skin deep. Both these constructions of race fail to recognize it as a socially constructed category and as a complex network of social relationships. Not only do students learn these flattened-out versions of race from us, as did the student who echoed the teacher's race-evasive construction of skin color, but they are also left with hollow understandings of their own experiences, cultures, and histories.

Deflecting discourses recognize that racism has a nasty sting but allow the speaker to avoid confronting his or her own role in its continued practice. These also flatten out race by posing relationships of dominance and subordination as polar relationships—we are either one or the other. Such conceptualizations ignore the complex dynamics of our subject positions. We are always raced, classed, gendered, and sexual beings, and we move along a continuum of power, our intersecting identities always mediating our experiences. Deflecting discourses oversimplify the workings of oppressive hierarchies and are employed to avoid confronting our own racism or our own privileged positions. Finally, individualist discourses reproduce white middle-class norms as common sense and leave students of color unable to explain their experiences as members of marginalized communities. These discourses leave students no way of understanding their experiences outside of themselves, even though they often experience discrimination and racism because of their collective identities. Like the boys who could not explain what happened at the interviews, individualist discourses leave students mute in the face of structural systems of domination.

Taken together, these discourses function to protect whiteness by leaving it unprobed and by simplifying the institutions of racism, removing it from a cultural context and minimizing the ways it shapes all of our lives. If we, white teachers, are to participate in antiracist pedagogy, we must begin by examining the discourses on race that frame our understanding of race and racism. As we deconstruct the discourses we employ, exposing the assumptions and privileges they hide, we must teach our students to do so as well, opening up race, including whiteness, for critical examination. Although this paper has focused on white teachers and students of color, the conclusions apply more broadly. Whether our students are white or students of color, we need to give them the analytical and critical tools to examine racism. When we work with white students it is easy to ignore these issues, particularly because when we protect our own privileges we are also protecting theirs. When we work with students of color, the impact of protecting white privilege is clearly detrimental to them. Nonetheless, if we are to work towards a more just world, we need to prepare all students to question the assumptions embedded in commonly employed discourses on race to prepare them to comprehend how race operates and how to begin to dismantle it.

REFERENCES

Delpit, L. (1993). "The Silenced Dialogue: Power and Pedagogy in Educating Other People's Children," in L. Weis and M. Fine (Eds.), *Beyond Silenced Voices: Class, Race, and Gender in the United States Schools.* Albany: State University of New York Press.

Frankenberg, R. (1993). *White Women, Race Matters: The Social Construction of Whiteness.* Minneapolis: University of Minnesota Press.

Johnson, L. (1992). *My Posse Don't Do Homework.* New York: St. Martin's.

Kohl, H. (1967). *36 Children.* New York: Signet Books,

Kozol, J. (1967). *Death at an Early Age: The Destruction of the Hearts and Minds of Negro Children in the Boston Public Schools.* New York: Bantam Books.

Paley, V. (1979). *White Teacher.* Cambridge, MA: Harvard University Press.

Sachar, E. (1991). *Shut Up and Let the Lady Teach: A Teacher's Year in a Public School.* New York: Poseidon.

Thompson B., and Tyagi S. (1993). "The Politics of Inclusion: Reskilling the Academy," in B. Thompson, and S. Tyagi (Eds.), *Beyond A Dream Deferred: Multicultural Education and the Politics of Excellence.* Minneapolis: University of Minnesota Press.

CHAPTER 11

Authority Is Not a Luxury
"Courageous Dialogue" in the Feminist Classroom

KIMBERLY KAY GUNTER

> *And how could I forget that fundamentally the*
> *purpose of my knowing was so I could serve*
> *those who did not know, so that I could learn*
> *and teach my own—education as the practice of*
> *freedom.*
> —BELL HOOKS (1989, P. 62)

Let me begin with a piece of lore, a pedagogical anecdote: In an introductory composition course that I taught at a mid-sized, southeastern regional university, my students and I were discussing providing evidence for arguments in upcoming papers and the kinds of evidence that were available to them. During our discussion, I asked students to pretend that they were writing a paper that argued for more funding for AIDS research and asked them what kinds of evidence they would include. Several students mentioned statistics about the number of HIV positive people and statistics about the increasing rates of infection. Others remarked that they could quote doctors like C. Everett Koop or famous personalities such as Magic Johnson or Elizabeth Taylor. One student then raised his hand and asked, "Could you write about homosexuals?" Both his smirk and his tone suggested his distaste of the topic, his deigning to speak of such an unseemly subject necessary only because of the hypothetical paper topic. It was as if he attempted to say "homosexuals" without the sound of the word actually touching the inside of his mouth: "ho-mo-SEX-u-als," followed by an unseen but clearly implied shudder. (I might note here that this particular student had issued several strongly conservative positions at this point in the semester, although never before in such a self-righteous, mocking manner.) As a young teacher and a self-identified lesbian, my first impulse was to avoid what was about to follow, to sum up his point in a tolerant way for him, and to bulldoze on past; yet as a feminist teacher, I did not want to misrepresent his position, and I also did not want to leave unacknowledged what was already a prejudicial slur. So, I asked him, "What about homosexuals?" His somewhat surprised response, his seeming not to believe that I might not understand the implication, marched out in four/four time: "Well, what they do." My rejoinder: "What do you mean exactly, Chris? That they go to work, that they go to the grocery store, that they go out to dinner? What exactly?" He floundered for a response, his face blotchy and also, I think, his reality questioned.

This moment and others before and since it where hate speech has been issued in my classes have spawned a crisis of faith for me. I strive to treat my students in the manner that I advocate for the culture treat all its citizens, respectfully, honorably, seriously. After all, part of my ideol/pedagogical mission aims at convincing the students themselves (they, as am I, are in part forming that culture) to do the same. But, if I aim at creating not just egalitarian classrooms but liberatory classrooms, hoping that in some small way such action pushes for an egalitarian, liberating culture, how do I, in a nonhypocritical way, interact with students who seek to subvert my objective? If indeed I am a feminist teacher who respects difference, should I not then respect difference of opinion and allow such speech to stand in my classrooms? If I squelch such hate speech, am I heaving my feminist principles just to prescribe beliefs that I hold, like some kind of patriarchal thought police? Do I subvert my own liberatory teaching theory when I judge what is ethically acceptable speech from my students and what is not?

As many feminist theorists have noted, one of the basic tenets of feminism is rejection of hierarchical authority. Cecilia Rodriquez Milanes and Carolyn Statler (1989) assert that "Feminism holds the breaking down of hierarchical authority as one of its most compelling values. . . . Feminists seek to foster cooperation, collaboration and collective process. . . . feminists strive for a sense of community. . . ." (p. 1). Andrea Lunsford (unpublished, n.d.) claims that authority is "exclusionary" and "functions as judgmental and as hierarchical" and that "its aim . . . has . . . been to control or to gain power over others" (p. 5). Sally Miller Gearhart (1979) even states that "any intent to persuade is an act of violence" (p. 195). Understanding feminism's adamant concern that hierarchical power relations be dispelled, I am troubled when I see myself as enacting oppression in my classrooms, not far-flung from my patriarchal predecessors and colleagues who seemingly easily continue to divide all thought into a binary of what is absolutely right and what is, if different, absolutely wrong (and, perhaps more complicated, what constitutes intelligence versus ignorance or what constitutes thoughtful speech versus reactionary lingo).

As I struggle with this issue, though, I think it ironic that feminist teaching, particularly in its rejection of authority, often enables students to proclaim the very hate speech that disputes feminist principles of equality and liberation, of the aforementioned "collaboration," "community," and nonviolence. Because feminist teachers do not position themselves as all-knowing bearers of truth and knowledge but instead as individuals grounded in a particular positionality (or perhaps as group members subscribing to a group positionality, although I think such group identity must be self-conscious so as not to be essentializing since just what is and is not feminist is often disputed within the fold) and because feminist teachers do not remain inaccessible behind their remote lecterns, hoarding their pearls of wisdom (read "power"), but rather seek to distribute power and authority among their students, urging them to discover or to fashion their own voices, our students take us up on the offer. Who are we to complain if our students do not, then, utter speech that we find agreeable? And for that matter, why should we be surprised that students do replicate the speech of the larger patriarchal culture when they (as we) are at least in part constituted by that culture? Yet I find it unsettling that feminist teaching might simply allow the power relations that are culturally dominant and that feminists seek subversion of these to realign themselves in the supposedly liberatory classroom. If we endeavor to empower students and thereby induce social transformation, such aims will hardly be achieved if we permit those students who possess power in the dominant culture to execute that power within the classroom, often silencing those who are already disenfranchised outside the classroom, particularly, I think, silencing those students whose patriarchal "flaw" is not visible, such as gay and lesbian students who are often so intimidated by institutionalized homophobia that they remain closeted within their classes.

With all of my angst stated, though, I am coming to believe more and more that I do not have to view hate speech in my classes as only a hazard or a failure of feminist teaching or as evidence of the impenetrability of patriarchy. If feminist teachers are set on sparking social change, hoping to educate students about cultural differences and a theory that engages differences, urging those students to enter the broader world more tolerant and respectful of those differences, we can expect our classrooms to be messy. We can expect resistance from our students, perhaps especially from younger, first-year students, who are often the enrollees of required composition courses. If acceptance of change to the hierarchical, oppressive status quo were concurred upon easily, our work would not be as important as it is and perhaps not necessary at all.

Although it is true that I would rather that hate speech not occur in my classrooms because I would rather that it not occur anywhere, if it is, in fact, going to occur, it seems to me that the feminist classroom provides a space where transformation can result.

Laurie Finke (1993) discusses the teacher-student dyad and claims that teaching is "a practice which, much like the analytic situation proceeds not progressively through time, but through resistance and through breakthroughs, leaps, discontinuities, regressions, and deferred action . . ." (p. 16). Although Finke focuses on students' resistance to student-centered classrooms, her theory might easily be applied to resistance that takes the form of hate speech as well. If students in our classes hold ignorant, bigoted views about any group of people and if feminist teachers want those students truly to learn and become more accepting, we as teachers must encounter those students' resistance. (And it is more likely that feminist teachers will encounter that resistance as they decenter the "generic" white male student.) Gregory Jay (1987) reminds us that student ignorance and student resistance are not forms of passivity or idleness but an "active dynamic of negation" (p. 789). If we as teachers are to do more than preach to the converted, we must engage this student opposition and contest it head on with feminist politics.

This conflict between feminism and bigotry as it transpires in the classroom returns me to the issue of authority and what a feminist teacher is to do about it. I believe that while we must move with great awareness as we consider our power position within our classes, we cannot and should not, as Finke and Jay imply, reject our authority positions. I feel this way for two reasons. First, we are teachers, and teachers necessarily have power over their students, as any student will tell you at the end of the semester, when she or he is awaiting final course grades. To think that we can shed that power is simply to delude ourselves. In fact, such a move might very well reinforce the power that we are steeped in by mystifying it. Second, to reject an authoritative position when hate speech is issued in the classroom is not to embrace a nonhierarchical feminist politics; it is an abdication of feminist politics. As feminists and as feminist teachers, we have a responsibility to prevent the same oppressive relations that form outside feminist classrooms from forming inside them, and we cannot fulfill such a responsibility if we have relinquished our authority, our critical silence sanctioning language of hate. I believe that claim with a kind of righteous morality that to some degree cannot be proven, any more or less, I suppose, than the claims of hate speech themselves. But that the playing field is no longer level as soon as hate speech is uttered because the speaker carries with him or her the validity of the entire patriarchal culture seems to me to once again minoritize and often silence marginalized students. "In such a context," Magda Lewis (1990) asserts, "a pedagogical approach that fails to acknowledge how such inequality silences, serves to reinforce the powerlessness of the powerless" (p. 478). By owning our authority and employing it in the cause of egalitarianism, we can see hate speech as an opportunity to, in bell hooks's (1989) words, make education more "real" (p. 51). If our goal is to expose the "real" oppression that the culture is based on, to confront it, and to overthrow it, hate speech provides a chance to do so, a classroom exercise where students and teacher can move away from the teacher's grandiose claims about liberation and indictments of subjugation and the students' bovine, note-taking agreement to "real" interaction in which everyone in the room has to confront the complicated realities in which we live. If we allow hate speech to just sit in the classroom as one viable opinion, however, it becomes just one more instance of patriarchal subordination and persecution.

I do not have all of the answers as to how to deal with hate speech in the classroom or how to achieve a balance of exercising authority while not replicating patriarchal power dynamics. I think, though, that Paulo Freire (1993) presents a place to start. In his *Pedagogy of the Oppressed,* Freire notes that liberatory education and social revolution can only transpire through dialogue:

> Dialogue with the people is radically necessary to every authentic revolution. This is what makes it a revolution, as distinguished from a military coup. One does not expect dialogue from a coup—only deceit (in order to achieve "legitimacy") or force (in order to repress). Sooner or later, a true revolution must initiate a courageous dialogue. . . . Its very legitimacy lies in that dialogue. It cannot fear the people, their expression, their effective participation in power. (p. 109)

It was partly because I had Freire in mind that I asked that student mentioned earlier what he meant about "homosexuals." I wanted him to move beyond the conventionally accepted prejudices of his statement and restate his ignorance in his own words (not the inherited accusations of patriarchy), to hear his own voice, and to then decide whether he wanted to continue to own such statements (trying to move beyond the process that many feminists describe as students "discovering" voices that lay hidden within them, for me an essentialist notion; instead urging students to realize the constant creation of their own "voice" and its mutability). I wanted the two of us to engage in a dialogue where he was challenged to examine what he really meant and to examine how truly valid his point was. (I did not, incidentally, leave that student floundering in front of his classmates. I eventually asked him if he meant homosexual sexual practices—he expressing a relieved "Yeah"—and I told him and the rest of the class that it might indeed be relevant to discuss transmission of AIDS through unsafe sex but that they should probably not focus on one sexual orientation, as the audience might assume they were being prejudicial or unjustly blaming a particular segment of the population for the epidemic.) I might add that it is through such dialogue that I have often learned from my students as well (the student who I've been using as my whipping post taught me quite a bit that semester). Such dialogue does not occur when teachers attempt to rid themselves of authority but when teachers use authority judiciously and fairly.

Some feminist theorists approach authority as if it were a bad word. Andrea Lunsford even goes so far as to suggest that we "give the term a rest, a time-out in our pedagogical and scholarly conversations" (p. 14). I have often wondered if such rejection of authority by some theorists is not entirely feminist but at least in part feminine and a means whereby we can rationalize ourselves into fulfilling more of our socially constructed role of "woman." After all, just because we oppose oppressive uses of authority and power, must we thereby reject all authority and power or even imagine that we can create classrooms in which such entities do not exist when they in fact pervade all aspects of the "real world." Perhaps such a rejection is even a way that we can make our lives easier in academia, assuring traditional administrators that we mean no harm: why, we don't even execute authority in our classrooms. I feel that authority is a tool to be used, yet justly and respectfully, and all the time knowing that our students may feel no differently after our dialogues than they did before.

One potential benefit of these dialogues is that we will model behavior that we as feminists encourage in our marginalized students (Buffington, 1993, p. 10). Once an atmosphere of open dialogue is created in the classroom, the horizontal relations in the room often take over, and students will question one another about their comments, particularly when hate speech is issued. Showing our students that conflict is neither good nor bad but exists and that people can converse about highly invested, emotional topics encourages students to come to or to create voices (depending on the slant of the pedagogue), speaking of their own realities and questioning others. That the classroom discussions sometimes do not come to neat closure supports hooks's goal of making education more real by inviting students to see the ever-contested ideologies they and others live by and under. It is when there are those silences, though, after issuances of hate speech, when no fellow student is offering a rebuttal (this often being the case when invisible minorities are being attacked—for instance, queers or students who are economically disenfranchised), that as a feminist teacher I feel the responsibility to speak, to engage in a dialogue, to be accountable to those very minority students who are often more damaged by higher education than empowered by it. (In the instance of hate speech I've been describing, if I had simply waited for a response from the other class members—and I did, briefly—I sincerely believe that none would have come, even from the gay student who had come out to me in a paper and in my office, as he sat staring at his desk top, unwilling to out himself or allow any oppositional speech to spawn such suspicions.) Creating the "safe place" that so many feminists write about in their pedagogical theory (for example, see Rodriquez Milanes and Statler), for students to question and make meaning, need not mean creating a space without conflict. It means creating a space where conflict can emerge between students who are valued as equals. Moreover, if we openly construct our classrooms around the fact that we are feminist and that the course will occur within a feminist environment, we do not dupe our students into agreeing with us. Rather, we acknowledge how all reality is socially constructed and is, therefore, capable of transformation. In such an atmosphere, we should not fear that our authority will trick our students, for we will have declared our politics openly, yet we should also not fear influencing our students, because that is at least in part our goal as feminist teachers: to convince our students that we do in fact live in a world in which only particular social constructions that contain some ten percent of the population are valued (McIntosh, 1989, p. 402), that we have in part been constituted by these constructions, but because they are constructions, they can be thrown off and a world that is more honoring and more accepting, more equitable and more loving can be achieved.

I am often reminded of one of Malcom X's analogies in which he compared Blacks who worked with Whites in civil rights struggles to ineffectual "house niggers" who were willing to settle for inequality simply because they stayed relatively warm in the winter and got decent, if leftover, food compared to their field slave brothers and sisters whose lives were harsher. I sometimes wonder if I am a kind of house nigger of the academy, proclaiming that I am working for change while I simultaneously pile up academic degrees and bemoan the lack of tenure-track positions. I can only believe that I am in fact working for change when I remind myself that I have not abdicated my debt to those who came before me and to those who are not in the privileged position that I now am and that I am in fact owning my authority as a teacher to push for a more egalitarian world. For me, rejection of authority is not a luxury in which I can afford to indulge. And, I believe, neither can any other feminist teacher who claims to be working for change.

REFERENCES

Buffington, N. (1993). *When Teachers Aren't Nice: bell hooks and Feminist Pedagogy.* (ERIC Document Reproduction Service No. ED 359 513).

Finke, L. (1993). "Knowledge as Bait: Feminism, Voice, and the Pedagogical Unconscious," in *College English, 55*(1), 7–27.

Freire, P. (1993). *Pedagogy of the Oppressed.* (M. B. Ramos, Trans.). New York: Continuum.

Gearhart, S. M. (1979). "The Womanization of Rhetoric," in *Women's Studies International Quarterly, 2*(2), 195–201.

hooks, b. (1989). *Talking Back: Thinking Feminist, Thinking Black.* Boston: South End Press.

Jay, G. S. (1987). "The Subject of Pedagogy: Lessons in Psychoanalysis and Politics," in *College English, 49,* 785–800.

Lewis, M. (1990). "Interrupting Patriarchy: Politics, Resistance, and Transformation in the Feminist Classroom," in *Harvard Educational Review, 60,* 467–488.

Lunsford, A. (1995). "Refiguring classroom authority." Unpublished essay, n.d.

McIntosh, P. (1989). "Curricular Re-vision: The New Knowledge for a New Age," in C. S. Pearson, D. L. Shavlik, & J. G. Touchton (Eds.), *Educating the Majority: Women Challenge Tradition in Higher Education* (pp. 400–412). New York: Macmillan, 1989.

Rodriquez Milanes, C., & Statler, C. (1989). *Feminist Pedagogy in Composition: Transforming Passive Receptors into Active Participants.* (ERIC Document Reproduction Service No. ED 331 065).

CHAPTER 12

Authentic Multiculturalism and Nontraditional Students
Voices from the "Contact Zone"

JUAN FLORES

One day my eleven-year old son asked, "Who decides what will be studied as history?" His question served as a reminder that the premise for a critical understanding of any historic event is through the authentic dialogue of all parties involved. Without authentic dialogue, knowledge must be imparted through the monocultural, that is, highly suspect soliloquy of one voice. Cultural inclusion in the loci of historical narrative sustains a "first-class seat" in mainstream culture, or what I have come to term for my freshman writers as "cognitive grace." Conversely, cognitive disgrace fosters oppression or exclusion from historical narrative, and its corollary is seen in the low educational success rate of Latino, African, and Native Americans. Remembering Socrates, the problem is that their lives seem unworthy of living because they remain unexamined.

The incorporation of multicultural literature in the writing classroom presents a perplexing riddle. Although our American paradigm earnestly seeks critical thought from our students, it simultaneously focuses on active learning situations that use culturally significant literature to develop critical reading and writing skills. But, as an educator with new anthologies in hand, I am frustrated by the unauthentic answer to the riddle: an ad hoc assembly of authors, too often looking suspiciously like the color palette of a paint-by-numbers kit. This new canonical tokenism is quickly seen as a ruse by minority students and teachers alike, who are circumspect and adept at uncovering such counterfeits.

In the February 1994 edition of *College English,* rhetoric and compositionalist Patricia Bizzell proposes that a new method of incorporating multicultural literature in the English classroom may be accomplished through the study of events in which cultures interact. Borrowing from Mary Louise Pratt, Bizzell categorizes these moments as "Contact Zones": instead of asking, for example, how to fit Frederick Douglass into an American Renaissance course, Bizzell writes that we should ask how to reconceive our study so that Douglass is naturally regarded as the important writer that he is (Bizzell, 1994). Applied as a pedagogy, this focused study circumvents canonical tokenism, while offering an authenticating direction for our discipline.

Counterfeiting authenticity is not foreign to south Texan Chicanos like me. As brown-skinned choir boys in grade school, we sang a fanfare of Texican songs, such as "Texas, Our Texas," designed to inspire a kind of monoculturalism: "We come your children true. Proclaiming our allegiance, Our faith, Our love for you." (*Texas Almanac,* 1994). Yet, no matter how I or my Chicano compadres tried to harmonize our feelings with words like these, something remained uncomfortable for us. Despite our own authentic, cultural contributions that sprang from names like Zavala, Hinojosa, and Gonzalez, we were not the authenticated and valued hosts whose white ancestries endorsed "historic inclusion." We had no connection with Davy Crockett, Jim Bowie, or Sam Houston. Any connection we thought we had concerned another side: history and movies told us so. "Our" was not inclusive of us; it was a left-handed "invitation" that encouraged in many of us Latinos a negative self-image and an internal resentment. Our melting pot is not so thin and soupy as many would think; it is big and chunky, embodying raw cultures of segregation and poverty.

There is, then, little question why many Latino students will not enjoy the passionate interest in Texican war heroes such as Houston or Jim Bowie. More abstractive and foreign extensions such as Charles Dickens, Dylan Thomas, or Robert Frost are in fact literary heroes whose voices do not echo the experiences of the Latino, the African, or the Native American. Like Bowie and Crockett, they contrarily embody a dominant culture's experiences, reminding many of us of color that we are without cognitive grace. As one African-American student once asked me, "How can I understand Dylan Thomas when I am not White nor Welsh nor male?" It is a question deeply rooted in her need to be socially and legitimately recognized—her need for authentication.

My experiences as an instructor of general education courses, adult literacy programs, reading-writing at a local prison, an English college instructor, and home-schooler have made me cognizant about placing carts before horses: sacrificing the practice of critical thought for the hardly significant knowledge of the variant, subsidiary models used to foster it. Our American system of education needs to seek real dialogue from all sides involved, both present and past, for such exchange not only authenticates the teacher's life but that of the student's as well. When lately, for example, my son asked me if I would listen to his new CD bearing a name having something to do with broken pumpkins, I waved him off and said, "I'll listen later." Yet I had faithfully asked him, as part of a home-schooling assignment, to listen to the works of Bach, Beethoven, and Mozart. He was seeking a personal inclusion in the contributory acts of our educational moments together, and I was denying him that right. In authenticating the personal as well as individual cultures of our students, men and women, boys and girls, we must seek the authentic dialogue of all participants from all sides and coming in all guises. We must place horses before carts. So long as the subject approach is inclusive of the learner, critical thinking is a more personal matter, and knowledge needs first to be personal before becoming integral to the learner.

Our statistical student profile at Del Mar College is vastly different from that of most academies. Take, for example, a typical Del Mar College student: an impoverished Latina, twenty-seven years old, who is a single-parent and the first of her family to attend college. Seven out of ten like her begin at developmental levels, and given four years, only one in ten will ever graduate. She is from the west side of Corpus Christi, where neighborhoods are addressed as "barrios" or "colonias"—the initial tie that extends beyond her family. She is a service industry employee at minimum wage, and college is an embarrassing dream that she is likely to quit due to work and child-care obligations. Hers is a world of different priorities: hand-to-mouth first; college study only when financial windfalls permit. In the internal makings of her familial home she has been nurtured with images of defeat; she is socially authenticated with freak-show media images of gang affiliation, third-world poverty, and recent statistics of genetic inferiority. From my years of teaching in south Texas, I understand her as a living irony, the epitome of the American paradox: "Pull your own self up by your own bootstraps—bootstraps you are not allowed to have."

My student profile is a living example of Pratt and Bizzell's contact zone, one of the many veritable human "arenas" in which diverse cultures have contended to interpret a historic placement. From a sociological perspective, she experiences diffusion, the acquisition of social elements from the dominant culture in order to survive. On a psychological level, she knows confusion, the state of being that seeks but is without cognitive grace. This absence of communal grace fosters little to no self-esteem in native Latino and African-American Texans, principally characterized by a personal sense of estrangement and ineptitude.

Hence, it was with the contact zone as a major theme that I constructed a yearlong pedagogical application of legitimizing "cultural literature," seeking not only to impart a global education to students of my contact zone classes, but to foster cognitive grace by reconstructing Western study to naturally include historic participants of color in the loci of chronicled events and thereby authenticate their contributions. Furthermore, student input concerning the direction of the course and its particulars was encouraged. It was no accident that our readings were sociopolitical in nature, selected to stretch the boundaries of a typical freshman writing curriculum to include psychology, sociology, American history, philosophy, and religion. My first *Accommodating Reader* began with the somewhat nostalgic "The Times They Are A'Changing," and in the fall and spring semesters of 1994 and 1995, I launched four freshman rhetoric and composition courses with the contact zone as theme.

First of all, we cannot ignore the study of the "mainstream," traditional, Western "canon." Entering community college students have little grasp of history and hardly any knowledge concerning Western thought. Hence, our comparative readings and discussions involved philosophy, religion, commercialization, industry, politics, and the revolutionary ethics instrumental in the West's political and economic metamorphosis. Since contact zones pivot on diffusive relationships, initially my concern was to model for students an era where such relationships were intense: the industrial metamorphosis of the twentieth century. I provided a review of Western thought with a special emphasis on ordinate relationships based on class, gender, race, ethnicity, and religious affiliation.

In the first portion of our semester, we discussed and read works by Max Weber, Charles Darwin, Frederic Jameson, E.L. Doctorow, Maxine Hong Kingston, and John Fowles. We made connections with Social Darwinism, Nietzsche, and Marxism. We made more extensive connections through Plato, Hobbes, Rousseau, Marx and Engels, Studs Terkel, and even Paulo Freire. In a sense, my classrooms were working think-tanks of researchers, all with separate but purposeful missions—to find and examine Western causal relationships wherever we could find them. Student essays, initiated from such rich assemblies, went beyond simple, canonical explication. And however laden with errors of grammar and logic, contact zone papers read with depth and passion that comes from authentic, academic discovery. The titles of their essays went beyond

what I normally see in composition classes: "An Explication on Nietzsche's Critical Statement That God Is Dead"; "A Comparative Analysis
of Modern and Postmodern Architecture"; and, "A Description of Natural Law Concerning Moral Values with Help from Rousseau and
Hobbes." Hilda Sanchez, a fifty-two-year-old Latina woman in my
course expressed in one essay that her own plight was similar to that of
Maxine Hong Kingston. From her abstract:

> Throughout history, culture has served as a medium for the representa-
> tion of feminine mystique. It is still very difficult to explain the mys-
> tery of woman as a separate self. The need for a woman to grow is no
> different than that of a man, yet the oppression that ensues reveals a
> limited image of womanhood. The actual basis for this "difference" is
> the fact that the possibility for a true self-realization has not existed
> until now.

Having established that ordinate relationships exist, we began the
second portion of our semester exchanging examples of cultural negotiation and authentication. The Americas have always been a cluster of divergent cultures grappling for domination, so culturally significant people
in literature and art are easily found. Historic, cultural figures such as
Pocohantas, Sacajawea, and Marina (Mexican spouse of conquistador
Hernando Cortez) were discussed. Dialogue and essays became pleas-
ingly analytical when we initiated our study with two eighteenth-century
viceregal paintings by Miguel Cabera and Jose Joaquin Magon over their
"Depictions of Racial Mixtures" (*San Antonio Express-News*, 1991).
Here we were debating authenticity as provided through social and political media. In Magon's painting, for example, there is the inscription,
"Spanish father and Mestiza mother produce a Quadroon daughter." In
the foreground of the painting there is a round table between a European
husband and his Mestiza wife holding their child: "the three figures necessary for the representation of 'mestizaje' [mixed family]" (1991). In an
essay, student Mark Bueno writes:

> Magon purposely divides his painting to show how husband and wife
> are from different cultures. On the left hand side . . . the man is sur-
> rounded by paper, pen, and ink indicating that he was raised to be edu-
> cated. . . . On the other side, the woman is surrounded with food,
> flowers, and pottery showing that she was raised in a culture that de-
> mands her to be home. . . .

Students like Bueno were fascinated by slides representing culture inter-
change. Dialogue indicated that they had identified not only the divergent cultures of the sexes and their social authentication, but also those of men and women from separate geographic realities and the subjectivity of the artist instilling the images. Dialogue and essay writing went beyond symbolism; we discussed the sociopsychological factors behind such historic artifacts. Some other students, like Jessica Bates, even pulled the boundaries back home into a more personal arena. In Bates's essay, "Women, A Subordinate Culture to Men," she writes:

> The subordination of women starts at an early age with girls being taught that their role is to be a wife and mother. This type of socialization is described in the poem "Barbie Doll" by Marge Piercy . . . This type of parenting was acceptable many years ago, but times are changing and girls need to be taught the skills they will need to survive in today's world.

Third, we initiated a study of Latino and Native American folk stories and poems. Contact zone pedagogy, of natural course, includes a plethora of cultural themes, imagery, symbols, irony—all the elements needed for literature analysis. I used Robert Frost's "Birches" and Jose Limon's "Frost in the Rio Grande Valley" to teach students that dominant images have a greater meaning than our initial perception (Trevino, 1977). From Robert Frost's "Birches":

> When I see birches bend to left and right
> Across the lines of straighter darker trees,
> I like to think some boy's been bending them.

Most south Texans have never seen a birch tree, much less an ice storm, although it is doubtful that many New Englanders have swung from thorny mesquites or tasted the smoky sweetness of its sticky sap.

In "Birches," the narrator negotiates from within. He daydreams, crosses reality with fantasy, but truth asserts its claims at the expense of his fancy (Hart, 1982). Though the narrator likes to think that "boy's been bending them," he knows that "ice storms do" that (Frost, 1972). With Frost's poem, definitions and explanations were anxiously fostered from my students, but they were all naturally adept at uncovering the symbolism, word puns, and irony built into Limon's poem:

When I see mesquites bend to left and right
Across the line of a straighter, darker river,
I'd like to think some boy's been swinging them.
But swinging doesn't bend them down to stay,
Only my ancestors did that,
Hanging,
Slowly
at mid-day,
In the glare of the suns of Texas.   (Limon 1977)

Limon's piece symbolizes "the harsh historical fact that numerous innocent Mexican-Americans were lynched in the Texas Valley, particularly during the early 1900s" (Trevino, 1977). Mesquites are large and thorny at the banks of south Texan rivers, and Limon, like Frost, likes to dream of them as bent by a "boy's . swinging them." There is, however, the harsher reality. In this same vein, but over the authenticity of the vaquero or cowboy, Richard Mondragon, in his final examination, wrote:

The original American cowboy originated from the Mexicans' traditions . . . *Cowboy* came from the word *Vaquero* . . . That's why the teaching, learning, and understanding of Bizzell's contact zone is essential to authenticating one's culture, to establish history as it truly is.

Cultural names and local folk stories were used as thematic study. One good example was La Llorana (Yo-rona), or Weeping Lady, who, according to legend, drowned her children because her European husband tried to take them. Remarkably, two other versions of the legend were offered by my students: in one, Llorona drowns her children because her lover does not want them, and in the other, Llorona drowns them because her spouse loved them more than he loved her. Thus, for students and teacher alike, the legend was enriched and deepened by the intrinsic sense of Freierean "dialogue" at the heart of my method.

Add to Llorona the conquistador Hernando Cortez and his Mexican interpreter Dona Marina, whose connections with Llorona are deeply metaphorical. Llorona is the mythical personification of Dona Marina, the Aztec woman who is despicably called by many Latinos "La Malinche"—the treacherous one—because she acted as an interpreter and guide for Cortez's conquest of Mexico. Like Llorona, Dona Marina marries the European Cortez; there are children. Hence, Marina's place is one of love, yet betrayal to her people. She is the mystical mother of Hispanics who is also the murderer of a culture. Contact zone studies of south Texas are a rich resource for multicultural literature. We discuss, as in any other monocultural literature course, contextual, personal, and cultural interpretations of literature. I know that my students have gained a wide range of connective knowledge. Recently, a student of mine suggested elemental items for a study that examines gay culture and the contact zone therein. As modern literature, that exploration seems tempting.

The question my home-schooled son asked me some time ago still bothers me like a Bosch painting: "Who determines what is written as history?" he asked. "Those in power," I answered. However far learning extends, initial and critical studies in composition need to stretch the current boundaries so that we are sure to justly authenticate the many voices of our world, and by doing that establish lives worth living, asserting the right to be cognitively graced with inclusion. Such inclusion needs to be carefully deliberated and planned, not with only some in mind, but with many in participation. I do not purport that my method here offers the only way—but it is one based in personal knowledge. Canonical tokenism, however, needs to be avoided, for no culture likes to feel like an unwelcome guest in its own home.

REFERENCES

Bizzell, P. (1994 February). " 'Contact Zones' and English Studies." *College English, (52)*2, 163–169.

Hart, J. (1982). Book Review. *National Review, 34,* pp. 305–307.

Lathem, E.C., & Thompson, L. (Eds.). (1972). "Birches." *Robert Frost: Poetry and Prose.* New York: Holt, Rinehart & Winston.

Trevino, A. (March 1977). "Teaching the Poem 'Frost in the Rio Grande Valley.'" *English Journal, 66*(3), p. 69.

Paledes, K. (Ed). (1991 March 31). "Mexico: Splendors of 30 Centuries." *San Antonio Express News,* p. 24.

WORKS CONSULTED

Ember, Carol R., and Melvin. (1985). *Cultural Anthropology.* 4th ed. Englewood Cliffs, NJ: Prentice Hall.

Estes, Clarissa Pinkola. (1992). *Women Who Run with the Wolves.* New York: Ballantine Books.

Lerner, Gerda. (1993). *The Creation of Feminist Consciousness*. New York: Oxford.

Polanyi, Michael. (1962). *Personal Knowledge: Forge a Postcritical Philosophy*. Chicago: University of Chicago Press.

Pratt, Mary Louise. "Arts of the Contact Zone." *Profession* 91. La Herencia Del Norte: Our Past, Our Present, Our Future. Ed. Pacheco, Ana. VI: Summer 1995. New York: MLA, 1991. 33–40.

CHAPTER 13

The Transformation of Silence into Language and Action
The Ideologies of Gender and Peer Response Sessions Perceived by a Teacher-Researcher

NANCIE BURNS-McCOY

> *I have come to believe over and over again that what is most important to me must be spoken, made verbal and shared, even at the risk of having it bruised or misunderstood. That the speaking profits me, beyond any other effect. . . . What I most regretted were my silences. . . . We can learn to work and speak when we are afraid in the same way we have learned to work and speak when we are tired. For we have been socialized to respect fear more than our own needs for language and definition, and while we wait in silence for that luxury of fearlessness, the weight of that silence will choke us.*
>
> —AUDRE LORDE

PART ONE: THE PROBLEM IN ITS CATERPILLAR STAGE

Composition instructors rely heavily on peer-response sessions in their classrooms—an interactive practice in which writing students bring their rough drafts to class, exchange drafts, and respond through either written or spoken comments to one another's texts. We use them for multiple purposes: to emphasize the social aspect of writing and to increase audience awareness—making this often abstract concept concrete; to facilitate task interpretation; to generate ideas; and to, in our wildest dreams, create an equitable environment. By establishing peer-response groups in composition courses, we strive to create a sense of community, a sense of shared goals. We strive to liberate student voices, to tip the power scales, decenter the hierarchy of the classroom. Indeed, these goals are crucial to my teaching, and peer-response sessions remain central to my classroom. I like the way they fill up my fifty-five-minute sessions with the sound of student voices instead of my own. And on the surface, because of the student rumbling of voice, these sessions do appear to decenter and empower. Too often, however, appearances can mislead. Consequently, I decided to look more closely at the dynamics of these small-group interactions. And when I looked, I was stunned.

Through close observation, I have noted again and again women participants' resistance to engaging in active literacy while involved in mixed-group, peer-response sessions. In other words, when I listen carefully to the timbre of the voices in my classroom, it hums deep and low. It is male. The women all too often remain silent. Hence, I'm experiencing a rip in the fabric of my teaching. Jean McNiff (1993) coins this rip between theoretical ideals and pedagogical circumstance a slippage: "The slippage rests in the experience of 'I' as a living contradiction, in that my values are not fully realized in practice" (p. 18).

Because I am convinced that much of what we do in the academy suits what has been construed as male socialization patterns best and female patterns hardly at all, I have worked at integrating feminist pedagogies into my writing courses. A particular branch of peer-response sessions does generate from the feminist revival of the 1960s. One composition specialist, Pamela Annas (1987), designed peer-response sessions as a feminist practice by modeling them after the response groups so popular during that revival, groups in which women shared a newfound social awareness through dialogue. Through these dialogues, many women gained social awareness that often led to action-taking and changed lives: bra burning was on the rise. Hence, Annas's aim was to break women's silences in order to liberate them as writers by refabricating these groups in her classroom. But I use peer-response sessions in my classroom, and there are no bra burnings there. Hence, I was forced to ask myself how peer-response sessions influence traditional (gendered) speaking and learning roles. Whom do they serve? And in what ways do they or do they not empower participants? To address these questions, I intend to situate my discussion and the necessity of it in my own classroom, locating my inquiry in my own practice.

Background to the Study

The theoretical underpinnings of this study are to be found in the work of feminist emancipatory discourses (Lather 1986a, 1991b; Gore 1993); the work of sociolinguists whose work explores conversational dynamics salient in male/female interactions (Fishman 1983, Tannen 1994); the social construction of knowledge (Bruffee 1983a, 1984b); and the social construction of identity (Belenky 1986; Gilligan 1982a, 1992). Patti Lather (1991) articulates my purpose for engaging in feminist methods when she asserts that an effective feminism is explicitly committed to critiquing the status quo and building a more just society. But I have found that my approaches to feminist practice have only accomplished the first half of this equation—critiquing the status quo—and fail to operate as agents of change. I have engaged in this pedagogical approach that employs peer-response sessions as a reaction against the "banking" mode of education (Freire,1990), but I have not looked carefully enough at whether this method disrupts or reemphasizes traditional learning patterns. A key assumption underlying this study is that knowledge-making and identity are indeed socially constructed affairs. However, social construction does not necessarily lead to equitability.

Some recent practical and theoretical work addressing peer-response sessions has emphasized the historicity of peer-response sessions. Jeff Jeske (1989) notes it as a writing tool reaching back to Ben Franklin's day. I would suggest, however, that writers have gathered together through the centuries to talk their "writers' talk" (Cain, 1994), to run their phrases before the eyes of others whom they respect and trust. In hopes of simulating the intimately social experiences of serious authors, teachers intent upon classroom equity incorporate peer-response sessions into English composition courses in order to expand learning beyond "teacher-centered and teacher-dominated forms of education" (Sommers, 1993, p. 1). Benefits of such groups can include an awareness of audience and a clear sense of writing purpose. This attention to writing as a social act shatters the myth of the writer as a gifted, muse-visited recluse, isolated in his or her ivory tower. To the contrary, peer-response groups suggest the social construction of knowledge and the answerability of the writer to society. Dialectics enter the picture as "writing instruction reflects a growing appreciation of the value of talk" (Herrman, 1989). Other intentions behind incorporating peer-response sessions into writing classrooms include an attempt to lessen writing anxiety and extricate students from isolated writing experiences (Murau, 1993), and it is an attempt to create a community, a particular environment that "brings teacher, student, and materials more nearly into balance" (Jeske, 1989, p. 1). Further, as noted earlier, some researchers and practitioners emphasize the potential of peer-response sessions as a tool to move women beyond silence (Annas, 1987).

The motives driving this teaching method are indeed noble. However, the literature regarding this practice remains nonreflexive. Little discussion exists regarding the roles students naturally assume based upon gendered socialization and conversational dynamics, roles that tend to reassert traditional patterns and often create an intense resistance to this potentially emancipatory teaching tool. Because of this lack of discussion, it appears that I am not alone in assuming that implementing pedagogy founded upon emancipatory principles automatically invites equity. In this study, I employ a teacher-as-researcher methodology—a distinct qualitative research strand—in an effort to reduce the slippage I experience between my theory and practice and shed light on specific writing classroom situations for myself, other professionals, and my students. Further, the purpose of my close observation is to move my pedagogy from merely critiquing the status quo to building a more just society. Originally, it was my intention and the aim of my study to find ways that invite female students to take a more active role in mixed-group, peer-response sessions without compromising their senses of selves. Ultimately, however, I've come to question both the ethics of employing peer-response practices and the ethics of presuming I might liberate anyone into active literacy.

Methods

In order to attain a clearer glimpse and a fuller awareness of the complexities of female students' participations in peer-response sessions and in order to attain a clearer glimpse of the ways I might unwittingly encourage traditional learning patterns, I have chosen teacher research as the approach that guides this study. Cochran-Smith and Lytle (1993) offer a working definition of this current research movement: "systematic intentional inquiry by teachers about their own school and classroom work" (p. 24). And Cathy Fleischer (1992) offers an honest account of this unruly though systematic approach to data collection, analysis, and interpretation: "It is not always neat; it tends not to be linear; it cannot be summarized easily; its conduct and its findings are, at times, confusing, even contradictory" (p. 87). And it is for these traditionally negative descriptions that I have chosen it. When has life ever been neat? When has life ever been linear? When has life not been confusing and contradictory? When has life ever been reducible to tight summary? This research strategy, I would argue, fits reality more closely than traditional research approaches. What's more, these basic principles of the teacher-as-researcher movement cohabits the world of feminist philosophy and is conducive to the socialization of women. To clarify, we are taught to value, nurture, and build relationships; we are taught to listen and empathize; we are taught from birth to connect (Gilligan, 1982). Yet traditional research methods demand a disconnection, demand a hierarchy of the knower (subject) raised above and speaking for the known (object). According to feminist philosophies, the research instrument as well as the researched are both acknowledged as subjects. Subjects, then, interact, construct knowledge, situate knowledge—based upon a certain place, time, and position—not generalizable but relevant to other places, other times, and other positions (Haraway, 1991). In this research paradigm, my students inform me as much as I inform them; it is a research model that reflects my reciprocal concerns as an educator: action, affinity, and agency.

Context of the Study

The university. Set in the midst of lush wheat fields, pleasantly removed from much of the chaos inherent in urban settings, the university where I teach is steeped in agricultural concerns. Traditional values and perspectives carry much weight. In different regions, gender roles in classrooms may be more fluid, but in the rugged northwest, last of the frontier, land of the hunter, wheat farmer, and cattle rancher, gender roles often remain rigid.

Writing course. Predominantly, students in our writing courses are male, the ratio of males to females running approximately two to one. Usually, class size remains below twenty-five students. Our composition courses run eighteen weeks, and we meet three times, three hours per week. These courses are designed to teach college-level writing and thinking skills. Recent writing pedagogy has influenced how these courses are taught. Indeed, cooperative learning/teaching techniques are employed eagerly, reflecting what has been called the paradigm shift, brought about by social constructivist theories that have influenced composition pedagogies since the seventies. We attempt to downplay the traditional aspect of teaching—the banking mode (Freire, 1990)—attempting instead to decenter the power structure of the classroom; hence, students often break into groups, not only in order to evaluate peer writing but to learn writing concepts and methods as well, thereby (supposedly) placing the instructor on the margins. The goal has become, in many college writing classrooms, to create a community (Beavan, 1977) in which students feel connected, supported, and confident to take risks.

Freshman essay writing. The course I taught while engaged in this study met at 8:30 A.M., in a stark, windowless room. There were twenty-three students in all—thirteen women and ten men. Five formal essays, numerous writing activities, and reading designed to generate writing content all led up to those essays. I began the semester engaging in a peer-response session for the first writing assignment, about two weeks after the course began. People were grouped together according to writing topics, three to four people in each group. Group participants would exchange papers, read, comment, and discuss concerns in light of clarity, organization, and development of each author's ideas.

Instrumentation and analytic procedures. I engaged in a case study in which my data collection took place throughout the spring semester of 1995. My purpose was to acquire as rich a portrait as possible of one student's reaction to peer-response sessions. In order to achieve this rich picture, I combined three research tools: observation, interviews, and text analysis. Achieving triangulation, "the data provided by text analysis served to add to, crosscheck, and refine the data generated by observation and interviews" (McCarthy, 1987, p. 236). Documenting changes both in my own reactions to this teaching practice and the participant's reactions, I analyzed transcripts and fieldnotes, looking for patterns, categories, and contradictions.

Participant observation. This data-gathering method invites participants to speak and researchers to listen. Wolcott (1990) suggests that participant observation allows "informants to speak for themselves . . . a bias in favor of trying to capture the expressed thoughts of others rather than relying too singularly on what I have observed and interpreted" (p. 130). During peer-response sessions, I recorded group interaction in my fieldnotes, paying careful attention to who spoke and who remained silent, the kinds of topics that were addressed (content versus surface concerns), and who addressed them. I also noted body language and facial expressions. Once the group appeared to have addressed their concerns, I would often chat with them about how effective they felt the session was. Engaging in a rather informal interview session with more than the study's main participant offered a sense of context both for my study and for the primary participant. Following these sessions, I analyzed those notes, developing rich layers of description, speculation, interpretation, and analysis (Bogdan and Biklen, 1992).

Interviews. Formal one-on-one interviews add another level of participation involvement and voice. Wolcott exemplifies the happy marriage between participant observation and interviewing: "The extent to which participant-observation and interviewing are a natural complement or get at quite different aspects of thought and action has always vexed experienced fieldworkers" (p. 130). I recorded these sessions, transcribed, analyzed, and interpreted them, seeking patterns and repeated themes. Once this process was completed, I discussed my ongoing analysis and interpretation with the interviewee in a second recorded interview session in which we together reflected upon our performances during the peer review sessions, our performances during the interviews, and our analyses of both, constructing meaning through negotiation with research participants (Lather, 1986).

Participants. Alicia: A nineteen-year old African-American from Alaska, she has eyes the shape of almonds, tilted up at the ends, dark as licorice, intelligent and soft simultaneously. Her dark hair is the texture of fine Merino wool still attached to the lamb. All too often she finds herself the only black face in a sea of white complexions. She's reserved, sitting as far away from me as she can get, comfortably hidden behind the student in front of her. When she speaks her voice is firm, certain, deep, and sure. She knows her mind. I invited Alicia to engage in this study for two reasons. The first and perhaps the most applicable reason for my choice was due to her utter hatred of peer-response sessions. On the first day of class I asked the entire group how they felt about this practice. Alicia's voice was angry and powerful. She appeared angry and resistant to both me and to the writing course in general as she spoke about her distaste of peer-response sessions and of her distaste of writing for English teachers. Hence, I used my research project as a means to work closely with her in hopes that her responses would shift enough to make learning possible.

Nancie: a forty-three-year-old, white, middle-class woman, mother of two daughters, and wife for twenty-three years. I perceive myself as a radical feminist intent on critiquing the traditions of how writing gets taught and committed to issues of equity. I have taught freshman writing courses, advanced expository writing, and literature courses at the university level for five years.

PART TWO: SPINNING OUR COCOON

> *Teachers always act like students don't have*
> *anything to teach them.*
>
> —ALICIA

Once again I state my research questions: How do peer-response sessions influence traditional (gendered) speaking and learning roles. Whom do they serve? And in what ways do they or do they not empower participants? What follows is the account of my attempt to answer these questions. But more than anything else, what follows is a tale that traces my metamorphoses from teller to listener, from teacher to learner. When I began to hear student voices responding to my pedagogy, I found myself compelled to reassess my goals, my very shape as a teacher.

During the previous semester, fall 1994, I had done enough close observation of peer-response sessions in my classroom to have developed reservations about their effectiveness. In other words, I noted that the women facilitated the conversation and the men, as recipients of facilitation, developed their ideas, claimed the subject position, and established control of the group (Burns-McCoy, 1995). Hence, this semester I was determined to empower the women in these groups, release them into active literacy, and help them take charge of these conversational dynamics (Fishman, 1983; Tannen, 1990). I was convinced that peer-response sessions served men best only because I hadn't quite learned how to use them as a means to empower female participants. Determined to do just that, I approached Alicia. Involving ourselves in a process that tested multiple approaches to peer-response sessions, we continued to check in with each other. But regardless of the method of peer-response we tried, Alicia's response varied little. She avoided these sessions at all costs.

> The larva attaches itself to a firm surface, appearing dormant
> but ready to spin.
> I employ the read-around.

Students, according to their topics, grouped together and engaged in a silent read around, passing each person's paper to the right. This was a short writing assignment, each paper only averaging about a page of typed, double-spaced text. Once everyone had silently read each person's paper, writers who felt they needed help asked the group for suggestions. Alicia's group was large. But the students seemed intent upon staying together. There were four men and four women. Once the group members appeared finished with their task, I sat down and asked some questions about the effectiveness of this group strategy. Not surprising, the four men found the group potentially helpful. Comments such as "I'll take their comments into consideration," and "Out of forty comments I might kinda pick up on one" summed up the male response. The female response, however, was loaded. Alicia's critique of this classroom practice was cutting:

> I don't trust their comments. I figure if they're taking this class they need it just as much as I do. They haven't gone to school to learn this. I hate it when they write on my papers. I want to stop them and say: What are you doing? (fieldnotes 2/3/95)

I was neither surprised nor alarmed at this response. Kenneth Bruffee assures us that students working in collaborative groups must learn a new language in order to talk effectively about writing (Bruffee, 1983). They have been used to viewing writing as a traditionally silent model. But the social model argues that writing is a form of talking, and Bruffee proposes that when students talk through their writing, they develop it fully. He further argues that:

> If thought is internalized public and social talk, then writing of all kinds is internalized social talk made public and social again. If thought is internalized conversation, then writing is internalized conversation re-externalized. (Bruffee, 1984, p. 641)

Thus, it is a given, such a perspective presumes, to make that internal conversation that is writing external. However, when I received Alicia's first writing assignment, I gained a fuller understanding of her distaste for collaborative evaluation. She has little confidence in her writing ability and fears not measuring up. In a cover letter addressed to me, Alicia attempts to explain her deep-seated reservations:

> I still write on a 103 [basic writer] level and that took me long enough to get there because of my English teacher from high school who ruined the small amount of self-esteem I had in my writing. (2/6/95)

Still convinced that my job was to empower this female writer in such a way that she could comfortably engage in peer-response sessions, still convinced that Bruffee was right, that building a discourse community was the ideal and peer-response sessions could do just that, I pushed on. I had yet to invite Alicia to participate in my study. And the relationship I had with her was anything but comfortable. Prior to submitting her first paper, she and a fellow student visited me in my office to gain clarification on the assignment, but she didn't talk to me. In fact, she didn't even look at me, offering only her dark and distant profile while her friend asked the questions.

One month later, the pupa is encased snugly in its first layer. I employ a read-around plus note-taking.

During this session, groups did not exceed four members. Each group member read the entire group's papers and took notes in response. The group was to discuss each paper together in light of some assignment criteria I had established as discussion guidelines:

1. Readers read for clarity. Where do you get lost?
2. What would you hope the writer addresses and does she/he indeed address your concerns?
3. Does the dialogue do more than skim the surface? Where could it dive deeper into the gaps of the primary text? (fieldnotes 2/24/95)

I had constructed these questions in order to offer participants a means to access this new language they were supposed to be acquiring, a language that would help them talk about writing with more ease (Bruffee, 1983). By offering a model, I had hoped to move women into substantial response and active literacy. It was my hope that such guidelines would give students permission to criticize (Danis, 1982). I was attempting to decenter the power structure of the classroom without abandoning students altogether (Flynn, 1982).

Lo and behold, Alicia did not show.

It was at this point that I began to suspect just how deep her distaste was of these groups. Still, I did not consider inviting her to participate in a study. Still, I did not presume to question the validity and necessity of my pedagogy. I did, however, attempt to make it ever more appealing to students. After watching one group closely, two men and two women, I felt I needed to restructure the groups. The female authors' papers were addressed first. In about eight minutes, discussion involving their ideas and concerns was completed. I then noted that the men turned their chairs around, showing their backs to the two women, and proceeded to respond for a half an hour to each other's texts. The girls leaned their heads against the wall and appeared utterly bored, entirely excluded, finding it unnecessary to engage with each other's projects and apparently impossible or unnecessary to attempt to break into the conversation with the men. The men, quite flagrantly, picked up the conversation ball and went elsewhere to play.

> A couple of weeks later, the shroud grows thicker, gaining bulk, but is
> battered by a high wind.
> I offer more group autonomy.

Once again, this session was situated around writing topics. Group size ran anywhere from three to five participants. Before students began to engage in peer evaluation, we, as a large group, generated reading criteria on the board. In other words, this time I attempted to help them form their own reading agenda that reflected their personal concerns. As they read, students were asked to comment in writing to the authors. Alicia didn't show. I must reiterate that this student was not chronically absent. She simply refused to engage in this community-building practice. But I pushed on.

I closely observed the session, speculating as to the effectiveness of this particular peer-response method:

> The room is quiet doing it this way. I feel somehow left out. But I think
> a lot is happening. They're doing close readings, thinking about the cri-
> teria as they move, probably applying the reading to their own works, I
> hope. (fieldnotes 3/15)

I found out later that this wishful thinking was hardly the case. One female student who I had interviewed after her group was finished bemoaned the lack of feedback from her group. And she negated my hunch that readers apply the criteria to their own work while reading their peer's work. When I asked her if she found the group helpful, she said: "No, these were the only things I got wrong." She showed me a couple of spots on her page where a student had marked punctuation. Students, then, simply see these groups as a replay of the traditional writing relationship that they experience with the teacher, except in this case, their peers are the graders. And, like Alicia said, "they haven't gone to school to learn this" (fieldnotes 2/3/95).

PART THREE: WOOING ALICIA, GROWING THE WINGS

It was at this point, nine weeks into the semester, that I finally considered calling Alicia and asking her to become a study participant. My field-notes say:

> Alicia didn't show up. I'm wondering why. I must call. I can see how including her as a part of my study will help us both. I'm determined that after spring break I shall woo her. (3/15/95)

I continued to view Alicia as a real challenge, noting her anger and her behavior patterns of resistance to writing and to me. I was yet to validate that resistance as cognitive choice on her part. Her papers were consistently Cs, but I knew those Cs weren't offering her the confidence she so desired. She continued to hide in the back of the room and avoid me whenever possible. Two days after the latest peer-response session, as she handed in her paper, she complained to me directly about English teachers' criteria: "They're all different, they all want different stuff." She told me that what I taught her about sentencing only confused her. She would have done it anyway if she was just left to her own devices. She claimed that she missed peer-response sessions because she never gets anything out of them. The overt message was that she gets nothing from my class, learns nothing from the assignments, from her peers, or from me.

Immediately after our conversation, I ran to a quiet place so that I could record our conversation and my reaction to it. Although I was hurt and frustrated, I sensed that because I offered her my ear, because I tried neither to defend myself nor my profession, miraculously we had a break through. But I didn't know where to go next. I jotted down a plan:

> What shall I do?
> 1. Interview: discuss learning
> 2. Value her knowledge and perspectives
> 3. Address her where she's at

I graded her paper early, offering interactive and positive remarks in the margins, attempting to encourage her to feel equipped. I returned it to her before I returned anyone else's, stating that I wanted to be sure and cater to those folks who worry most about the grading policy, and I invited her to revise up to a B, but told her she must meet with me first. Approaching me after class, her demeanor had shifted. She seemed honestly open to learning writing strategies from me and claimed that she had chosen her next paper topic because it would let her blend a narrative voice along with intellectual rigor, because that's what I had suggested—first positive comments. But as I processed her response, I couldn't help but wonder just who was being empowered here. I had set the goals, and Alicia responded exactly as Joan Bolker (1979) suggests female writers have been trained to respond to authority: "programmed to please" by a society that values subservient female roles.

Because Alicia's and my relationship seemed on more stable footing, I decided to invite her to participate in my study on April 7, sending her a note of explanation that reflected my goals to value her knowledge and perspectives and address her where she was at:

Dear Alicia,
    How would you feel about being a participant in my doctoral study? There are three reasons why I'd like to work with you on this project. First, you don't like peer response sessions. Second, you are so articulate and full of wonderful stories. Three, I like the excuse to get together with you so we can work on writing consistently. (4/7/95)

Immediately after class, she agreed to participate, and I was utterly aware of the power differential at play here. Although I gave her much encouragement to decline my invitation, I was fully aware of just how dangerous it is for a student to reject a professor. Be that as it may, together we attempted to compose a writing/reviewing policy that would serve Alicia and prepare her for group interaction. The plan was that she would write her rough draft, work with me during office hours to sharpen it, thereby ensuring a confidence level when sharing her work with her peers. I continued to see great value in attempting to move Alicia, already articulate and forceful when the need arose, to engage in formal writer's talk with peers in her composition classroom. Alicia agreed to trust me when I insisted that this procedure would improve her writing and was part of the writing process.

Extended Interview with Alicia, 4/18/95

I found a quiet room in which Alicia and I might engage in conversation without interruption. Equipped with tape recorder, fieldnotes, Coke, and pretzels, I sought to understand Alicia's history as a writer and communicator in general in order to construct reader-response groups that would cater to her background. What I heard during that hour opened up new knowledge for me and in many ways changed me as an educator. For the first time, I began to understand how teachers tend to take an awful lot for granted, for example, that everyone is basically the same, with the same pasts, the same needs, the same educational desires. I designed my interview questions from Lynn Z. Bloom's (1985) taxonomy that accounts for students' intellectual, artistic, emotional, and social contexts.

To begin, I asked Alicia if her family participates in active group conversations about controversial topics. I was beginning to suspect that much more than gender affected a group participant's ability or inability to engage actively in writing groups. She claimed that, although her family is well to do, in the communication department they are dysfunctional. Rarely does anyone speak to anyone else without a shouting match. Hence, as she put it, "I don't open my mouth for fear of being misunderstood and talked over." This environment reflects Alicia's primary experience with group dynamics and goes far to explain a dimension of resistance she holds to peer-response sessions.

My next question attempted to address her sense of self as a writer and the historical construction of that sense. How well do you feel your high school experience prepared you for your college writing courses? When you reflect on past writing experiences, do you have a positive view or a negative view? This particular set of questions elicited an emotional wash for which I was ill-prepared. She began by describing an English teacher with whom she suffered through both her junior and senior years of high school English instruction. Apparently, this instructor chose favorites. Alicia was not one of them. In an attempt to build a relationship with this teacher, she would visit her after school, share her writing, ask for suggestions, and then receive ridicule during class periods. She was placed in a peer-response group with the teacher's "favorites" so that they could "fix" her remedial prose. Her attempt to build a relationship in which learning and growth became possible and pleasant was met with teacherly arrogance (ah, we're an arrogant lot) and disappointment. And I am reminded of Belenky et al.'s assertion that women come to know through connection and intimacy, an intimacy that peer-response sessions ostensibly encourage but realistically violate.

Next came a question that attempted to address writing as personal investment and how that personal investment interacts with social realities. What kind of writer do you perceive yourself to be: artistic or more conventional? How so? How might this propensity affect your peer-response engagements? Alicia imprints her very self upon the page. She sees herself as an artistic writer, writing as an act of composing herself on paper: "How can someone in a group say 'hey, this is wrong' when I know this is the way it is and they don't even know me? They weren't there. They can't know."

> The silken bundle is brutalized by a late frost: I offered alternatives, take-home responses.

Based upon the information that Alicia shared, I worked hard to restructure the final peer-response session of the semester in such a way as not to violate a student's sense of privacy and autonomy. I was still at it, still spinning that sticky, opaque cocoon, determined to make this practice work, as it had become a convention, a given, in every writing classroom taught on my campus and other campuses across the nation for the last ten years. For this session, students were to bring three copies of their rough drafts and exchange papers with their groups. With whom they worked I left entirely up to students. I also isolated two different types of responses and asked students to take the papers home, read them twice, respond in the margins first as readers and second as teachers, and during the following class sessions reconvene and discuss reader/teacher comments. I was attempting to disrupt the notion of peer-response as "correction," fully aware that they had never been given any other roles but teacher/student to play. The reader role asked the students simply to tell the writer what the writing did to them—made them laugh, confused them, interested them, and so forth. Knowing full well that simply asking them to turn off the teacherly voice was much too simplistic, I instead asked them to separate it from the readerly voice. Once again, I was attempting to offer means by which they might engage in talking about writing in such a way as to create a discourse community. But this time I was attempting to do so in a less threatening way in order to accommodate students like Alicia with high anxiety toward these sessions.

To equip Alicia to participate in this session with confidence, we scheduled a meeting to discuss her rough draft three days prior to the paper exchange. She, however, skipped her meeting.

> She called me and rescheduled prior to my 8:30 class on the same morning the paper exchange was to take place. So I ran to meet her this morning, expecting to pour over her working draft and found her still

attempting to make sense of the assignment. No draft. Paper exchange
in 20 minutes. It seems she will go to any length to avoid the peer-
response sessions that trouble her at so many different levels. I have
made headway, however, for she has agreed to be present to ask her
peers questions about her focus and goals: first time this involvement
has happened. (fieldnotes 4/21/95)

She also claimed that she planned on asking Paul and Brandon, two men
from our composition class, to review her text once it was written. She
wanted Brandon's feedback because "He'll give me opposition." She
knows these two students on a personal level, outside of the classroom;
hence, she feels more comfortable asking for response. Obviously, she's
experiencing a greater sense of control. Obviously she's demonstrating
an active literacy: announcing her needs and pursuing them. Isn't this
peer-response? Yes, indeed. But it is not institutionalized peer-response.
"Perhaps the least studied of the widespread uses of collaboration in
writing groups is that informal network of assistance and support that
goes on in residence halls, study rooms, coffee shops, and libraries. . . ."
(Harris, 1992, p. 370). What kind of community can we build in an eigh-
teen-week period? Meeting three times per week for less than an hour is
hardly conducive to building mutually trusting relationships. My key
point here is that peer-response as a method appears viable only when
the writer controls where it happens, when it happens, and with whom it
happens. I don't believe, however, that we can replicate, institutionally,
this experience for them.

PART FOUR: THE PRACTICE WON'T FLY

I'm most aware of how I am controlling writers' talk, institutionalizing
yet another part of the writing process, all in the guise of empowering
students and decentering my own power. Although I would not likely
seek to exchange my ill-shaped drafts with a group of strangers I neither
trust nor respect, I continued to believe that just such an exchange was
beneficial, even necessary, to my students' writing precesses. I respond
to painful student cries such as Alicia's with reassurances such as:
"You'll get used to the exposure" (Hale, 1988); "the exchange is not
meant to humiliate"; "it's designed to help your writing gain clarity and
to increase your audience awareness" (Harris, 1992); "the exchange is
not for you but for your reader as it helps to hone her critical thinking
skills" (Gere and Abbott, 1985). I've responded to student discomfort

much like my mother did to my resistance to swallowing spinach. "Eat it, it's good for you." But I have been convinced through the years that I can acquire my iron and vitamins through other sources that don't violate my palate to such an extreme. Likewise, listening to Alicia has convinced me that my students can attain clear prose, a sense of audience awareness, and critical thinking skills without undergoing a process that seems to violate many students' sense of privacy.

How Do Peer-Response Sessions Disrupt Traditional Learning Roles?

Quite frankly, they don't. Students have learned to employ two roles when participating in classroom activities: the teacher role and the student role. In many ways, they tyrannize each other just as teachers in the past have tyrannized them, scribbling copious notes in the margins of each other's papers, crossing out entire lines of text. Or, when assuming the role of the students, they resist commenting whatsoever, lacking the training and confidence to do so with authenticity. Many students, students like Alicia, experience a sense of victimization from the more assertive students engaged in their teacher roles. These groups do not decenter the hierarchy. The power structure has not dissipated in the least. Rather, it has simply reestablished itself in more insidious ways (Ashton-Jones, 1995). Some proponents of peer-response practices claim that students involved in such sessions experience writing and revising for less threatening audiences than the teacher (Berkenkotter, 1984). To the contrary, Alicia's experience and my observations negate such a naive presentation of community.

Who Do Peer-Response Sessions Serve?

Why, the teacher, of course. Because I forced myself to scrutinize how I used peer-response sessions and what my goals were for them, I arrived at the uncomfortable conclusion that they are not the student-empowering, student-centered practice our field enjoys believing (Harris, 1992). By employing this classroom strategy, I gain ever-more control of students' writing practices (Heilker, 1994). I have captured Alicia in my Foucaultian gaze, and through this exploitative gaze I've constructed my classroom, my scholarship, and her. Fifteen years ago, students at the end of a writing assignment owed me a single paper, a product. No longer merely in control of that final product, I involve myself in every event leading up to that product. Writers' talk, not just writers' products, has become institutionalized. I control how that talk happens, where it happens, when it happens, and why it happens. I also insist that it must happen (Mullin, 1994). And through this usurpation of students' writing processes I, and others like me, have constructed a field—composition theory—in which we speculate about the processes we isolate and impose. Our academic reports are directly dependent upon the scope of students' processes we can discuss. This, I would argue, is not student-empowerment but researcher-empowerment, teacher-empowerment.

Further, to assume that it is somehow my job to move women from their silences into language, into active literacy, is promoting literacy as violence (Stuckey, 1991), a violence that gobbles up the quiet announcements of students like Alicia. It is to presume that I know what's best for her, to presume that I know her group needs better than she does. It is, ultimately, to disempower her yet again. On the one hand, I am as committed as ever to making salient ideological values that dictate women's facilitative speech roles and males' active ones. I'm as committed as ever to helping women move from silence into language during mixed-group interactions. But to attempt to do so without the student's permission or to attempt to do so by employing a convention that has become a norm, a law, a given, such as peer-response sessions, is to renounce the very critical pedagogy I attempt to embrace.

> My concern is that when discourses of critical or feminist pedagogy present themselves in a fixed, final, founded form, that form soon protects them from rethinking and change. It turns what was once "critical" in their work into a kind of norm or law—a final truth, a final emancipation. For Foucault that is just what critical "truth" cannot be. As a teacher educator practicing critical and feminist pedagogy, I have wanted to believe that what I am doing is right—it is certainly more difficult to live with uncertainty. But now I am inclined to agree with the function and ethic for the intellectual Foucault proposes: that is, the attempt to constantly question the "truth" of one's thought and oneself. (Gore, 1993, p. 11)

Becoming sensitive, open to student voices is, I now believe, the only way for a teacher to check the truth of her thoughts, the ethics of her pedagogy, the integrity of her praxis. However, there are indeed dangers. Research that invites students to speak is, at its very core, emancipatory, offering students access into defining what takes place in their writing classrooms. It is only right that their voices announce what works and what does not. But to manipulate student voices (and yes, I do mean manipulate, because we do so with all of our data) without engaging in self-reflection, without scrutinizing why we enact the theory, practice, and research that we do, is, I believe, the opposite of empowering. It is unethical. Mini Orner says it beautifully when she claims that:

> Educators concerned with changing unjust power relations must continually examine our assumptions about our positions, those of our students, the meanings and uses of student voice, our power to call for "students to speak," and our often unexamined power to legitimate and perpetuate unjust relations in the name of student empowerment. (p. 77; emphasis added)

I've called for Alicia to speak, both in my classroom and in my research; I'm using her voice to construct meaning. But I am concerned about what I have not let her say, what I was not able to hear.

On a final note, Alicia didn't blossom into the confident writer that we both would have liked her to become. She passed my course with a C, but she can no longer claim that "Teachers always act like students don't have anything to teach them."

REFERENCES

Annas, P. (1987). "Silences: Feminist Language Research and the Teaching of Writing," in C. Caywood and G. Overing (Eds.), *Teaching Writing: Pedagogy, Gender, and Equity* (pp. 3–17). New York: Basic Books.

Ashton-Jones, E. (1995). "Collaboration, Conversation, and the Politics of Gender," in L. Phelps and J. Emig (Eds.), *Feminine Principles and Women's Experience in American Composition and Rhetoric*. Pittsburgh: University Press.

Beaven, M. (1977). "Individualized Goal Setting, Self-evaluation, and Peer Evaluation," in C. R. Cooper and L. Odell (Eds.), *Evaluating Writing: Describing, Measuring, Judging* (pp. 135–136). Urbana, IL: National Council of Teachers of English.

Belenky, M., Clinchy, B., Goldberger, N., & Tarule, J. (1986). *Women's Ways of Knowing: The Development of Self, Voice, and Mind*. New York: Basic Books.

Berkenkotter, C. (1984). "Students Writers and Their Sense of Authority Over Texts." *College Composition and Communication, 35*, 312–319.

Bloom, L. (1985). "Anxious Writers in Context: Graduate School and Beyond," in Mike Rose (Ed.), *When a Writer Can't Write* (pp. 119–133).

Bogdan, R., & Biklen, S. (1992). *Qualitative Research for Education: An Introduction to Theory and Methods.* Boston: Allyn and Bacon.

Bolker, J. (1979). "Teaching Griselda to Write." *College English, 50,* 906–908.

Bruffee, K. (1983). "Writing and Reading as Collaborative or Social Acts," in J. L. Hays, et al. (Eds.), *The Writer's Mind: Writing as a Mode of Thinking.* Urbana, IL: National Council of Teachers of English.

Bruffee, K. (1984). "Collaborative Learning and the Conversation of Mankind." *College English, 46,* 635–652.

Burns-McCoy, N. (1995). "Expressionist Pedagogy and the Politics of Form." Paper presented at CCCC, Washington, D.C.

Cain, M. (1995). *Revisioning Writers' Talk: Gender and Culture in Acts of Composing.* Albany: SUNY Press.

Cochran-Smith, M., & Lytle, S. (1993). *Inside/Outside: Teacher Research and Knowledge.* New York: Teachers College Press.

Danis, M.F. (1980). "Peer-response Groups in a College Writing Workshop: Students' Suggestions for Revising Compositions." *Dissertation Abstracts International, 41,* 5008A–5009A.

Fishman, P. (1983). "Interaction: The Work Women Do," in B. Thorne et al. (Eds.), *Language, Gender, and Society* (pp. 89–101). Rowley: Newbury House.

Fleischer, C. (1994). "Researching Teacher-research: A Practitioner's Retrospective." *English Education, 26*(2), 87–124.

Freire, Paulo. (1990). "The 'Banking' Concept of Education," in D. Bartholomae & A. Petrosky (Eds.), *Ways of Reading: An Anthology for Writers* (pp. 206–222). Monclair: Boynton.

Flynn, E. A., et al. (1982). "Effects of Peer Critiquing and Model Analysis on the Quality of Biology Student Laboratory Reports." Paper presented at the Annual Meeting of the National Council of Teachers of English, Washington, DC (ERIC Document Reproduction Service No. ED 234 404).

Gere, A. R., & Abbot, R. D. (1985). "Talking about Writing: The Language of Writing Groups." *Research in the Teaching of English, 19,* 362–381.

Gilligan, C. (1982). *In a Different Voice: Psychological Theory and Women's Development.* Cambridge: Harvard UP.

Gore, J. M. (1993). *The Struggle for Pedagogies: Critical and Feminist Discourses as Regimes of Truth.* New York: Routledge.

Hale, C., & Wyche-Smith S., (1988). "Student Writing Groups: Demonstrating the Process" [videotape]. Tacoma: Public Wordshop Production, Inc.

Haraway, D. (1991). *Simians, Cyborgs, and Women: The Reinvention of Nature.* New York: Routledge.

Harris, M. (1992). "Collaboration Is Not Collaboration Is Not Collaboration: Writing Center Tutorials vs. Peer-response Groups." *College Composition and Communication, 43,* 369–383.

Heilker, P. (1995). "Discipline and Punish and Process and Paradigms (or Foucault, Visibility, [Dis]empowerment, and the Construction of Composition Studies)." *Composition Studies, 21*(2), 4–13.

Herrmann, A. (1989). *Teaching Writing with Peer Response Groups.* ED 307-616.

Jeske, J. (1989). *Peer-response Groups: Answering the Critique.* ED 309 446.

Lather, P. (1986). "Research as Praxis." *Harvard Educational Review, 56*(3), 257–277.

Lather, P. (1987). "Educational Research and Practice in a Postmodern Era." Paper presented at the Ninth Conference of Curriculum Theory and Classroom Practice, Dayton, Ohio, 1987.

Lather, P. (1991). *Getting Smart. Feminist Research and Pedagogy with/in the Postmodern.* New York: Routledge.

McCarthy, L. P. (1987). "A Stranger in Strange Lands: A College Student Writing across the Curriculum." *Research in the Teaching of English, 21,* 233–265.

McNiff, J. (1993). *Teaching as Learning: An Action Research Approach.* New York: Routledge.

Mullin, J. (1994). "Feminist Theory, Feminist Pedagogy: The Gap between What We Say and What We Do." *Composition Studies, 21*(2), 14–24.

Murau, A. (1993). "Shared Writing: Students' Perceptions and Attitudes of Peer Review." ERIC ED 367 138.

Orner, M. (1992). "Interrupting the Calls for Student Voices in Liberatory Education: A Feminist Poststructuralist Perspective" (pp. 74–89), in C. Luke & J. Gore (Eds.), *Feminisms and Critical Pedagogy.* New York: Routledge.

Sommers, E. (1993). "Student-Centered, Not Teacher Abandoned: Peer Response Groups That Work." ERIC ED 307 616.

Stuckey, E. (1992). *The Violence of Literacy.* Portsmouth: Boynton/Cook.

Tannen, D. (1994). "I'll Explain It to You: Lecturing and Listening," in P. Eschholz (Ed.), *Language Awareness* (pp. 389–403). New York: St. Martin's Press.

Wolcott, H. (1990). "On Seeking—and Rejecting—Validity in Qualitative Research," in E. Eisner & A. Peshkin (Eds.), *Qualitative Inquiry in Education: The Continuing Debate* (pp. 120–152). New York: Teachers College Press.

CHAPTER 14

Cultural Studies (Alone) Won't Do It
Strategic Reform of Academic Departments in the University[1]

SCOTT SHEPARD

As we prepare to enter the new millennium, we ask ourselves if multicultural and countercultural thinking is penetrating the great American university's canon of necessary truths and ideas, or if the Anglo-centric legacy has actually regrouped and solidified its position. Are the marginalized, the oppressed, the people of color, and all those with progressive insights on truth and beauty reconstructing the concept of a "liberal" education, or a "degree-worthy" education, or are the voices along the margins being brushed aside still? Although what I call "multicultural programming"—for want of a more precise term—proliferates in colleges and universities all over the country, I suggest here that this has not meant that white power reality in higher education is being dismantled or even remodeled by the rainbow coalition. I think what has happened is that white power at college has learned how to deal with multicultural activism, its intellectuals, its noise makers. Multiculturalism[2] has made it onto the campus, which counts for something, but has not found a home inside those buildings where the ivy grows thick on the walls; the registrars and the advisors and the deans don't sweat it; and the president and the trustees don't even see it. The university has ghettoized its multiculturalists, and this is manifested in a two-track educational system—one track consisting of "the core" material, which emerges in and is sustained through "required" courses, and the other track, the "alternative" (multicultural) material, which, like what is taught in cosmology or flight attendant school, is meaningful for a few, but not required of and representing little of significance to anybody else. I don't mean to belittle the books, ideas, or personnel associated with multicultural education as

measured against "traditional" education—especially since my sentiments and loyalties are there among the multiculturalists; nor am I belit-
tling cosmology. I am distressed that after a quarter century of cultural
studies programming on many campuses, we continue to find that the experiences, creations, and contributions of and about folks of color are
treated by those in power as something one can choose to study or
choose to ignore without doing injury to one's education; and material
that encroaches on or is threatening to white power reality remains
among the electives rather than the requirements. It is inconceivable that
someone would suggest that the contributions of Homer, Shakespeare,
Roosevelt, Descartes, or Freud were optional, not terribly critical components of undergraduate education. Yet the texts of artists and intellectuals of color, those American or those from cultures around the world,
continue to be treated as add-ons to what really matters, rather than as ir-
replaceable pieces of what higher learning ought to be in the twenty-first
century. And it is getting worse, I suggest, because the activist scholars
who might make a difference in the traditional departments are continu-
ously migrating into the scholarly ghettos that we think of as cultural
programs.[3]

It is time to rethink the migration of progressive scholars out of the
university's "traditional departments"—English, history, sociology, and
others—and into specialized programs. While some archconservatives
regard English departments as a sanctuary for campus radicalism, in fact,
English has been a toothless tiger when it comes to ideas that directly
challenge the white patriarchy in which it was founded. English would
defend Ezra Pound on the issue of anti-Semitism; but it will not make
Black or feminist literature a requirement for graduation. This is important, because, until a course or subject area becomes required in the university, it simply does not exist as material that the student body need
take seriously; not having your course required is like being a New York
cab driver who doesn't own a medallion: you can sit in your car but
you'll never carry any passengers. And English continues to be a chilly
place for the feminist and/or colleague of color at the faculty meetings.
That is why white women and people of color have been transferring out
of English departments as fast as the alternative programming slots have
been appearing. Although escape probably feels better to the individuals,
this approach can be counterproductive if one's larger goal is reform of
the university.

Through a little story, let me illustrate the disturbing pattern I have
witnessed, symbolizing the lost ground in the struggle to reform the uni-

versity power structure: imagine that the English department of a prestigious university hires a reform-minded Black woman—let's call her
June—to teach ethnic American literature. The department has a high
proportion of white males, most with years of continuous service in the
same program. June is not told that an ethnic literature slot was created,
more for the reason that department members felt they "ought to" offer
such courses rather than because they really wanted to offer them. She is
the only person of color in the department. She is not told of the Asian-
American woman who had transferred out of the department and into
Women's Studies a year earlier, although she will pick this story up eventually. An idealistic young woman, June applied for the position in English for the same reason she did her graduate work in English—because
of an appreciation of words, because literature somehow turns painful
stories into something beautiful. She arrives on campus fired with fresh
ideas for an old department, but quickly becomes disillusioned that so
few of her colleagues share her interest in change. Everyone defers to
June as "the" multicultural expert, though this unsought ranking does not
result in their acting on her views or her advice to do something differently than they did before. Deeming her the multicultural expert seems to
be a justification to dump into her lap any multicultural project, event,
activity, and responsibility, along with the assumption that she will mentor all students of color and supervise any theses and dissertations that
engage writers of color. Although she was hired on a two/three teaching
load (two courses one semester, three the next), not only has this to include one graduate course each semester, but all of the sections of undergraduate multicultural literature. When she insists that the department
needs additional faculty to keep up with the demand for course offerings,
her colleagues start to roll their eyes. One colleague, perhaps a white
woman, shares many of June's views, and speaks out—but more tenta-
tively than June, and the department does everything it can to foment distrust between the two reformers (such as inviting one to serve on a
desired committee but not the other). Some of June's white students can
not grasp the issues that emerge in the ethnic literature she was hired to
introduce them to, and they make her the scapegoat of their frustrations.
Perhaps she is challenged as well by students from other racial or ethnic
groups when she teaches a work by a writer whose ethnicity she does not
share. After seeing a few nasty course evaluations, the department wonders if this new professor has bad communication skills. The tenure
struggle looms. But June has made a friend in the Ethnic Studies program, and when the possibility of a transfer emerges, it seems to June to

be both attractive and sensible. Colleagues in the English department, who had found themselves challenging her on so many other matters, are only too willing to help June to make the transfer; June's departure is treated as a no-fault divorce. Tranquillity returns to the English department. In her new program, June finds support and encouragement for some of the same things that met with such resistance over in the other department. Perhaps she has even been offered the chance to start a program herself (San Juan writes of the administration's use of titles and offices to seduce and to neutralize "superstar" reformist scholars whose effectiveness frightens them).

In her new office, June is too busy learning new ways, courses, and coworkers to keep up with what is going on back in the English department—although she meant to. Some of the Black students who had gotten excited about English because she had been their teacher, lose interest after she is gone. Or they follow her to Ethnic Studies, assuming that the English department no longer needed their services—as it no longer needed June's. The "other" reformer back in English feels as outnumbered as she had before and retreats back into her shell.

In a semester or two, a new search gets underway for a teacher of multicultural literature, and the process begins again. Gerald Graff writes that "the structure of patterned isolation defuse[s] academic conflicts by keeping warring factions in noncommunicating departments, fields, and course areas" (p. 134). "Noncommunicating" because there is more than enough to do just to keep business running in one's own department or program. Our young professor, who has moved from English to Ethnic Studies, teaches most of the same texts she would teach in the other, although her (new) colleagues and students engage the literature just a little differently than was the case in English. There is a little more interest in the history in the texts and a little less in the artistry, but she does not really like sacrificing the art. Some of the confrontational spirit June brought with her to English is reoriented into a bunker mentality, for now she is trying to protect the jewel—her new program—she has been handed. She is no longer surrounded on a daily basis by intractable white male colleagues or resistance to her every course, her every idea; and she enjoys this. Part of her thinks—"I know that white male intractability is still out there (undefeated), but do I really want to leave my warm building to go out looking for it?" At the height of her frustration while in the English department, June had planned to ask advice from that Asian-American woman who had started in English and transferred to Women's Studies. Perhaps they could compare experiences and strategize institutional reforms. But now that she is making a fresh start in a new program, June is simply busy again, and her priority is with what goes on in Ethnic Studies, not with what happened with someone who used to be in English, or how it is going for someone who is in Women's Studies. The dean, who administers over Women's Studies, Ethnic Studies, as well as English, funds each at a different level, approving a hire here, refusing one there. In each department there is an uneasy sense that the dean's favoritism is extended toward the other.

The guardians of the Anglo-centric legacy in places such as the English department have actually solidified their position recently, because the scholars who would have been reforming it are taking their voices, their ideas, and their committee votes into other offices. Thus, multicultural programming on campus, while doing a lot of other necessary things well, has actually inhibited strategic reform of Anglo-centric hegemony. For many Anglo Americans in the university, support for such programming proves that they are not racist. Apart from what actually is taught in an Ethnic Studies program (which they ignore), Anglo American traditionalists have co-opted the term *multiculturalism* and defined it in terms that work for Anglo America. Anglo American multiculturalism bears closer resemblance to *cultural tolerance*, according to which Anglos are not required to acknowledge or share any of their disproportionate power and privilege or to participate otherwise in meaningful change of the society. Anglo American multiculturalism largely consists of a willingness to attend an Asian food festival and a read-in on Martin Luther King, Jr.'s, birthday. An Anglo American multiculturalist defers without question to the essentialist knowledge of a Black faculty member on the topic of African-American literature and generally stays out of his or her way as much as possible, while ignoring without serious engagement the opinions of that same faculty member on departmental affairs and program vision. Anglo American multiculturalism usually means vaguely endorsing the creation of cultural programs of study on campus, such as a Black Studies Center, and agreeing not to inhibit or interrogate on scholarly grounds anything a Black faculty member does over there. It means an Anglo professor's willingness to include Dr. King's "I Have a Dream Speech" in his syllabus for freshman comp and Maxine Hong Kingston's *The Woman Warrior* on the syllabus for a contemporary literature survey without submitting to any particular training to teach either one. What Anglo America typically makes of *multiculturalism* is what has made so many people of color distrust the term.

At a glance, the emergence of cultural studies projects on campus seems to indicate that the powers that be have finally acknowledged the worthiness of the voices and ideas of formerly marginalized communities; it seems to show that when the marchers came and the bullhorns blared that the academic elite waved the flag of surrender to this people's revolution; surely it means that we have the facilities to prepare the courses we have always needed, do the research we have always wanted, and initiate the reeducation of our students. When it comes to the full needs of higher education, diversity programming thus far has meant, in fact, much less than it should have. Veterans of the battles over multicultural study know that culture studies programs were initiated, in large part, to pacify noisy minorities and feminists; the real question comes down to whether the marginalized are able to mine enough gold out of these programs to justify ignoring the white supremacy being marketed in the traditional departments. In *Beyond the Culture Wars,* Gerald Graff contends that those in the centers of power have been manipulating reform movements without appreciably giving ground to them:

> Whereas the old college had avoided controversy by excluding dissenters, the new university avoided it by keeping dissenters apart. Whereas the old college had blindly resisted innovation, the new university painlessly absorbed the most threatening novelties by the simple device of adding new components to an ever-expanding aggregate. (p. 133)

Similarly, Epifanio San Juan sees university versions of multiculturalism as "the latest reincarnation of the assimilationist drive to pacify unruly subaltern groups" (p. 60). For San Juan, the struggle of the underempowered has never been a matter of tolerance or of "cultural differences"— the notions that have recently caught fire; rather, San Juan keeps his eye on the "the inescapable centrality of power relationships" and the inequality that has defined them in our historic context. Graff and San Juan are skeptical of the way in which multicultural programming has been unfolding on the campus (although not long ago, having been in a position to choose between teaching in an English department and teaching in an Ethnic Studies department, San Juan chose Ethnic Studies). When I was in graduate school in the English department, graduate students talked subversively about making the switch over to Ethnic Studies or Women's Studies, in part because we saw our mentors in English talk the same way.

    While I have discussed some scenarios in which a frustrated scholar flees her department when it seems she can play no role in its reformation, I might briefly visit another situation, in which, rather than transfer out of an Anglo-centric department, the progressive scholar stays in (for example) English, but "checks out" of the department mentally. Sometimes, after enduring months of resistance and stupidity in the company of her colleagues, the maverick scholar becomes petulant, vowing never to allow herself to be so insulted at another departmental meeting, ignoring whatever "they" do from then on, and pouring her real efforts into her scholarship. The activist/intellectual becomes full-time intellectual. "I'll show them," she thinks, imagining that the strength of her ideas will percolate down from her published writings and into the consciousness of the scholarly community and eventually overwhelm her oppressors by their sheer brilliance. Or, perhaps it is not so much that she is thinking: "I'll show them," as it is: "To hell with them; I'm going to look out for my career" (since I can't produce any changes in this department anyway). This is a variation on the former attitude; she may not hold any hopes that her scholarship will revolutionize anything, but if she just keeps cranking out articles, they won't be able to say that she is a slacker. Losing oneself in one's scholarship or writing projects can be another kind of transfer out of a situation that seems only to frustrate. Those who have chosen to lose themselves in their specialty may have cultivated a working community that is not in their department, or even in the same university; theirs is an extended community, shared with colleagues dotted all over the globe, who happen to share the same scholarly focus. Except at a conference or two each year, these specialists do not debate with each other at the staff meetings or at the mailboxes; they debate through published articles, in much the same way that some play chess through the mail. If June, our reformer, becomes one of these kind of scholars, she may become less quarrelsome in the department meetings and prefer small talk to debate at the mailboxes (that is, if you happen to catch her at the meetings or near the mailboxes). She has given up on making a difference in her department, and she will no longer fight with them about whatever they want to do. She will teach her classes, get back to her word processor, and wait for the MLA Conference. No doubt some of our best scholarship comes from scholars whose focus is on a "long distance" community of specialists. And perhaps these great ideas eventually steer the ship of knowledge just a bit more in a desired direction. But what else happens is that the only reform being generated by June here and by that brilliant professor at a university over there is happening at the top of the ivory tower, in the pages of dense and heavily endnoted journals. Back down at the level of where students and the faculty and staff actually work—in academic departments at universities on either side of the country—no pressure for change is being applied by two who were most suited, by intelligence and energy, to give it. Indeed, in the department where June (quietly) works every day, her colleagues may scarcely even know that somewhere in a journal she has been waging a holy war against much of what they believe. And just as we graduate students bad-mouthed the department if our mentors did, we became convinced that cool professors didn't worry about what their own departments did; they worked on their publications. In no time at all we incorporated bad-mouthing and self-preoccupation into our own styles—if this was the be-havior that we saw in the professors we admired.

At the Conference of Asian American Studies last spring in Wash-ington, D.C., Elaine Kim confessed that even a diehard revolutionary can become distracted by the attainment of a little power. After years of dis-tinguished service on behalf of Asian Americans, when Kim became chair of Ethnic Studies at U.C. Berkeley, she found herself worried about office space, paychecks, and graduate assistants. Peter Kwong, at the same conference session, agreed that the same Asian American scholars who once carried picket signs in front of the administration buildings can, after going on the payroll of the university, become preoccupied with protecting their professional lives. For Kwong, writing articles will not save the world. "I am a materialist," he insisted, who sees the enemy as the traditional "cultural superstructure; to beat it, you don't [just] write about it, you mobilize against it."

In this, the era of both civil rights and student loans, the emergence of diversity programming in universities has coincided with the in-creased presence of women, of people of color, among the student body, faculty, and staff. Members of marginalized groups were instrumental in the push for the programming, and the programming in turn helped to in-crease the enrollment among those groups. Perhaps the administrators outsmarted us right from the beginning, because, while culture studies programs were initiated, they have never acquired the legitimacy that mainstream departments, texts, and ideas enjoy. And departments that were all white and mostly male in the 1960s, such as English and history, continue to be mostly white and largely male.

In hindsight, we can observe that diversity programming not only gives revolutionaries a place to go after they become frustrated with their "regular" departments, it also allows departments like English and soci-ology "off the hook," in terms of meaningful change. It may be counter-productive that alternative programs provide a "pressure release," a pain-free solution to those on both sides of the problem: white men, who do not want to listen to or tenure a solid but meddlesome associate, can evade responsibility for wanting her out by helping her to make the sideways move, so she can become someone else's problem; the upstart professor is happy as well, to escape an office battle in which she was outnumbered and instead be "delivered" to a scholarly space she can participate in creating. Since statistics and anecdotal evidence suggest that women and people of color are tenured at lower rates than are white men, it would seem an act of self-preservation for those who get the opportunity to choose transferring to another department over being forced out of the university altogether. Still, one has to wonder if the availability of options, such as culture studies programs and specialty projects, has made it easier for those protective of white power reality to act with impunity toward talented upstarts. Even the most productive and talented of scholars with reform agendas can be forced out of the department, without her enemies having to cast the ballots to accomplish this. The scholar who is forced or invited into an attractive lateral move in the same university is more likely to take the new job and put her grief behind her than to refuse the position and challenge her treatment by her colleagues in court. All this preserves the appearance of civility on the campus, but it is not the way revolutions work. In one sense, it would have been better if the guardians of the old school had been forced to express in hard votes their hostility toward change, toward multiculturalism in the curriculum, or toward opinionated people of color in the department; perhaps it would have been useful to compel such faculty to take responsibility for tenure decisions that might not stand up well under scrutiny. This is not to suggest that a review committee would grant tenure to or otherwise retain (for example) a Black professor simply to avoid an appearance of racism or reactionary politics; every year we read of well-known universities failing to tenure a progressive scholar under suspicious circumstances. But if we accept for argument's sake that some worthy and productive scholars find themselves regarded as "misfits" in a department, owing to gender, color, values, politics, or all of the above, were there no alternative departments or offices in place to relieve both sides—the Anglo-centrists and the new blood—of discomfort, tenure committees might find themselves far more regularly faced with having to vote out objectionable colleagues whose strong credentials might make that awkward. If they had no other options, perhaps some of those who believed that they were denied tenure unfairly would challenge the decision in ways that would embarrass the department and the university. If it seems that what I am insisting upon is confrontation rather than accommodation, it is because the university establishment seems to have responded to demands for multiculturalism with "separate but equal" curriculum. To this point, separate but equal in the university has worked much the same as it used to with toilets, restaurants, and public schools: business is conducted by members of the outcaste in a place safely apart from that of the majority, and an aura of illegitimacy and inferiority always surrounds these separate facilities. The traditional forces do not expend much energy critiquing what their (onetime) colleagues teach over in the cultural studies programs, but they do not require their students to take those classes in order to graduate, either; that, for example, some substantive exploration of African-American literature is not regarded as necessary for an undergraduate English major at most universities speaks volumes about what the true crisis in higher education is. It is more than whether or not a couple of professors have the right to teach courses they believe in, or that they control a little office space and employ a work-study student; it is about being cut off from participation in the defining of our civilization.

Although the traditional departments can become a hell for the scholar of color or for a white woman with a reformist agenda, what concerns me is that we are postponing rather than undertaking the serious debate over what will be defined as the great ideas required of educated people. If the faculty of color and other progressivists who begin careers in the English department continue migrating out into separate and unequal cultural studies programs, it will continue to be difficult to convince students of color and others on the margins that English is not a white person's discipline. When I was in graduate school studying English, both of the Black women who started in the program around the time that I did gradually shifted their allegiance and their course of study to the Ethnic Studies program, located in a building on the other side of the grassy mall; in an English department dominated by white men, these students felt that neither the selection of literary texts and classes nor the "office climate" reflected their experiences or suitably defined the America in which they grew up. Although I came to appreciate their concerns (but stayed in English) and found a number of friends and allies in the Ethnic Studies program, I am convinced that the English department that my two Black colleagues drifted away from was a lesser place for their loss. Graduate students influence the direction of their graduate programs in a number of indirect ways, including that of voicing concerns to their teachers and participating in the selection of next year's student applicants.

When sites frozen in Anglo-centricism lose reformers it becomes even harder to attract future reformers. Thus it is becoming easier—not more difficult—for a white professor in one of the traditional departments to go through an entire semester without having to face a person of color in a situation in which he will have to negotiate some issue of power and change; easier for him to avoid having to defend his position on the best direction for the future of the department; and to hold onto some plum of privilege without having to at least wrestle someone for it. While scholars over in cultural studies offices and classrooms study and discuss ways to challenge white supremacy, in the old brick buildings on another part of the campus, white supremacy is finding confrontation increasingly infrequent.

Over the past twenty years, there seems to have been a tactical and philosophical turn in the focus of a reform movement whose origins began in the streets in the 1960s. In the early days of the young movement, African-Americans, Asian-Americans, Latinos, white men and women, in a brief, shining moment of informal partnership, targeted specific sites of inequality—particularly on the college campus—demanding change. At the very least, "we" were united by the fact that we were in the streets, and the forces of "our" oppression were in the buildings, maintaining the wheels of the Anglo-centric power machine. Higher education's establishment managed to co-opt the revolution in part by doing exactly what the revolutionaries wanted—by letting them into the buildings—or, more precisely, by initiating the new generation of academic programs that are separate by equal. Once the protesters began to be absorbed into the system as scholars themselves, the pressure for massive reform dissipated. Once inside the walls, each cultural community detached itself from others, trying to establish its own credibility and worthiness, according to terms that the intellectual establishment recognizes. The collective energy of disjunctive constituencies had concentrated on the guardians of white power; and then, suddenly, the collectivism was fragmented, with each one focusing inward toward self-theorization. In his review of the first twenty-five years of Asian-American Studies, for example, Stephen Sumida uses such terms as *self-definition, validation,* and *legitimization* to describe program parameters and goals over the years—terminology we could likewise associate with the objectives of other cultural studies programs. The street-level, confrontational stance that marked Asian-American activism in 1969, when there was nothing the establishment could take away, put the college administration on the defensive. With the creation of cultural studies programming, Asian-

Americans were back to defending their membership as Americans, their literature, their theories. This is not to suggest that there has been something "wrong" with Asian-American Studies, which, from an educational standpoint, has taken some of the invisibility out of the Asian-American experience and enriched countless lives in its quarter century. The point is that no community that has been historically marginalized should be made to feel that it must invest years validating itself to its oppressor in exchange for a sliver of equity. Asian-American protesters in 1969 did not have the benefit of the critical foundations of Sau-Ling Wong, King-Kok Chung, and Frank Chin before they took to the streets—but they did not need journal articles to tell them they were getting a raw deal, and they marched demanding change. At the 1996 Asian-American Studies Conference, Peter Kwong insisted that the original goal in Asian-American Studies was not "identity and who I am," but the fight against racism in order to "transform conditions oppressing all people."

Although it was unacceptable gaps in what was taught that necessitated the creation of cultural studies programs in the first place, the traditional departments in which those gaps existed are losing the "opportunity" and have evaded responsibility in having their futures redirected by those most equipped to do so, when the best of the progressive scholars gravitate out. In my rhetorical collapsing of a broad assortment of situations over twenty-five years in the colleges, I do not mean to "damn by anecdote." None who have invested their skills and energies into diversity programs has done so out of a crusade for personal glory. It has been the intransigence and insider politics of white power in higher education that has precipitated the fractionating of teaching areas in the college in the first place. Scholars of color have been getting pushed long before they jump out of traditional departments. At the time I began research on this article, three Latina professors had recently transferred out of the sociology department at the University of Colorado at Boulder to escape what they described as "a hostile environment" (Cage, A-18). Two of the three former sociology professors went on to teach in a new multicultural program, Boulder's Center for Studies of Ethnicity and Race, and the third went to Boulder's fine arts department. Good for them, good for the newly created center; but it was precisely in its sociology department that Boulder needed these scholars and their fresh ideas most of all.

However understandable the expansion of programming may be, accompanying this expansion is the dissolution of reformist scholarly talent over an ever-widening plane. Often because they are the least patient with the oppressive status quo, the persons most equipped to rejuvenate an "old" department are the ones most likely to wind up in a new cultural studies office. What we see is that it is the frustrated and oppressed who do the most moving, while the white men remain rooted in the traditional departments. The excitement and the revolutionary thinking may be going on over in the new offices, but that probably has little bearing on where the university's political power is located. The activist scholar who has removed herself from an "old" department will have a harder time learning the ropes of the influence game, since those equipped to mentor her in these ways (or at least to allow her to observe) are not in the specialized programs.

In too many instances on the campus, marginalized group members have allowed themselves to be caught up in the white supremacist's trap: they believe that there is an absolute and limited size to the slice of the power pie available to nonwhite males; accepting this to be true, the best any marginalized group can do is to fend off competitors—other marginalized groups—for the largest bite of this finite slice. An example of this kind of thinking was on display at San Francisco State College in 1991, when Oba T'Shaka, chair of the Black Studies department, supported student disruptions of the classes of a Black history professor named Smith, who had begun teaching a course called "Black Politics." T'Shaka saw Smith as part of a veiled attempt by the administration to put him out of business, by encouraging other departments to offer courses already available in Black Studies. If, as Smith insisted, his course was very different from the version of the course taught in Black Studies, then T'Shaka was guilty of just the kind of territorialism that I have lamented in this article. Cultural studies programming was never supposed to give its faculty a corner on the market in the study of previously neglected groups. One of the hopes had been to stimulate or embarrass the other departments into reevaluating their offerings and getting themselves up to date. Those in the cultural programming offices should not be sending the message that there is only one "authorized" version of a marginalized group's history: that available in a cultural studies class. Perhaps—if approached—Dr. Smith would have been willing to join Dr. T'Shaka in a challenge of the administration and the deans over just how much Black history an undergraduate ought to be required in order to earn a degree. In any case, on a campus that already has too few faculty of color, students of color should not be caught up in a misdirected campaign by one Black professor trying to discredit another Black professor. The problem is not that there are too many versions of Black history for one state university; the problem is that the university makes too few course requirements of its students when it comes to multicultural materials and ideas. Given the limited requirements, students may feel that they ought to either take Smith's class or a class in the Black Studies department rather than both. That is an issue that T'Shaka and all of us should pour our energies into—correcting the rules governing course requirements. No department head should operate on the defeatist principle that since the pool of students who will take a course focusing on a marginalized community is limited and unchangeable, the right to offer such courses must be jealously protected.

Similarly, in August 1995, Northwestern University's Law School found itself in an uproar during an effort to make a long overdue "minority hire"; the leading candidate was Maria Hylton, whose father is Australian-Irish and whose mother is African-Cuban. Hylton found herself under fire from Latino students; from the school's only Black law professor, Joyce Hughes; and from the Black Law Students Association. It seemed that the university was representing Hylton as Black or as Latina, depending upon the audience, and neither constituency was satisfied that her "first loyalties" or affinities were with them (Sege). The point was not whether the university was attempting to make a "double score" with Dr. Hylton (Black, female) or even a "triple score" (Black, Latina, female) in its efforts to reach minority hiring goals. We see that kind of politics played all the time. Nor was the point that Hylton may not have seemed as politically militant on behalf of one group or the other. It is regrettable that Dr. Hylton's record of scholarship and service with regard to Blacks and Latinos would not have dominated the evaluation of whether she was a reasonable choice rather than having her skin color be the factor of greatest interest. But what is most important and disturbing was the conviction shared by Dr. Hughes and Black and Latino students that Northeastern was only going to make one nonwhite hire, so the candidate had better meet a supreme standard of ethnic or racial and political purity; that is, Dr. Hylton had to be superhuman, because she would be taking "the slot" reserved for a faculty member of color.

Perhaps you have witnessed or participated in a comparable faculty search on your campus, in which it was understood that a person of color would be hired, and after that hiring, neither students nor faculty better expect to see another person of color brought into the same department until or unless the previous one leaves. A variation on this practice that many of us have observed is that if, for example, one Latino or one Asian Indian has been brought into the department, it is understood that that particular community has been "covered," and so, should another nonwhite be hired in the future, he or she will not belong to that group; while the tacit understanding is that the reason that there is usually a one-Latina or one-Asian-Indian rule in effect is that department members are trying to include a number of different voices with their hiring practices; the underlying reason for the practice is the fear by the white faculty that two Latinas or two Asian Indians would become fast political allies and turn their energies against the majority and its policies for the department.

It is in large part the history of what has happened in America and at universities that would prompt Dr. Hughes at Northwestern and Dr. O'Shaka at San Francisco State to feel protective of the "minority" slices in their departments. I would suggest, however, that strategic multicultural advocacy calls for us to challenge the white supremacist hiring tendencies that impose limits on the number of nonwhites who will be hired in a given department or office or institution. The alternative and defeatist path, the one followed at Northwestern with Dr. Hylton, is for persons of color who find themselves in a position to influence hiring to play directly into the hands of white authorities. Such persons vent rage that they really feel toward the white power structure on innocent and unsuspecting candidates of color, who are guilty of no crime, but are made to feel as though they are. In a page right out of the book written for slaveholders centuries ago, it is the marginalized people who have been duped into putting the candidates through interview hell, while the white authorities file their nails. Rather than waiting for the man to announce he is ready to solicit "minority" views because the powers that be have decided it is time to hire a person of color, marginalized students and faculty members ought to push for continuous participation in employment at the institution; they should be speaking out on the subject of the hiring committees that, season after season, departments and offices all over the campus create to conduct searches; they should be demanding to know why such committees are generally composed entirely of whites, who are mostly interviewing and hiring other whites. Contrary to what your white colleagues might tell you, there are qualified applicants of color with culturally diverse experiences who apply for these positions; it is too often that the nearer the search gets to the hiring stage, the whiter the "serious" candiates tend to become. Conscientious, reform-minded members of the campus community need to keep unceasing pressure on the institution to take far more seriously the interviewing and hiring of candidates who do not necessarily fit within the Anglo-centric comfort zone. We need to work to reach a point where each hiring of a faculty member or staffer of color is not a miraculous event, each search a search for the perfect cultural representative.

Iris Marion Young ("Social Movements and the Politics of Difference") might dispute my notion that the most effective challenge to white supremacy would mean that cultural communities work in concert with one another right now, given her contention that "members of oppressed groups need separate organizations . . . in order to discover and reinforce the positivity of their specific experience . . . [and] their specific needs and interests" (205–206). Young is skeptical of those she calls "liberal humanists," whose idea of emancipatory action is the transcendence of group differences toward some new homogenization. But figuring out how to work with someone who is different from you in order to challenge a common enemy is far from a new homogenization. I believe that there are situations in which it is vital for communities to cloister or regroup, to build strength and a knowledge base; and there are other times when members of those groups need to work in strategic alliances with those of other groups. We work all day with people different from ourselves, and then we go home at night. Usually when I have suggested to Black activists or Asian-American activists that they ought to put more energy into collaborative action, at least one horrified member will respond, "How can we help (or understand) them when we can't even help ourselves yet?" I strenuously reject the idea that cross-community alliances are something that should come about only after members of both communities have reached some breakthrough or plateau of self-understanding or orderliness: such plateaus are never reached. As we look more closely into our community, we discover not a diminishing number of interesting complexities about it, but rather variety that ever increases. All the months and years that we engage in self-contemplation, the power disparity between the Anglo-centric mainstream and the communities on the margins glaringly persists. Furthermore, postponing cross-cultural alliances suggests an unwillingness to grow beyond old prejudices and rivalries that have historically kept Blacks, Asian-Americans, and Latinos from effective collaborations against white supremacy.

Edward Said disputes the quality of critical thinking generated by groups of people who too intimately share deeply held beliefs, and who are not developing thought through interaction with people, organizations, and theories outside their like-minded nucleus. "On its own," Said writes in "The Politics of Knowledge," "ethnic particularity does not provide for intellectual process" (26). Said claimed that,

> If you are weak, your affirmation of identity for its own sake amounts to little more than saying you want a kind of attention easily and superficially granted, like the attention given an individual in a crowded room at a roll call. (24)

If I am critical of the strategic political effectiveness of subdividing and self-defining, this is not to say that I am a customer of the Anglo-American multiculturalism peddled by some college administrations and faculty. Iris Young is right to be contemptuous of a campus diversity based on a principle of "one common culture above conflicts." Nor should we put any faith in campaigns of "toleration," in which Anglocentric culture has the most to gain. The essence of cultural tolerance, Anglo-style, is "I will tolerate your ethnic holidays if you will tolerate the existing distribution of power and resources in America and around the world." Toleration campaigns, like efforts of validation, put the activists and revolutionaries on the defensive, when it is white supremacy that should be on the defensive.

Another model of multiculturalism that does not work is based on the idea that we ought to visualize all of the individuated communities of America and the world as coexisting equally on a level playing field. As San Juan complains, this theory of natural and "pure difference" "denies the centrality of racism and exploitation. . . . It explains away political and economic antagonisms as [simply] the effects of [the] natural cultural legacies" (66). Pure cultural difference says that Native Americans and African-Americans are as different from one another as both are different from Anglo Americans. Such a conceptualization dissolves away the historically documented ways in which Anglos have inflicted themselves upon the other two for four hundred years. It is not in the interest of those in marginalized communities to focus on distinctions that separate them from all other groups at the expense of focusing on the ways that their distinction from the Anglo-American mainstream exceeds that of their distinction from any of the other marginalized communities. Although some who belong to marginalized communities like being treated as if they possess an understanding of their group that is essential and exclusive, replete with secrets unfathomable to outsiders, we ought to approach notions of essential wisdom cautiously. First, whites who concede essential realities to other groups can and will turn it around to insist upon an essential reality to whiteness—and the components that these whites will lay exclusive claim upon will inevitably include intelligence, hard work, honesty, cleanliness, and so on. This is precisely what sociologist John Rex found being practiced by white South Africans, who have tried to use their "cultural distinctiveness" to reassert their superiority over Black South Africans. Second, conceding essentialism is a way of absolving oneself from having to try to understand the position of another, since it has already been agreed that only insiders can know what the community is like. If only Blacks can understand Blacks, then white students should not takeBlack studies classes, since it would not be possible for them to learn anything, and Black students should not waste their time and money on Latino studies classes for the same reason. Furthermore, Black men will not be able to understand the essential experience of Black women, and so should not delude themselves by trying, and heterosexual Blacks need not bother to try to figure out homosexual Blacks. As long as we indulge in the conceit that there are secret storehouses of truths, we do not have much need for education at all, since the truths are already programmed in, according to one's group and experience. When I have participated in workshops on racism, and some whites have insisted that it is impossible for them to imagine what it is like to be Black or to be continually harassed or to be the object of stereotypes and ridicule, folks of color have reacted with disbelief, and I share this disbelief; why is it that some folks exercise a selective lack of empathy when it comes to the persecution of a group toward whom they feel (but won't admit) hostility, while these same people can be reduced to tears while watching a movie that includes the death of a dog? Yet some of the same folks of color who cannot believe whites "can not imagine" and strongly think whites ought to try, become apprehensive if they see a white student enrolling in an ethnic studies class and disturbed at the thought of a white student making ethnic studies his or her field of study. Should we not be pleased that there are persons concerned enough to dedicate their college careers and perhaps their professional careers to the study and understanding of experiences outside of their own familiar and secure space?

As a result of community self-ghettoization, too often on college campuses we find members of one oppressed group silently hanging back while members of another group weather the blows of some racist humiliation. Each group looks at the other's agony and thinks: "It isn't my problem." It was a shame that in 1995 so few (if any) Asian-Americans and Latinos joined Black students at Rutgers University who staged a sit-down strike at center court during half-time at a Rutgers-UMass basketball game. Blacks had been enraged by comments the Rutgers' president had made about the genetic inferiority of African-Americans, and they shrewdly recognized a school sports event as being a suitable site at which to bring public attention to the racist thinking of the highest levels of the university. The next morning, many U.S. dailies carried a dramatic photograph of that first African-American woman who made it down from the stands to sit, stone-faced and cross-legged, in the middle of the basketball court. While Latinos and Asian-Americans at Rutgers—who could not have missed the issue boiling on the campus for days—evidently thought "It's not our beef," how could they think that a university president who traffics in genetic racism when looking at Blacks is suddenly open-minded when matters shift to those of other races? If Asian-Americans and Latinos resent that whites typically do not worry about political pressure from their communities, and so they both ignore and exploit them, Asian-Americans and Latinos will have to stop waiting for African-Americans to stick their necks out first each time white supremacy strikes a blow at all persons of color; they will have to stop forcing Blacks to carry the whole burden and risk of political action. On the other hand, African-Americans and Asian-Americans have been conspicuously quiet in California, during the recent years of white nativist hysteria over illegal aliens and immigration policy. Whether it is in the labor market (as in hiring committees and their minority searches) or civic affairs, San Juan, Avakian, Graff, hooks, and many others insist that it is a loser's strategy for individual groups to wait for their community to be insulted or abused before acting out or for one community to imagine that their position can actually be strengthened if another community is knocked back. Marginalized groups are not each other's competition for bites of the sorry slice of the pie that white supremacy sets on the table; until they resist the situation, however, they are the collective chumps in white power's immoral, inequitable, and despicable apportioning scheme, a scheme that continues to reserve ninety-five percent of the wealth and power for itself. If the marginalized communities do not make inroads against the Anglo-centric power base collectively, no constituency among them will succeed in doing so on its own.

We need to get beyond the idea that marginalized groups "need" to indulge in separatist proclivities on the campus since each requires a "safe" space. Dormitories should be the safe spaces, not those places in which scholars are conducting their business; we need to sleep and to recreate in safe spaces, and for this reason I fully support the desire of some students to be housed with others like themselves rather than to be melted into the university's dormitory pot, as part of some ill-conceived, round-the-clock integration program. The place we sleep at night should be a safe place; the place we wage the revolution during the day should be the real place: the site of the oppression itself. bell hooks in *Teaching to Transgress* will not distinguish between the bad or counterproductive separatism of right-wing conservatives and that practiced by groups who

see themselves as oppressed. Nor does she have patience with a preoccupation with "safe spaces" at the college, writing:

> I enter the classroom with the *assumption that we must build* [empha-
> sis added] community in order to create a climate of openness and in-
> tellectual rigor. Rather than focusing on issues of safety, I think that a
> feeling of community creates a sense that there is a shared commit-
> ment and a common good that binds us. (40)

I have no doubts that it can feel safer and more reassuring for a marginalized student to spend four years hanging out at the Ethnic Studies
offices, studying and sharing with the Ethnic Studies professors, who
also enjoy the comparative peace. But in the U.S. university, an environment in which white power exerts a near monopoly on what passes for
required truth and wisdom, the maintaining of peace could only mean
that white power is being left unchallenged and unthreatened. But we
need not approach our clash of ideas grimly, as if it is a punishment, according to Edward Said, who borrows from Aime' Cesaire's poem
"Cashier d'un Retour" to call for "a place for all at the rendez-vous of
victory" (24). As reassuring as home is, we need to put ourselves at least
somewhat at risk in order to grow. Said argues that we should cultivate a
disposition of "worldliness" which, he says, "can only be accomplished
by an appreciation, not of some tiny, defensively constituted corner of
the world, but of the larger, many-windowed house of human culture as a
whole."

Over the next decade I would like to see more of the focus and energy that reformist scholars currently invest in their (personal) research
projects channeled into contesting Anglo-centricity in the departments of
English, sociology, history, philosophy, psychology, and so forth. I
refuse to see the traditional departments as "lost causes," as far as multicultural reform is concerned. We must reject the cynical view that having
gotten control of some cultural studies programs, we might as well surrender to white power influence our interest in the traditional departments. Scholars with multicultural perspectives need to become at least
as concerned with the curriculum requirements at their institutions as
with how fairly colleagues treat them, because the more the curriculum is
liberated of Anglo-centricism, the more the people who study and work
there will be, too. Significant expansion of the multicultural course work
required in all departments must become a priority; but overhaul of undergraduate course requirements at a given school will not come as a

consequence of having a cutting-edge cultural studies program or having published a groundbreaking article in an elite journal (whatever else good results from such accomplishments); it will come only from relentlessly and skillfully working the systems within the institution. Beyond providing good teaching, writing good articles, and developing rigorous programs, multicultural scholars need to move outside of their territories—to increase their presence at all levels of policy formation within the institution; they need to cultivate relationships with the deans, the vice presidents, the trustees, and all those who shape the vision of the school. White power would often prefer to say no to reformers from the margins, it is true; so we need to put the agents of white power into the position of having to say no over and over and over again, until they realize that only by saying yes more often can they be relieved of some of the pressure.

NOTES

[1] This paper was inspired by a conversation I had with Dr. Bonnie TuSmith in 1995 when I was one of her graduate students—although I assume complete responsibility for any faulty reasoning or errors in the written product.

[2] The "shorthand" that space constraints force me to work in compels me to employ generalizations, characterizations, and misleading associations at times. To set up a dichotomy between multicultural classes, ideas, and teachers, on the one hand, and on the other, "mainstream," "canonized," "traditional," "white power," "Anglo-centric" classes, ideas, and teachers, implies that every Black teacher, every Latino studies class, and every poem by an Asian-American writer is united as part of a collective of wisdom that has transcended faulty, narrow-minded, and racist thinking that characterizes everything else; that would be as grossly unfair to educators and cultures and materials that have been marginalized as it would be to much of Western civilization, a lot of good (white) teachers, and a lot of worthy books. While the scholar of color in this article, and the so-called "cultural studies" course will tend to be "lumped" in with references to "progressivism," and "reform" for the purposes of this article, I would not suggest that all progressives are of color and all of color are progressives. Or that study of Native Americans by itself constitutes "progressivism" whereas study of Anglo culture constitutes "regression." Nor would I mean to suggest that no white men are progressives.

[3] Some might see me as implying that all that is done in a cultural studies program could and should be done in "traditional" departments; secondly, that the faculty of cultural studies programs all began their careers in the traditional

departments before moving over (and down) into cultural studies. What I mean to suggest is that some of what is done in cultural studies programs could be done in the traditional departments—for example, the study of literary texts by writers of color—but this is not to suggest that all the approaches to multicultural study and the research and projects undertaken there could simply be farmed back over into the "old" departments. Nor do I insist that what is done in traditional departments is qualitatively superior to that done in the younger cultural studies programs. I believe that—as a long-term goal—decisions about how the curriculum should be divided up or unified within the institution should be reached on an academic rather than political basis.

REFERENCES

Avakian, Arlene. (1991). "Armenian American Women: The First Word . . ." In Johnnella E. Butler and John C. Walter (Eds.), *Transforming the Curriculum: Ethnic Studies and Women's Studies* (pp. 271–301). Albany, NY: SUNY Press.

Butler, Johnnella E. (1991). "The Difficult Dialogue of Curriculum Transformation: Ethnic Studies and Women's Studies." In Johnnella E. Butler and John C. Walter (Eds.), *Transforming the Curriculum: Ethnic Studies and Women's Studies* (pp. 1–20). Albany, NY: SUNY Press.

Carey, James W. (1992). "Political Correctness and the Cultural Studies." *Journal of Communication, 42* (2), Spring, 56–72.

Cage, Mary Crystal. (1995). "Three Hispanic Professors Have Transferred Out of the Sociology Department at the University of Colorado At Boulder." *The Chronicle of Higher Education,* 31 March, A-18.

Graff, Gerald. (1992). *Beyond the Culture Wars: How Teaching the Conflicts Can Revitalize American Education.* New York: Norton.

Hayes, Floyd. "Politics and Education in America's Multicultural Society: An African American Response to Allan Bloom." *The Journal of Ethnic Studies,* 17:2. 71–83.

hooks, bell. (1994). *Teaching to Transgress: Education as the Practice of Freedom.* NY: Routledge.

Joyce, Joyce A. (1991). "Black Woman Scholar, Critic, and Teacher: The Inextricable Relationship between Race, Sex, and Class." *New Literary History, 22,* 543–565.

Kim, Elaine. (May 1996). From comments during a panel discussion: "Rethinking Academic Activism: Asian American Studies and the Institutionalization of Radicalism." The Thirteenth National Conference of the Association for Asian American Studies, Washington, DC.

Kwong, Peter. (May 1996). From comments during a panel discussion: "Rethinking . . ." Asian American Studies Conference, Washington, DC.

Magner, Denise K. (1991). "Push for Diversity in Traditional Departments Raises Questions about the Future of Ethnic Studies." *The Chronicle of Higher Education*, 1 May, A–11,

Mattai, P. Rudy. (1992). "Rethinking the Nature of Multiethnic Education: Has It Lost Its Focus or Is It Being Misused?" *Journal of Negro Education*, Vol. 61, 65–77.

Olaniyan, Tejumola. (1994). "The Role of African-American Studies in English Departments Now." *Callaloo*, 17:2, 556–568.

Preston, Rohan. (1995). "Battle to Keep Black Professor Leaves Bruised Egos and Reputations." *New York Times Education Section*. 8 March, B-8.

Robbins, Bruce. (1991). "Othering the Academy: Professionalism and Multiculturalism." *Social Research*, 58:2, Summer, 355–372.

Said, Edward. (1991). "The Politics of Knowledge." *Raritan*, Summer. 17–31.

San Juan, Epifanio, Jr. (1994). "Problematizing Multiculturalism and the "Common Culture." *MELUS*, 19:2, Summer, 59–84.

Sege, Irene. (1995). "Not Black Enough?" *Boston Globe*. 9 February, 63.

Spivak, Gayatri Chakravorty. (1990). "The Making of Americans, the Teaching of English, and the Future of Culture Studies." *New Literary History, 21*. 781–798.

Sumida, Stephen H. (1994). "Centers Without Margins: Responses to Centricism in Asian American Literature. *American Literature, 66* (4) December, 803–815.

Takaki, Ronald. (1993). "Multiculturalism: Battleground or Meeting Ground?" *The Annals of the American Academy* (ANNALS), 530, November, 109–121.

Young, Iris Marion. "Social Movements and the Politics of Difference" from *Campus Wars, Multiculturalism and the Politcs of Difference*. John Arthur and Amy Shapiro, eds. Boulder: Westview Press, 199–225.

CHAPTER 15

Synthesizing Gramsci and Freire
Possibilities for a Theory of Transformative Adult Education

PETER MAYO

INTRODUCTION

This paper focuses on two of the most cited figures in the radical debate on education, namely Antonio Gramsci (1891–1937) and Paulo Freire (1921–1997). It is a preliminary attempt on my part to discover the extent to which the combined insights of these two writers, admittedly engaged in different projects but, nevertheless, concerned with what can be regarded as an unmistakably left-wing politics of social transformation, can contribute to the development of a theory of radical adult education. I consider such a theory as one that affirms the idea of pedagogy as a site of cultural politics (Giroux, 1992; Simon, 1992). It is a theory that therefore affirms the political nature of all educational interventions. It is also a theory that calls for socially transformative adult education initiatives that focus, in J. E. Thomas's words, "upon change at the roots of the systems" (1991, p. 11). Those engaged in such initiatives do not confine themselves to dealing with symptoms of what are perceived, from the vantage point of those seeking to end all forms of injustice, as structurally determined forms of oppression.

These considerations give rise to a series of questions that, to my mind, should form the basis of an assessment of the potential that an educationist's work can have for incorporation in a theory of radical, transformative adult education. It is my view that such a theory should be grounded in a critique of mainstream educational systems. The question that arises, therefore, is: Does the work contain a "language of critique" (Giroux, 1985: XIV)? And by a "language of critique" I mean a process of analysis that ties educational systems to systemic and structural forms of domination in the wider society, without denying these systems a "relative autonomy." It also entails a form of dialectical engagement that exposes the contradictions that lie behind the veneer created by the dominant, hegemonic discourse. A related question would be: In what way is the view of education, posited in the work, different from conventional, mainstream ones? This question calls for an assessment of the extent to which education is politicized in the work and, therefore, the extent to which the author exposes it as not being "neutral," relating it to the dominant power interests and configurations in society.

The next stage would be to determine whether the work contains, to use another prominent Giroux phrase, a "language of possibility." Does the work allow room for agency? And I would submit that, when dealing with the issue of agency in adult education, what Allman (1988) refers to as a "critically conscious agency" (p. 95), one should inquire: Who is(are) the agent(s)? The question can, in my view, be answered in terms of an identification of the type of adult educator who can act as an agent of social transformation. It can also be answered in terms of: Are there larger agencies that can promote the cause of these social categories more effectively? If so, does the work being examined recognize and draw out the implications for the role that radical adult education can play within the context of this larger agency? This brings us to issues of party and social movements, the latter increasingly being considered, in the literature (cf. Bocock, 1986, pp. 12-13), as the more likely agents of social change. One also notices the existence of a growing literature in the area of adult education and social movements (cf. Lovett, 1988; Finger, 1989). In terms of radical adult education, one would perforce have to determine in what ways the kind of pedagogy being proposed is different from that which prevails in contemporary society and what the ramifications for such a change in pedagogical approach would be. I would submit that the analysis, in this regard, would have to be done in terms of sites of practice, content, and social relations. My focus on sites of social practice is born out of a recognition that education should be viewed in its wider context, beyond the boundaries of formal institutions and, in its widest sense, as a concept. It is also based on a recognition that processes of learning, whether in support of or against the existing power relations in society, take place in different instances and different contexts throughout our life (cf. Adamson, 1980, p. 142), as will be indicated when I discuss the issue of hegemony in the section on Gramsci. An effective strategy of counterhegemonic adult education initiatives should therefore involve as wide a range of social practices as is possible. I consider a separate focus on content to be appropriate for the purposes of this exposition because one of the central themes in the proposed project would be the issue of culture and, more specifically, whose culture should constitute the basis of the learning process.

I also consider the separate focus on social relations to be an important one because it is in this area that power manifests itself. In my view, forms of power should not be reified, viewed as "things," but should be regarded as complex sets of social relations. In changing the social relations that are constitutive of a particular form of power, one would therefore be changing its very basis. Educational initiatives characterized by radically democratic social relations can, if supported by similar action in other social spheres, contribute towards altering the symmetrical social relations that are a characteristic of the capitalist social formation.

It ought to be underscored that all three elements are interrelated in a process of radical adult education. Their separation, in this discussion, is therefore being done in the interest of organizing and presenting clearly the material at hand.

It is in terms of the above questions that I shall be examining, in this paper, the respective potential contributions of Antonio Gramsci and Paulo Freire for the development of a theory of radical adult education.

ANTONIO GRAMSCI

Antonio Gramsci sought, in his scattered writings, which mainly consist of cultural reviews, journalistic pieces, letters, political pamphlets, and a wide range of cryptic and by no means completed studies (written under trying circumstances in prison), to formulate a revolutionary strategy for social transformation in Western Europe.

It is common knowledge that Gramsci was, in terms of affiliation, first a socialist and eventually a communist militant whose goal was, ultimately, proletarian revolution. His politics were, therefore, comprehensive, involving an analysis of class politics in a variety of its forms. His was a project that extended far beyond an analysis and discussion of educational issues, even though one might argue that education, in its wider context and conception, played an important role in his overall strategy for social transformation. It is accorded an important role in his particular formulation of the theory of hegemony, which is a concept he borrowed from Lenin (Morrow, 1987; Morgan, 1987). *Hegemony* has been defined, in the strictly Gramscian sense, "as a social condition in which all aspects of social reality are dominated by or supportive of a single class" (Livingstone, 1976, p. 235). I would go along with this definition. However, since my concerns, with respect to exploring possibilities for a theory of radical adult education, extend beyond class, I would substitute the words "dominant groups" for "a single class," in order to stress the multiple facets of power (not necessarily unrelated) in a given society.

These aspects of social life are generated among, and made to be accepted by, human beings through the exercise of influence and the winning of consent (Morgan, 1987, p. 299). This involves a process of "learning." For Gramsci, every relationship of hegemony is essentially an educational relationship (Gramsci, in Hoare and Nowell Smith, 1971, p. 350). The agencies that, in his view, engage in this educational relationship are the institutions forming *Burgerliche Gesellschaft* (civil society), which constitutes the cultural bedrock of power. He argues that, in Western society, the state is surrounded and propped up by a network of these institutions that are conceived of as "a powerful system of fortresses and earthworks" that makes its presence felt whenever the State "trembles" (Gramsci, in Hoare and Nowell Smith, 1971, p. 238). As such, social institutions such as schools and other educational establishments are not "neutral" but serve to cement the existing bourgeoisie. Implicit throughout Gramsci's writings on "the state" and "civil society" is a critique of educational establishments. Contained in his writings are elements for an analysis of the politics of education in the Western capitalist social formation. Education is thus perceived as playing an important role in cementing the existing hegemony. It is crucial in securing consent for the ruling way of life, one which is supportive of and is supported by the prevailing mode of production. Compulsory initial learning mandated by the capitalist Italian state during the years of Fascist rule is problematized by Gramsci in his critique of the Riforma Gentile and the kind of streaming it was intended to bring about. His critique of the Fascist regime's proposed separation between "classical" and "vocational" schools strikes me as being well within the radical tradition of opposing any kind of differentiation made on the basis of "meritocracy" when, in effect, the whole process is one of selection made on the basis of class. In short, Gramsci's writings, of relevance to education, are imbued with the "language of critique." Is there a "language of possibility"?

I would submit that such a language makes its presence felt throughout Gramsci's work. Gramsci was no economic determinist. As a matter of fact, his work is generally regarded as having marked a decisive break with the official Marxism of the time. He rejected the views regarding social change that emerged from the Second International, views one associates with such key figures as Plekhov, Bukharin, Kautsky, and the Italian, Achille Loria (Broccoli, 1972, p. 28; Merrington, 1977, p. 144; Adamson, 1980, p. 75). He likened the fatalism that such views generated to a "theory of grace and predestination" (Gramsci, 1957, p. 75). A strong sense of agency is conveyed throughout his writings. This sense of agency can be discovered in his theoretical formulations concerning hegemony and the state. For Gramsci, hegemony is characterized by a number of features, one being its dynamic nature (it is constantly open to negotiation and renegotiation, therefore being renewed and recreated). It is also incomplete and selective (Williams, 1976), and there exists moments wherein the whole process undergoes a crisis (La Belle, 1986, p. 49; Carnoy, 1982, p. 88). All this indicates that there can be room for counterhegemonic activity, which can be very effective at highly determinate moments. There are also excluded areas of social life that can be explored by people involved in such counterhegemonic activities.

For Gramsci, the terrain wherein hegemony can be contested is the very terrain that supports it, namely that of the civil society, which is conceived of as a site of struggle. He argued that, because he regarded it as being propped up by the institutions of civil society, the state cannot be assaulted frontally by those aspiring to overthrow it in order to bring into place a new set of social relations—what he calls a "war of maneuver." The process of annihilating the state and its coercive apparatus must, in Gramsci's view, precede, rather than follow, the seizure of power (Lawner, 1973, p. 49). People working for social transformation—in Gramasci's case, the proletariat seeking to overthrow the bourgeois state, had to engage in a "war of position," a process of wide-ranging social organization and cultural influence. It is for this reason that Gramsci underlined the cultural basis of educational activity and was instrumental in rendering the emphasis on culture and education as one of the important features of the Ordine Nuovo group (Buttigieg, 1990, p. 19), the revolutionary group named after the periodical of socialist culture, which it launched on May 1, 1919 (ibid.). It is through this process that the group creates, together with other groups and sectors of society, a *historic bloc,* the term Gramsci uses to describe the complex manner in which classes or their factions are related (Showstack Sassoon, 1982, p. 14).

> Every revolution has been preceded by an intense labor of criticism, by
> the diffusion of culture and the spread of ideas among masses of men
> [sic] who are at first resistant and think only of solving their own

immediate economic and political problems for themselves who have no ties of solidarity with the others in the same condition. (Gramsci, in Hoare and Matthews, 1977: 12)

The primacy of cultural activity for the revolutionary process is therefore affirmed by Gramsci, an idea that reflects the influence of a number of people, notably Angelo Tasca, a syndicalist of Turin (Marks, 1957, p. 192) and one of Gramsci's socialist friends who had emphasized the importance of cultural activity for the working class in a speech delivered at the Socialist Youth Congress in Bologna in 1912 (Clark, 1977, p. 49). As a crucial area of "civil society," adult education has an important role to play in this "war of position," entailing a wide-ranging counter-hegemonic cultural activity (cf. Armstrong, 1988, p. 257, 258). Indeed, there is historical evidence to show that it has played such a role in a pre-revolutionary context, albeit one that, going by Gramsci's criteria for his distinction between "war of maneuver" and "war of position," should have lent itself more to the former than the latter strategy. Accounts of the Nicaraguan revolution (cf. Arnove, 1986) indicate how popular education carried out, among others, by priests belonging to the "liberation wing" of the Church, helped create the climate for revolution prior to the Sandinista seizure of power in 1979. Gramsci's Ordine Nuovo group directed a lot of its energies during the revolutionary climate that prevailed in Turin, prior to the Fascist takeover, towards the Factory Council Movement that was, in effect, an adult education movement in which workers were "educated" as producers rather than simply as "wage earners" (Merrington, 1977, p. 158) and initiated into the process of industrial democracy. The Factory Council was conceived of as a "politically educative institution" (ibid.). This movement brought Turin, regarded by Gramsci as "Italy's Petrograd," close to a revolution—the main reason for its ultimate failure being that its activity was not carried out in the context of the kind of alliance called for by Gramsci through his formulation of the historic bloc. In retrospect, Gramsci noted that the insurgents in Turin were isolated (Adamson, 1980, p. 60).

While on the issue of agency, it would be pertinent at this stage to determine who, in Gramsci's view, are the agents of social change. With respect to adult education, the issue can be discussed in terms of an identification of who the adult educators are and whether there exists a potential target learning group with whom the responsibility for agency lies. The agents who, in Gramsci's view, play a pivotal role in the "war of position" are the intellectuals. These can be of two types. There are those "great" intellectuals, such as Gramsci's mentor, Benedetto Croce, who fashion the cultural climate of the age, a climate that would be commensurate with the hegemonic group's interests in a given society (De Robbio Anziano, 1987, p. 28). Then there are the subaltern intellectuals, such as teachers, priests, or functionaries, who, by and large, work in favor of the prevailing political system (ibid.). Gramsci suggests a new way of looking at intellectuals. He writes in terms of organic intellectuals—cultural or educational workers who are experts in legitimation. They emerge "in response to particular historical developments" (Ransome, 1992, p. 198) as opposed to "traditional intellectuals," whose "organic" purpose ends when society enters a different stage of development (ibid.).

The organic intellectuals can, if they are organic to the dominant class/group (e.g., managers), serve to mediate the ideological and political unity of the existing hegemony (Merrington, 1977, p. 153) or, if they are organic to the subordinated group or class aspiring to power, engage in the war of position that enables them to secure the alliances necessary to succeed. Adult educators engaging in counterhegemonic cultural activity are to be conceived of, according to the Gramscian conception, as intellectuals organic to the subaltern groups aspiring to power. This implies that they should be politically committed to those they teach. Unless this occurs, there can be no effective learning. One of the reasons why Gramsci did not consider the Italian "popular universities," institutions similar to those of the WEA in the United Kingdom (Hoare and Nowell Smith, 1971, p. 329), to operate in the interest of the proletariat was that the intellectuals involved were not organic and therefore committed to this class (Broccoli, 1972, p. 41). For this purpose, Gramsci argued that it is imperative for the working class, the social category to whose cause he was committed, to produce its own intellectuals or else assimilate traditional intellectuals, the process of assimilation being a crucial aspect of the "war of position" itself. It is most likely that a social group's endeavors, in this regard, would be characterized by a combination of both processes. Furthermore, as Holub (1992) points out, there are instances when it is strategically expedient for these intellectuals to forge alliances, "communicative links" with "intellectual communities" whose political project may be different (p. 163). The case of Gramsci's links with the liberal intellectual, Piero Gobetti, is cited. Both Gramsci and Gobetti appealed to the "democratic imaginary" (Laclau and Mouffe, 1985) that was severely undermined by Mussolini's Fascist regime. This is something that radical adult educators will have to deal with in liberal, bourgeois democracies, especially if they are working "in and against" the system. This may be all part of the "war of position" in which they may have to engage.

As for the issue of whether there exists, in Gramsci's theories, a social category with whom the responsibility for agency lies, one can argue that, despite his first-hand knowledge of the peasant-dominated south, it was to the industrial proletariat, located in Turin, that he looked for revolutionary potential. Although he attempted to deal, at some depth, with the southern question (cf. Gramsci, in Ferrara and Gallo, 1964, p. 797–819) and advocated an historic bloc characterized by a "national-popular" alliance between the proletariat and the peasantry, he ascribed to the former the role of leadership or dictatorship *(direzione)* in the alliance:

> we favored a very realistic and not at all "magic" formula of the land for the peasants, but we wanted it to be realized inside the framework of the general revolutionary action of the two allied classes under the leadership of the industrial proletariat [emphasis added]. (Gramsci, 1957, p. 30; Gramsci, in Ferrara and Gallo, 1964, p. 799)

His view would easily be regarded by such writers as Laclau and Mouffe (1985) as an essential one, hardly removed from the classical Marxist tradition of ascribing agency to the proletariat, hailed as the "universal class" with a historic mission to accomplish. This is not to say that he did not ascribe agency to other groups or movements. As a matter of fact, Bocock (1986) points out that Gramsci attached importance to national liberation movements as active agents in history-making processes (p. 106). However, most of Gramsci's writings that are of relevance to adult education focus on the educational needs of the industrial working class. The issue of adult literacy, an important concern for anyone dealing with adult education in the southern Italian regions, where illiteracy ran rampant, is given lip service in Gramsci's writings—a very short piece explaining the causes of peasant-class resistance to compulsory education being one of the very few extant pieces, if not the only piece (Gramsci, in Ferrara and Gallo, 1964, pp. 235–236). In short, there is an identification in Gramsci's writings of a specific adult education clientele, and this can be explained by the fact that these writings are the product of his first-hand experience as activist, organizer, and adult educator, whose experience was confined to the city of Turin. He therefore wrote specifically about the area in which he was directly involved.

A discussion on the issue of agency in Gramsci's writings would be incomplete without reference to the fact that he conceived of his proposed revolutionary and educational activities within the framework of a movement or alliance of movements. These movements constitute the larger agency in relation to which socially transformative activities would be carried out. Arguably, the most revolutionary period in Gramsci's life is that related to the Factory Council Movement (cf. Clark, 1977). What we discover during this period is cultural action that is carried out within the context of a movement coordinated by the Ordine Nuovo group. This appears to suggest that a "war of position" would have a good chance of success if carried out within a movement. The inference that one draws from Gramsci's Factory Council experience is that this must be a movement that, unlike the one in Turin, should be broad enough to extend its activities into various spheres of social life and beyond the locality in question. Gramsci's bitter final experiences with the Turin Factory Council Movement and his subsequent writings, with respect to the creation of a historic bloc, appear to call for this. *L'Unita'*, the name of the PCI (now, PDS) daily, chosen by Gramsci, who is also recognized as the paper's founder, represents the idea of an alliance—a unity of all the popular forces in a new historic bloc, achieved through the acquisition of a large consensus (Amandola, 1978, p. 39).

The issue that now remains to be addressed, as far as Gramsci's writings are concerned, is the type of adult education that he proposes. I shall discuss this issue from the standpoints of sites of practice, social relations, and content.

Sites of Practice. In keeping with the idea of a "war of position," that is to say, a cultural offensive on all fronts, Gramsci's writings convey the idea that different sites of social practice can be transformed into sites of adult learning. In point of fact, his scattered writings reflect a lifelong effort to engage in counterhegemonic activities in all spheres of social life. Gramsci comes across in these writings as an indefatigable organizer and educator who would leave no space unexplored to educate members of the subaltern classes. The area of industrial production becomes an important site of learning. These workplace educational experiences are to be sustained, according to Gramsci, by cultural centers. The Club Vita Morale, which he helped organize in 1917 and wherein workers read works and gave presentations to each other (De Robbio Anziano, 1987, p. 124), was one such center. Another center was the short-lived Institute of Proletarian Culture, which was inspired by ideals similar to those of the Russian Proletkult (Caprioglio, 1976, p. 216) of which it became a section (Buttigieg, 1992, p. 75). The Institute was also inspired by the group associated with the French journal Clarté, including Romain Rolland and Henri Barbusse (Broccoli, 1972, p. 47). The latter had, in fact, delivered a lecture on the movement at Turin's Casa del Popolo (People's Home) in December 1920 (Buttigieg, 1992, p. 75). Some of Gramsci's writings reveal a yearning on his part for the creation of a cultural association for workers, one that creates space wherein workers can debate all that is of interest to the working class movement. He may have been inspired, in this respect, by the writings of Anatoli Lunacarskij, who had an article on the issue translated into Italian and published in *Il Grido del Popolo*, a periodical for which Gramsci wrote articles. Lunacarskij (1976, p. 362) had insisted on the creation of a network of socialist cultural circles. The importance of such circles must have been recognized by Gramsci for a long time. Indeed, there is evidence that the young Gramsci had, in 1916, delivered talks to workers' study circles in Turin on a variety of topics, including Marx, the Paris Commune, Romain Rolland, and the French Revolution (Buttigieg, 1992, p. 68). His engagement as an adult educator therefore started at an early age, during which time he was also greatly involved in journalism (ibid.).

The ongoing commitment by Gramsci to explore opportunities for proletarian adult education is reflected in his efforts, despite obvious physical and external constraints, to create and teach (between November 1926 and January 1927) in a prison school, "scuola dei confinati," at Ustica (De Robbio Anziano, 1987, p. 125). At this "school," which he helped set up with Amadeo Bordiga, and through the "external" help of his longtime friend Piero Sraffa (professor of Economics at the University of Cagliari and later Cambridge University), who established, at a Milan bookshop, an open account for books to be forwarded to Gramsci (Buttigieg, 1992, p. 86), different courses relating to different levels of study were held (Lawner, 1973, p. 66). This idea spread to all other prisons in Italy where potential detainees could be found (ibid., p. 68). For Gramsci, therefore, transformative education can take place in a variety of sites of social practice, and this strikes me as being well within the tradition of radical, nonformal adult education, particularly the tradition that incorporates the efforts of movements seeking structural change.

Social Relations. Allowing for the fact that there are scattered references to adult education in his letters and cultural writings, I would submit that his greatest contribution to the development of theory in this area lies in his writings on the Factory Council Movement. The emphasis in these writings is on the acquisition of industrial democracy, the backbone of the workers' state. According to Merrington (1977), this is one area where "democracy was crucially denied in a capitalist society" (p. 158). The sense of democracy is conveyed throughout Gramsci's writings on the Factory Council Movement, with their emphasis on the generation of an environment characterized by a "collaboration between manual workers, skilled workers, administrative employees, engineers, and technical directors" (Gramsci, in Hoare and Matthews, 1977, p. 110). Through such collaboration, the worker was to experience "the unity of the industrial process" (ibid.) and, as such, acquire complete mental control over the production process to "replace management's power in the factory" (Gramsci, in Mancini, 1973, p. 5).

One assumes that the educational program that the Factory Councils had to provide in order to render workers capable of exerting such control must mirror the spirit of democracy and collaboration it is intended to foster in the workplace and, eventually, in the envisaged democratic workers' state (cf. Gramsci, in Hoare and Matthews, 1977, p. 66). The kind of environment generated by the Factory Councils was intended to prefigure that of the socialist state (ibid.). The democratization of relations in the sphere of production must therefore have been regarded as an important step towards democratizing those wider social relations that constitute the state, the state being conceived of by Gramsci, in this context, not as a "thing"—a reified object—but, as Corrigan, Ramsay, and Sayer (1980) would argue, as a relation of production. In my view, the logical conclusion to be drawn from the foregoing is that the social relations of adult education between worker educators and worker learners must be participative and radically democratic if the councils are to prove effective in their prefigurative work.

That Gramsci was concerned with mitigating hierarchical relations between those who "educate" and "direct" and those who learn can be seen from his writings concerning hegemony and the role of intellectuals. He advocates a relationship that has to be "active and reciprocal," one whereby "every teacher is always a pupil and every pupil a teacher" (Gramsci, in Hoare and Nowell Smith, 1971, p. 350). I take this to mean that Gramsci favored a relationship between intellectuals and the masses wherein the former act in a directive capacity with the latter on the basis of the former's theoretical formation, and, at the same time, allow the latter some directive capacity. They would therefore learn from each other in a reciprocal, communicative manner. In her excellent bibliography of Gramsci, Laurana Lajolo (1985) indicates how he engaged in such a process during discussions with workers at the Club Vita Morale or at his Avanti! office (p. 35).

The same applies to his views concerning educators. In his piece "On Education," which led certain authors to argue that he advocated a conservative education (cf. Entwistle, 1979; Senese, 1991) or elements of such an education (De Robbio Anziano, 1987) for working class empowerment, Gramsci refers to the teacher who limits himself or herself to a straightforward transmission of facts as "mediocre" (Gramsci, 1971, p. 141; Gramsci, in Hoare and Nowell Smith, 1971, p. 36). Such a teacher is closely associated with the "old school," which, according to Gramsci, has its merits. He underlines these merits to move to one extreme in order to expose the shortcomings of the other, in this case, the Gentile Reforms. This school was, nevertheless, considered wayward enough by Gramsci to justify the struggle for its replacement (Gramsci, 1971, p. 141; Gramsci, in Hoare and Nowell Smith, 1971, p. 36).

The point Gramsci seems to be making in the relevant passage is that dialogue and other elements of a participative education, not grounded in information and rigor, would be detrimental to the working class. Any dialogue taking place would merely be rhetoric. He underlined the merits of the conveyance of facts, an aspect of the old school, in reaction to what he perceived to have been the emerging practice of carrying out dialogue in a vacuum. The implication for adult educators seems to be that a certain degree of instruction needs to be imparted to render any dialogical education taking place an informed one. This point is topical in the debate on adult education, in which it is being argued that mere facilitation, without critical analysis, keeps the learner locked in the same paradigm of thinking (cf. Brookfield, 1989, pp. 209, 210). The inference that I would draw from the foregoing, for a theory of radical adult education, is that the adult educator can bolster a participative and dialogical education by conveying information within the context of democratic social relations. The pedagogy is directive (it is intended towards a political goal), and the organic intellectual/adult educator is equipped with a body of knowledge and theoretical insight that, nevertheless, needs to be constantly tested and renewed through contact with the learners and the masses. This explains Gramsci's advocacy of a dialectical relationship between adult educators/organic intellectuals and the learners/masses. The reciprocal educational relationship that he advocates (and that was cited earlier)

> exists throughout society as a whole and for every individual relative to other individuals. It exists between intellectual and non-intellectual sections of the population . . . (Gramsci, in Hoare and Nowell Smith, 1971, p. 350).

Content. Gramsci focuses in his writings on both aspects of the conventional and problematic "high" and "low" culture divide. He does this as part of a constant search for a synthesis between the potentially emancipatory aspects of both, with a view to providing the basis for a proletarian culture. For this reason, he expresses great interest in works like Dostoyevski's novels, which draw on serial fiction and, in so doing, reveal the interplay between the "popular" and the "artistic" (Forgacs and Nowell Smith, 1985, p. 12). For this reason, elements of the "canon" were not discarded by Gramsci but were considered relevant to the needs of the working class. The inference that I draw is that such knowledge should be featured in a program of cultural preparation of workers developed along Gramscian lines. This knowledge should not, however, be treated unproblematically. The process involved is one of critical appropriation. This is central to the emergence of a new "subaltern" and, in his case, proletarian culture. The issues of critical and selective appropriation of the dominant culture as well as of its mastering in order to transform it constitute the basis of Henry Giroux's (1988, pp. 201, 202) and Michael Apple's (1980, pp. 437, 438) critiques of Harold Entwistle's book (1979) with respect to this feature of Gramsci's work.

The issue of mastering the dominant culture in order to transform it is also developed in other aspects of Gramsci's work. For instance, Gramsci advocates mastery of the dominant hegemonic language for members of the "subaltern" classes not to remain in the periphery of political life. This has implications for adult literacy programs. In the short piece dealing with illiteracy, referred to earlier, he emphasizes the need for peasants to learn the standard language to transcend their insular environment by what would be regarded in Italy as *campanilismo* (parochialism) (Gramsci, in Ferrara and Gallo, 1964, 236).

For Gramsci, it is not only the dominant culture that has to be mastered in processes of adult education but also knowledge of history. As with the canon, which has its roots in the past, history too needs to be confronted and transformed. History should be a feature of working-class adult education. He states:

> If it is true that universal history is a chain made up of efforts man [sic] has exerted to free himself [sic] from privilege, prejudice, and idolatry, then it is hard to understand why the proletariat, which seeks to add another link to the chain, should not know how and why and by whom it was preceded or what advantage it might derive from this knowledge. (Gramsci, in Hoare and Nowell Smith, 1971, p. 41)

I consider the issue of a critical appropriation of the dominant culture as central to an exploration of the potential contribution that Gramsci's writings can make to the development of a theory of transformative adult education. There are, however, other issues, insofar as content is concerned, that are emphasized by Gramsci. The earlier discussion on workplace democracy highlights the importance that Gramsci attached to the workers' sharing of knowledge of the entire production process and of their learning economic and administrative skills. Being first and foremost a Marxist, Gramsci must have considered important a process of education through praxis. And the notion of praxis that comes across in his writings is one that entails an absolute fusion between education and the world of production. It is for this reason that he revealed a fascination for forms of art that stressed the relationship between human beings and industry (his letters to Trotsky on futurism are indicative of his preoccupation with this issue) and affirmed, somewhat idealistically, that:

> The worker studies and works; his labor is study and his study is labor [sic]. In order to be a specialist in his work [sic], the worker on average puts in the same number of years that it takes to get a specialized degree. The worker, however, carries out his studies in the very act of doing immediately productive work [sic] . . . Having become dominant, the working class wants manual labor and intellectual labor to be joined in the schools and thus creates a new educational tradition (Gramsci, in Forgacs and Nowell Smith, 1985: 43).

PAULO FREIRE

Paulo Freire is widely regarded as one of the leading figures in the area of critical pedagogy (McLaren, 1989), that particular type of pedagogy that is concerned with issues of voice, difference, and social transformation. Unlike Gramsci, he writes from the standpoint of an educationist rather than from that of a political analyst. Despite his involvement as Education Secretary in São Paulo (Freire, 1991, 1993; Torres, 1993, 1994; Torres and Freire, 1994) on behalf of the Brazilian Workers' Party (PT), his writings do not contain formulations for a comprehensive party strategy. For the most part, they concentrate on issues pertaining to education, even though these issues are addressed within the framework of wider and more general discussions concerning forms of oppression and possibilities for social transformation. Like Gramsci, however, Freire underscores the strong relationship that exists between education and politics: "It is impossible to deny, except intentionally or by innocence of the political aspect of education" (Freire, 1976, p. 70).

Freire's writings are therefore grounded in a critique of traditional educational methods. Giroux's phrases "the language of critique" and "the language of possibility" were used in relation to Freire's work (Giroux, 1985, p. IV; 1988, p. 108) Originally drawing on his experiences in Latin America, Freire projects a vision of society as being characterized by relations of power and domination. The focus is placed on the ideological means whereby those in a position of privilege and power (the oppressors) exert their control over those whom they exploit (the oppressed). The social relations between the oppressors and the oppressed are prescriptive in nature. This process of prescription is facilitated by a variety of means, including traditional mainstream education. "Banking Education" (Freire, 1970, p. 58), a "top down" process of transmitting knowledge, constitutes an important feature of mainstream education. Through this process, the teacher is the sole dispenser of knowledge, with the students being its passive recipients (Goulet, 1973, p. 11). Under such conditions, the learner is "object" rather than "subject" (Freire, 1995, p. 20). As I have indicated elsewhere (Mayo, 1991, p. 21), deference to authority, an uncritical consumption of knowledge, and an immersion in what Freire calls the "culture of silence" characterize this process. The prescriptive mode of pedagogy alienates learners from the material to be learned. It also facilitates a process of what Freire calls "cultural invasion" because the learner is uncritically exposed to ideas imposed from above, namely, ideas that form part of the dominant culture, and from without, the latter occurring within a process of "cultural imperialism" (Mayo, 1991, p. 21).

Given this affirmation of the strong connection between education and dominant political interests, Freire argues that education cannot be neutral. It is perhaps this aspect of his work that renders it diametrically opposed to conventional, mainstream educational theories. He demands of educators an important choice: "Educators must ask themselves for whom and on whose behalf they are working" (Freire, 1985, p. 80). This is a recurring theme throughout his writings and, in one of his publications in English, he argues that neutrality is a "convenient alternative to saying that one is siding with the dominant" (Freire, in Horton and Freire, 1990, p. 104). As with other radical educators, he advocates commitment to the cause of social transformation, an issue that is given prominence in the transcribed conversation with Myles Horton in which the experiences of brave, popular educators in Nicaragua, who risk life and limb for the cause, are reflected upon (Horton and Freire, 1990, p. 224). The stress on commitment indicates a conviction, on Freire's part, that social transformation is possible. This makes reference to his work relevant for the purpose of establishing the basis for a theory of radical adult education. The message conveyed throughout Freire's writing is one of hope (Freire, 1994)—a vision that, in Henry Giroux's (1988) words, is the product of "the spirit and ideological dynamics that have both informed and characterized the Liberation Theology movement that has emerged primarily out of Latin America . . ." (p. 113).

This is very much a theology that emphasizes the role of human agency in the permanent struggle against oppression and social injustice for the creation of the Kingdom of God on earth (ibid.). It is a sense of agency, the means of "counteracting reproduction" (Freire, in Escobar et al., 1984), that derives from the influence of other sources, including Marxist humanist thought (Youngman, 1986), Hegelian dialects, and phenomenology (Torres, 1993, p. 120), whereas, as far as pedagogical principles go, it emanates from a variety of other sources, and it has recently been argued that such sources include the *l'éducation nouvelle* tradition (Taylor, 1993, pp. 37–39). Because he accords great importance to the transformative potential of human agency, Freire repudiates the overly deterministic and mechanistic theories of reproduction associated with "vulgar Marxism," arguing that these theories convey a sense of "liberating fatalism . . . a liberation given over to history . . . It will come no matter what" (Freire, 1985, p. 179). The idea of "the inexorability of a history that will come in a predetermined manner" is vehemently repudiated by Freire (1994, p. 101).

As in the section on Gramsci, I consider it pertinent at this stage to inquire: Who are the sources of such agency? Freire regards adult education and, given his Latin American background, that particular kind of adult education known as "popular education," as an important source of agency. Needless to say, adult educators play an important role in this context. These educators are conceived of by Freire as adult-learning facilitators. Their task is to facilitate processes whereby educators and educatees are to learn together. The task of the facilitator is to promote learning through dialogue. This process is contrary to the notion of the teacher as the sole dispenser of knowledge and is intended to render the learners active participants in the process of their own learning, to render them "subject." The culture of the learners increasingly becomes the basis of the learning process. Through a "pedagogy of question" (Freire, in Bruss and Macedo, 1985, p. 9), rather than a prescriptive pedagogy, the facilitator enables the learners to reflect on the codified versions of their "reality" (their own world of action) in a process of praxis. The codification serves its purpose in distancing the learners from their world of action so that, through reflection, the educatees begin to see it in a different, more critical, light. It is the process whereby one is allowed to move beyond the popular, everyday ("basist") knowledge, the "knowledge of living experience" (common sense) to "the knowledge emerging from the more rigorous procedures of approach to knowable objects" (Freire, 1994, p. 83).

Because the process throughout is a dialogical one through which the educator learns from the educatees in the same way that the latter learn from her or him, the roles of educator and learner become almost interchangeable. In what has become a classic formulation, Freire (1970) wrote:

> Through dialogue, the teacher of the students and the students of the teacher cease to exist and a new term emerges: teacher-student with students-teachers. (p. 67)

One may argue, therefore, that both educators and educatees are agents in this process. This is not to say, however, that they are completely on an equal footing within the educational process. In a rather late formulation, Freire emphasizes the directive role of the educator (Freire, in Shor and Freire, 1987, p. 103), a role similar to that ascribed by Gramsci to the organic intellectuals. This is an acknowledgment on Freire's part that the educators have a political vision and a theoretical understanding that guides their pedagogical action. This denotes a certain competence, on their part, from which their authority derives.

Freire's acknowledgement of this authority on the part of the teacher appeared, interestingly enough, in a "talking book" published a year after Youngman's (1986) critique of his pedagogy. Youngman had argued that Freire does not admit that educators can have a theoretical understanding that is superior to that of the learners and that is an indispensable condition for the growth of critical consciousness (ibid., p. 179). In according the educator authority, Freire underlines the importance of this authority not degenerating into authoritarianism, the latter being the hallmark of "banking education": "the democratic teacher never, never transforms authority into authoritarianism" (Freire, in Shor and Freire, 1987, p. 91). Freire reiterates the point in his "talking book" in the English language, asserting that "Authority is necessary to the freedom of the students and my own. The teacher is absolutely necessary. What is bad, what is not necessary, is authoritarianism, but not authority" (Freire, in Horton and Freire, 1990, p. 181).

Freire has even gone so far in his work to concede that there are moments, especially during initial meetings with learners who are accustomed to prescriptive teaching methods and therefore not used to risk taking, when the facilitator must show discretion in her or his teaching style, being "50 percent a traditional teacher and 50 percent a democratic teacher" (ibid., p. 160). This may be taken as a belated recognition by Freire of the fact, often pointed out with respect to his advocacy of a dialogical education, that such adult learners would not be disposed to partake of transformed social relations of education overnight. Elements of the "old" pedagogy can, when absolutely necessary, be incorporated into the new one, the main proviso being that the prevailing spirit in the teaching process be one of democracy.

When dealing with the issue of educators as change agents, or to use Giroux's terminology, "transformative intellectuals" (Giroux, 1988), Freire places the emphasis not only on a democratic teaching style but also on something akin to an "organic relationship," in the Gramscian sense of the term, between facilitators and the class or group of people with whom they are engaged. He has used in this regard words like *growing* (1971, p. 61) and *in communion* (Freire, in Freire and Faundez, 1989, p. 56) with the group. According to the Freirean conception of the relationship between educator and educatee, differences between facilitators and learners have to be mitigated as much as possible. Freire is no doubt aware that facilitators/teachers can possess a "cultural capital" that is very different from that of the learners. This can constitute a powerful force of domestication in the learning situation (cf. Torres, 1990, p. 280). As such, repeating a phrase attributed to Amilcar Cabral, Freire writes/speaks about the possibility of intellectuals, including facilitators, committing "class suicide" to integrate themselves with the masses (Freire, 1978, p. 104; Freire, in Freire and Faundez, 1989, p. 56).

Having given an account of Freire's view regarding the role of facilitators as transformative agents, I now attempt to identify whether there exists, in Freire's writings, a specific social category with whom the agency for social transformation lies. Unlike Gramsci, much of the focus in Freire's early work deals with the campesinos in Brazil and Chile. His work concerning the former Portuguese colonies in Africa also deals with peasants. All this indicates that the agency for change does not lie specifically with the industrial proletariat, a view that is not in keeping with the classical Marxist position according to which this class is viewed as the "universal class" with a historic mission to accomplish. Walker (1981), referring to Freire's early work, states that, like Mao, Freire finds greater revolutionary potential in the peasantry than in the urban proletariat. He quotes a passage by Freire to this effect in order to confirm this view:

> large sections of the oppressed form an urban proletariat, especially in the more industrialized centers of the country. Although these sectors are occasionally restive they lack revolutionary consciousness and consider themselves privileged. Manipulation with its series of deceits and fertile promises usually finds fertile soil here (Freire, in Walker, 1980, pp. 137, 138).

The emphasis shifts somewhat in his later works, when Freire engages in dialogical exchanges with prominent U.S. or U.S.-based critical pedagogues (Freire, 1985; Shor and Freire, 1987; Freire and Macedo, 1987; Horton and Freire, 1990). In these works, we discover references to the plight of a variety of oppressed groups whose cause is advanced by social movements. Viewing his work in its entirety, I would submit that Freire's oppressed vary from context to context. For instance, when referring to his work as Education Secretary in São Paulo, he identifies the oppressed as women, who constitute the majority of illiterates in the city and who face a double workload. They also include in-migrants from the impoverished northeast who end up as auxiliary workers in the area of civil construction (Freire, in Viezzer, 1990, p. 6). Most of the social categories mentioned throughout his works are class categories. Nevertheless, the emphasis on different groups, such as gays/lesbians, Blacks, ethnic minorities, and women, in his "talking books" seems to confirm Giroux's (1988) view that "with the notion of difference as the guiding thread, Freire rejects the idea that there is a universalized form of oppression" (p. 109). In a conference session on the work he carried out in São Paulo (Freire, 1991), Freire confirmed that view, arguing that one cannot reduce everything, that is, all forms of oppression, to class struggle: "I have never labored under the misapprehension that social classes and the struggle between them could explain everything, right down to the color of the sky on a Tuesday evening" (Freire, 1994, p. 90).

The emphasis on social movements apparent in his books and in his work in São Paulo indicates that, for Freire, they constitute the larger context within which transformative educational initiatives can be effectively carried out. In the "talking book" with Ira Shor, he advocates that

educators striving for change "expose themselves to the greater dynamism, the greater mobility" found "inside social movements" (Freire,
in Shor and Freire, 1987, p. 39). He reiterates this view in his taped conversation with Antonio Faundez (Freire, in Shor and Freire, 1989, p. 66).

Having underlined the sense of agency present in Freire's work and
having outlined issues related to it, I now focus on the type of adult education that Freire proposes. In the section on Gramsci, I discussed this
issue in terms of sites of practice, social relations, and content. I feel that
the issue of social relations in Freire's work has been explored in sufficient depth for the purposes of this essay in the section dealing with
agency and the role of facilitators. I therefore confine myself, in this section, to questions of sites and content.

Sites of Practice. Like Gramsci, Freire engages in a "war of position," and, therefore, his chosen sites of educational practice are numerous. Although he is strongly associated with adult literacy work in
nonformal settings, I would argue, going by his formulations, that Freire
favors working both within and outside the system. In his view, no space
should be left unexplored in what should be a lifelong effort for social
transformation. In contrast to, for instance, Myles Horton, who would
have no truck with formal social institutions, Freire argues:

> I think politically, every time we can occupy some position inside of
> the subsystem, we should do so. But as much as possible, we should
> try to establish good relationships with the experience of people out-
> side the subsystem in order to help what we are trying to do inside.
> (Freire, in Horton and Freire, 1990, p. 203)

The notion of having one foot in the system (he calls schooling a
subsystem of a larger system—education) and the other outside appears
to have been a feature of his efforts as an educator. For instance, as Education Secretary in São Paulo, he operated "within" the system; in connection with agencies, such as the social movements, he was engaged
"outside" the system. Thus, he was "tactically inside and strategically
outside" the system (Freire, 1991; cf. Freire, 1994, p. 90).

Content. Paulo Freire's work is erroneously associated with adult
literacy programs. It is true that his work in northeast Brazil, as well as in
Chile, dealt with literacy. The need to become literate was essential, in
such contexts, for the oppressed peasants not to remain at the periphery
of political life. Even so, I would submit that adult literacy, though it

served an important purpose in Brazil in that it enabled the learners to vote, was availed of by Freire only as a vehicle for the more important process of political conscientization. It was therefore only a means to an end. It is for this reason that attempts at using the "Freire Method" without its political ingredients for the purpose of spreading literacy constitute a travesty of Freirean pedagogy (cf. Kidd and Kumar, 1981).

Freire's concern is with the attainment of political literacy, the means of reading the world (cf. Freire and Macedo, 1987). Therefore, the codification/decodification method—the means whereby people are enabled to detach themselves from their world of action to reflect upon it and gradually begin to view it in a different, more critical light (praxis)—can be applicable to contexts in which the participants are *literate,* in the conventional sense of the term. It can constitute an effective method to reconsider critically taken-for-granted aspects of one's reality, therefore converting one's "common sense" to "good sense."

Unlike Gramsci, Freire does not focus in his writings on culture on both sides of the conventional and problematic "high" and "low" divide. There seems to be no attempt, judging from his works in English at least, to explore the possibilities for critical appropriation of aspects of the dominant culture, with a view to incorporating them in a transformative adult education program. The only exception in this regard would be the learning of the dominant language, which, Freire feels, ought to be learned, in a problematizing manner, so that subordinated groups would no longer remain at the periphery of political life (Freire, in Shor and Freire, 1987, pp. 71–73).

Otherwise, the emphasis throughout his work is on elements of the "popular culture," elements he regards as providing the basis for a transformative adult education program. Like Gramsci, he is wary of not overromanticizing such culture, and he acknowledges the presence within it of such potentially disempowering elements as superstition, magic, and traditional religious beliefs.

GRAMSCI AND FREIRE: COMBINED INSIGHTS FOR A THEORY OF RADICAL ADULT EDUCATION

The question that arises in the light of the two expositions is: What can be appropriated from Gramsci and Freire with a view to developing a theory of radical adult education? In venturing a preliminary answer to the question, I attempt to suggest a framework for integrative work regarding their adult education insights.

Commitment

The first and obvious point that emerges from their writing is that adult education, as is true of all education, is not neutral and is very much tied to the hegemonic/counterhegemonic interests within a given society. A theory of radical adult education should be born out of a recognition of this point and should be inspired by theoretical perspectives that highlight the strong relationship that exists between knowledge, culture, and power, rendering the kind of knowledge provided by mainstream institutions and the manner of its dissemination problematic. Radical adult education initiatives, therefore, underline a commitment to a cause. The common cause in Gramsci's and Freire's writings is imbued with a "language of possibility" and emphasizes a strong commitment to the emancipation of subaltern groups from hegemonic domination. Gramsci focuses, for the most part, on the issue of class domination. Freire's notion of oppression extends beyond the issue of class—which, as he himself acknowledges (Freire, in Freire and Macedo, 1993, p. 172; Freire, 1994, p. 90), was the main concern of his earlier works—and beyond the issue of the proletariat to a wider recognition of social difference and oppression. It ought to be remarked, however, that he does not go beyond universalized forms of oppression (cf. Macedo, in Freire and Macedo, 1993, p. 172). In combining their insights, I would argue that, regardless of whether they focus on single- or multiple-issue politics, radical adult education initiatives should be rooted in a commitment to confronting oppression in its different forms. Therefore, adult education initiatives directed towards the emancipation from oppression of a particular social category should be carried out in a manner that does not perpetuate the subordination and domestication of another. As Corrigan, Ramsay, and Sayer (1980) stress:

> Any system of representation which signifies (by silence or by positive branding) some group as less than fully human has to be transformed on the road—a long and winding road—of socialist construction. (p. 22)

Agency

Both writers recognize that cultural activity plays an important role in the consolidation or transformation of power relations in a given society, especially in Western capitalist social formations. Dominant groups exercise their power not merely through coercion but also, and perhaps most importantly, through consent. Mainstream cultural and educational activities help generate such consent through the promotion of legitimating ideologies and social relations. Both Gramsci and Freire conceive of the terrain of such cultural activity as a site of struggle. There is a strong sense of agency in their work, and radical cultural and educational initiatives are accorded importance in this respect. Radical adult education initiatives can play an important role in this struggle by problematizing "taken for granted" notions concerning what is defined as "reality," exposing their hidden ideologies and promulgating democratic and dialogical social relations in opposition to the conventional, asymmetrical relations that are supportive and reflective of the "legitimized" power relations in society.

Social Movement

The sense of agency accorded to radical adult education initiatives becomes even greater if these initiatives are carried out not in isolation but within the context of a social movement or, better still, an alliance of movements. This alliance can develop out of a recognition of the different forms of oppression that exist in present-day society and of the need to create a radically democratic society characterized by an equitable share of power along class, gender, race, and ethnicity lines. This goal would lead the different social movements, promoting struggles against different forms of oppression, to engage in solidarity with each other, creating a new "historic bloc." The movement or alliance of movements should develop enough strength to sustain counterhegemonic efforts, including radical adult education ones, in as wide a range of institutions of "civil society" as is possible. Movements could therefore sustain efforts in the area of nonformal education as well as the efforts of committed adult educators who operate within the state system (cf. Freire, in Horton and Freire, 1990, p. 203), carrying out their day-to-day tactical work within the context of a long-term strategy for social transformation.

The issue of working within and outside the system leads to an important consideration concerning radical adult education, to which authority can be lent by both Gramsci and Freire. As indicated earlier, both explored possibilities for a transformative education and action in different spheres of public life, in keeping with Gramsci's advocacy of a "war of position" entailing an attack on all fronts. The implication that one draws from this for a theory of radical adult education is that such a theory should guide practice carried out not only in a specific site but in a multiplicity of sites. It acknowledges the potential of different sites of social practice to become sites of counterhegemonic and, therefore, transformative, learning. Committed adult educators working in state institutions can become mediating influences in the process of cultural transmission, reinterpreting mandates in the light of their own hidden, radical agendas—being "in and against the state" (cf. London, Edinburgh Weekend Return Group, 1979, p. 80). I would submit that these adult educators are more likely to prove successful in their endeavors in sites where there is a concentration of people from a particularly oppressed social category (e.g., work with the unemployed). This was the case with Gramsci in his "prison university" at Ustica, where the learners were political detainees.

Adult Educators

Gramsci's views concerning organic intellectuals and Freire's views regarding facilitators can be combined to project the image of the adult educator, working in the context of a radical adult education program, as a person who, equipped with a theoretical understanding of the adult learners' predicament, engages in a directive form of adult education. The sense of authority that she or he possesses as a result of the competence derived from an understanding of the logic governing different forms of systemic oppression does not degenerate into authoritarianism. On the contrary, every effort is made to promulgate democratic social relations and to render the learners "subjects" of the learning process. The culture of the learner makes its presence felt through a dialogical teaching process. The educator's task is to facilitate the means whereby this culture is examined critically by the learners themselves, so that the "common sense," which is a hallmark of this culture, is converted to "good sense." Freire's codification/decodification process, which can be applied not only to literacy education but to different forms of knowledge dealing with different aspects of social life, can be one of the vehicles for the conversion of common sense to good sense. Through a dialogical process, it is not only the learners who begin to consider that which they "know" in a more critical light, but also the adult educator, who constantly modifies his or her theoretical understanding through contact with the adult learners. This is akin to Gramsci's notion of the intellectuals testing their theories through a dialectical engagement with the masses. Whatever knowledge the adult educator possesses at the outset of the learning process is relearned through dialogical contact with the learners (Freire, in Shor and Freire, 1987).

Gramsci's ideas concerning the instruction-education nexus (Gramsci, in Hoare and Nowell Smith, 1971, p. 36) combine with those concerning dialogue in Freire, in a view of adult learning facilitation that does not preclude the possibility that a certain amount of "teaching" occurs when absolutely necessary (Freire, in Horton and Freire 1990, p. 160; Freire and Macedo, 1995). Instruction can be necessitated by the need for adult educators to interrogate some of the opinions being expressed. It could also be necessitated by some of the dynamics at play within the learning circle. One would be naive to assume that adult learners readily accept processes of a dialogical education. Years of experience of banking education cannot be shrugged off overnight. There will, therefore, be moments when the radical facilitator will have to show discretion in the choice of teaching style, also engaging in a process of negotiation of meaning. Both Gramsci (in Hoare and Nowell Smith, 1971, p. 37) and Freire (in Gadotti, 1994, p. 157) emphasize the seriousness and rigor involved in good teaching/learning situations. Such teaching should, however, be carried out in a manner that in no way undermines the spirit of democracy that should characterize the social relations of education within the learning group.

The image of adult educator that emerges from their combined insights is that of a person totally committed to the learner's cause. Implicit in Gramsci's concept of organic intellectual (Gramsci, 1971; Gramsci, in Hoare and Nowell Smith, 1971) and Freire's insistence that the adult educator experiences her or his "Easter," therefore committing, in Cabral's terms, "class suicide" (Freire, 1978; Freire, in Freire and Faundez, 1989), is an awareness of the strong possibility that the much hoped for process of emancipation can be severely undermined and can degenerate into one of domestication if the educator brings into play a "cultural capital" that is at odds with that of the learners.

Culture

The discussion concerning a Gramscian/Freirean synthesis has hitherto centered around the issue of process. In this final part of the section, I shall focus on content and, more specifically, on questions of culture. Both Gramsci and Freire attach importance to popular culture in their writings, although whereas Freire uses the popular as the basis of his conscientization process, Gramsci provides little sustained analysis of this particular form of culture in his writings except for the serial novel. I have shown that there exists, in Gramsci, a systematic and wide-ranging analysis of the dominant culture. A similar wide-ranging analysis is not to be found in Freire, although the Brazilian educationist does attach great importance to one aspect of the dominant culture—language. I consider it possible to derive insights for the purposes of developing a theory of radical adult education from a synthesis of Gramsci's ideas regarding the dominant culture and those of Freire concerning popular culture. I would submit that, while radical adult education should serve as the vehicle whereby esteem is accorded to popular culture—which should nevertheless be examined closely for the purposes of distilling it of its potentially disempowering elements—canonical works should not be discarded. They too should be subjected to close and critical scrutiny in the interest of selective appropriation for the subordinate groups' ends. Cultural studies programs, engaged in outside traditional academic settings, in what Giroux, Shumway, Smith, and Sosnoski (1988) refer to as the "public sphere," can constitute an important type of radical adult education and therefore provide the context for such appropriation. Cultural studies, over which Gramsci's writings have exerted considerable influence (cf. Turner, 1990; Morrow, 1991), would therefore be taken back to one of its old sites, that of adult education. This is the terrain wherein it originated in at least one country: Britain (Williams in McIlroy and Westwood, 1993, p. 260; Scholle, 1991, pp. 124, 125). In these programs, canonical and noncanonical objects are examined against the background of the learners' conditions of existence (Giroux et al, 1988, p. 150) and in a manner that admits no disciplinary boundaries: hence, no "strong classification" (Bernstein, 1971).

The key issue of "critical appropriation" applies to all aspects of dealing with the dominant culture, including that of teaching the dominant language. Going by Gramsci's and Freire's insights, this is one aspect of the dominant culture that needs to be learned so that the subordinated groups will not remain at the periphery of political life. I would, however, reiterate for the purposes of a theory of radical adult education that Freire insisted that the dominant language be taught by radical adult educators in a problematizing manner. This view is not shared by Gramsci, whose pieces argue that subordinated people should learn the dominant language in order to survive the power struggle. Combining their respective views, I would argue that radical adult educators should not overlook critically appropriate elements from the dominant culture in their attempts to empower learners to engage successfully in a "war of position" with socially transformative ends in mind.

CONCLUSION: ANY LIMITATIONS IN GRAMSCI AND FREIRE FOR FORMULATING A COMPREHENSIVE RADICAL ADULT EDUCATION THEORY?

I consider it appropriate after a preliminary attempt at synthesizing their ideas to expose some of the limitations that I feel one must be wary of when attempting to incorporate their work in such a project. These limitations will have to be addressed by going beyond their work and taking into account other literature, most notably that produced by authors who have critiqued their work. Owing to limitations of space, I shall confine myself to what I consider to be two important lacunae in their work for the purposes of its incorporation into such a theory.

In the expository section, I have shown that Gramsci focuses primarily on the role of the industrialized proletariat as the agent of change. The peasant class is in no way overlooked in his writings, and it constitutes the subject of an unfinished study. Nevertheless, the limited references to the issue of adult literacy in his writings and his constant focus on cultural activities that emphasize the written word, even in his discussion on popular culture (e.g., the serial novel), indicates that the educational requirements of the industrial proletariat were uppermost in his mind. The industrial proletariat was concentrated in the Piedmontese area, where illiteracy was down to 11 percent (Coser, 1977, p. 414). Illiteracy characterized southern Italy, where most of the people led a peasant life. In Sardinia, the level of illiteracy affected 90 percent of the population (Hoare and Nowell Smith, 1971, p. XXV).

Gramsci saw the role of the peasant class as secondary in importance to that of the northern industrial proletariat. So there are priorities in Gramsci's analysis, even with respect to social classes. One finds little in the Factory Council Theory concerning social difference among workers. Although 40 percent of the workforce in Turin consisted of women, who were in the forefront of all proletarian upheavals between 1912–1920 (Hoare and Nowell Smith, 1977, p. XXV), one derives little, if any, indication regarding how traditional unequal power relations between male and female workers can be improved through a process of education for industrial democracy. Neither does he address adequately the issue of race in this context, even though he was confronted by the issue of whether southern workers, with a recent peasant past, gained acceptance in a workers' environment located in the north of Italy. To what extent did the traditional north-south form of racism rear its ugly head in the Turin factories?

Any organization representing the interests of subaltern groups has to deal effectively with the issue of difference if it is to be an agent of social transformation. Dealing effectively with difference also implies confronting racism, homophobia, and patriarchy, as well as any form of harassment (cf. Taking Liberties Collective, 1989, p. 124) related to each of these issues. I would argue that, unless such differences are considered, there would be limits to the extent in which adult educators acting as organic intellectuals can help mitigate potential barriers between them and the learners. They may be organic to them in terms of class but estranged from them, or, at best, a number of them, in terms of gender, race, ethnicity, or sexual preference. Failure to account for such differential location can lead to elements of domestication emerging from ostensibly emancipator practice.

Unlike Gramsci, Freire takes account of differences in his writings. As indicated, his conception of oppression extends beyond the notion of class. However, it has been a standard critique of Freire that, despite his constant references to social movements in his English language publications, there are few sustained analyses of gender (the "blind spot" or "flaw" in his work, according to bell hooks, 1993, p. 148), race, and sexuality issues. These issues and movements are mentioned only in passim, although he is pushed hard on the gender issue in his 1993 and 1995 interviews with Donaldo Macedo (Freire and Macedo 1993; Freire and Macedo, 1995; Freire, 1994). In his "revisiting" of *The Pedagogy of the Oppressed* (Freire, 1994), Freire dwells at length on the various reactions by feminists to his major work, which was characterized by the use of the male referent throughout. He states that their letters made him realize "how much ideology resides in language" (Freire, 1994, p. 67) and that he considers gender oppression as a form of colonization. In this respect, there is a marked difference between Freire's most recent works and his earlier ones.

When he deals with the issue of differential location between educators and educatees, he does so primarily in terms of class. His solution to the problem is class suicide. To what extent can such suicide be carried out? Couldn't there be barriers, including one's "habitus," that continue to locate educators differently from the learners, despite the former's political pedagogical commitment? Can the concept of "suicide," as used by Freire in *The Pedagogy in Process,* be applied in the contexts of race, gender, and sexuality, especially in situations wherein, for instance, men teach women, whites teach Blacks, and heterosexuals teach gays and lesbians (Mayo, 1993, p. 18)? There is little in Freire that deals with such an issue. Weiler (1991) has recently critiqued Freire on these grounds, arguing that Freire's dichotomy of "oppressor" and "oppressed" is somewhat simplistic and reveals a failure on his part to indicate the multiplicity of subjectivities involved in the learning process. She points out, therefore, that a person can be oppressed in one situation and be an oppressor in another. Ball (1992) stresses this point with respect to feminism: "There has often been a failure by feminists to respect differences between women, of racial origin and social class" (p. 8). I would submit that failure to take account of the complexity of the nature of oppression and of the interchangeability of roles between oppressor and oppressed is one of the lacunae in both Gramsci's and Freire's writings. A radical adult education theory would have to address this issue in a substantive manner. It would therefore have to go beyond their work to take into account the writings of Weiler (1991) herself, a host of other writers in the areas of feminist and antiracist education, including people who draw on either Gramsci (e.g., Holub, 1992) or Freire (e.g., hooks, 1989, 1993), and, to a certain extent, Henry Giroux's work (Giroux, 1992).

One other limitation concerns the issue of global capitalism (cf. Ross and Trachte, 1990). I would argue that global capitalism can have a devastating impact on the allocation of public funds to social programs, including adult education ones, intended to establish, in Carnoy and Levin's (1985) terms, the state's democratic basis. In Ross and Trachte's (1990) terms, the "rhetoric of the business climate" (p. 68) would take precedence over concerns for democracy. To what extent can radical adult education contribute successfully to a process of social transformation, given such a scenario? With regard to Gramsci's theory of power and the state, as well as its pertinence to contemporary reality, is it still useful to talk in terms of surrounding the locus of power through a "war of position" engaged in and across the entire complex of "civil society," in which the locus of power has to be seen in the context of larger, international forces? Given such a scenario, would there be validity in the suggestion that Gramsci's concept of a historic bloc must transcend its "national-popular" character to begin to signify an alliance of movements across national boundaries? I would argue that, if there is validity in this suggestion, social movements appear to be the ideal change agents to form such an alliance, given that they, at least the most prominent ones, have an international character. I would also argue that transformative adult education would prove even more effective if sustained by an alliance of international social movements.

In my view, the questions just raised need to be addressed adequately in a transformative adult education theory inspired primarily by the writings of Antonio Gramsci and Paulo Freire, but also by those of other writers who deal with crucial, pertinent issues that the two theorists overlooked.

REFERENCES

Adamson, W. 1980. *Hegemony and Revolution.* Berkeley: University of California Press.

Allman, P. 1988. "Gramsci, Freire, and Illich: Their Contributions to Education for Socialism," in Lovett, T. (Ed.), *Radical Approaches to Adult Education.* London: Routledge, pp. 85–113.

Amendola, G. 1978. *Antonio Gramsci Nella Vita Culturale e Politica Italiana.* Naples: Guida Editori.

Apple, M. 1980. "Antonio Gramsci: Conservative Schooling for Radical Politics," by Harold Entwistle (Book Review). *Comparative Education Review, 24* (3), 436–438.

Armstrong, P. 1987. "L'Ordine Nuovo: The Legacy of Antonio Gramsci and the Education of Adults." *International Journal of Lifelong Education, 7* (4), 249–259.

Arnove, R. F. 1986. *Education and Revolution in Nicaragua,* New York: Praeger.

Ball, W. 1992. "Critical Social Research, Adult Education and Anti-Racist Feminist Praxis." *Studies in the Education of Adults, 24* (1), 1–25.

Bernstein, B. 1971. "On the Classification and Framing of Educational Knowledge," in Young, M. F. D. (Ed.), *Knowledge and Control.* London: Collier–Macmillan.

Bocock, R. 1986. *Hegemony.* New York: Tavistock.

Broccoli, A. 1972. *Antonio Gramsci e l Educazione Come Egemonia.* Firenze: La Nuovo Italia.

Brookfield, S. 1989. "Teacher Roles and Teaching Styles," in Titmus, C. J. (Ed.) *Lifelong Education for Adults: An International Handbook.* Oxford: Pergamon Press, pp. 208–212.

Bruss, N., and Macedo, D. 1985. "Toward a Pedagogy of the Question: Conversations with Paulo Freire." *Journal of Education, 167* (2), 7–21.

Caprioglio, S. (Ed.). 1976. *Antonio Gramsci, Scritti 1915–1921.* Milan: Mozzi Editore.

Carnoy, M. 1982. "Education, Economy and the State," in Apple, M. (Ed.). *Cultural and Economic Reproduction in Education.* Boston: Routledge and Kegan Paul, pp. 79–126.

Carnoy, M., and Levin, H. 1985. *Schooling and Work in the Democratic State.* California: Stanford University Press.

Carnoy, M., and Torres, C. A. 1987. *Education and Social Transformation in Nicaragua 1979–1986.* California: Stanford University Manuscript.

Clark, M. 1977. *Antonio Gramsci and the Revolution That Failed.* New Haven: Yale University Press.

Cooper, G. (1995). "Freire and Theology." *Studies in the Education of Adults, 27*(1) 66–78.

Corrigan, P., Ramsay, H., and Sayer, D. 1980. "The State as a Relation of Production," in Corrigan, P. (Ed.). *Capitalism, State Formation and Marxist Theory.* London: Quartet Books, pp. 1–25.

Coser, L. 1977. *Masters of Sociological Thought.* New York: Harcourt, Brace and Jovanovich.

De Robbio, A. I. 1987. *Antonio Gramsci e la Pedogogia del Impegno.* Naples: Ferraro.

Elias, J. (1994). *Paulo Freire. Pedagogue of Liberation.* Florida: Krieger.

Entwistle, H. 1979. *Antonio Gramsci: Conservative Schooling for Radical Politics.* London: Henley, Routledge, and Kegan Paul.

Escobar, M., Fernandez, A. L., Guevara-Niebla, G., and Freire, P. 1994. "Paulo Freire on Higher Education. A Dialogue at the National University of Mexico." Albany: SUNY Press.

Ferrara, G., and Gallo, N. (Eds.). 1964. *2000 Pagine di Gramsci,* (Vol. 1), Milan: Il Saggiatore.

Finger, M. 1989. "New Social Movements and Their Implications for Adult Education." *Adult Education Quarterly, 40* (1), 15–22.

Forgacs, D., and Nowell Smith, G. (Eds.). 1985. *Antonio Gramsci. Selections from Cultural Writings.* Cambridge: Harvard University Press.

Freire, P. 1970. *Pedagogy of the Oppressed.* New York: The Seabury Press.

Freire, P. 1970. "To the Coordinator of a Cultural Circle." *Convergence, 4* (1), 61–62.

Freire, P. 1972a. "Education: Domestication or Liberation?" *Prospects, 2* (2), pp. 173–181.

Freire, P. 1972b. *Cultural Action for Freedom.* New York: Penguin.

Freire, P. 1973. *Education for Critical Consciousness.* New York: Continuum.

Freire, P. 1976. "Literacy and the Possible Dream." *Prospects, 6* (1), pp. 68–71.

Freire, P. 1978. *Pedagogy in Process: The Letters to Guinea Bissau.* New York: Continuum.

Freire, P. 1981. "The People Speak Their Word: Learning to Read and Write in São Tome and Principe." *Harvard Educational Review, 51* (1), 27–30.

Freire, P. 1985. *The Politics of Education.* Massachusetts: Bergin and Garvey.

Freire, P. 1991. "Educational Policy and Social Change in Brazil. The Work of Paulo Freire as Secretary of Education in São Paulo." (AERA Annual Meeting), an audio tape. Chicago: Teachem, Inc.

Freire, P. 1993. *Pedagogy of the City.* New York: Continuum.

Freire, P. 1994. *Pedagogy of Hope.* New York: Continuum.

Freire, P. 1995. *The Progressive Teacher.* De Figuereido, C., and Castaldo, D. (Eds.). "Paulo Freire at the Institute." London: Institute of Education.

Freire, P., and Macedo, D. 1987. *Literacy: Reading the Word and the World.* Massachusetts: Bergin and Garvey.

Freire, P., and Faundez, A. 1989. *Learning to Question: A Pedagogy of Liberation.* Geneva: World Council of Churches.

Freire, P., and Macedo, D. 1993. "A Dialogue with Paulo Freire," in McLaren, P., and Leonard, P. (Eds.). *Paulo Freire: A Critical Encounter.* New York: Routledge.

Freire, P., and Macedo, D. 1995. "A Dialogue: Culture, Language and Race." *Harvard Educational Review, 65* (3), 377–402.

Gadotti, M. 1994. *Reading Paulo Freire. His Life and Work.* Albany: SUNY Press.

Geras, N. 1987. "Post Marxism?" *New Left Review,* No. 163, pp. 41–82.

Giroux, H. 1985. "Introduction," in Freire, P. *The Politics of Education.* Massachusetts: Bergin and Garvey.

Giroux, H. 1988. *Teachers as Intellectuals.* Massachusetts: Bergin and Garvey.

Giroux, H., Shumway, D., Smith, P., and Sosnoski, J. 1988. "The Need for Cultural Studies," in Giroux, H. *Teachers as Intellectuals.* Massachusetts: Bergin and Garvey, pp. 143–157.

Giroux, H. 1992. *Border Crossings.* New York: Routledge.

Goulet, D. 1973. "Introduction," in Freire, P. *Education for Critical Consciousness.* New York: Continuum, pp. VII–XIV.

Gramsci, A. 1957. *The Modern Prince and Other Writings.* New York: International Publishers.

Gramsci, A. 1971. *Gli Intelletuali e l'Organizzazione della Cultura.* Roma: Editori Riuniti.

Hoare, Q., and Nowell Smith, G. (Eds.). 1971. *Selections from the Prison Notebooks, Antonio Gramsci.* New York: International Publishers.

Hoare, Q., and Matthews, J. (Eds.). 1977. *Antonio Gramsci, Selections from Political Writings* (1910–20). New York: International Publishers.

Horton, M., and Freire, P. 1990. *We Make the Road by Walking: Conversations on Education and Social Change.* Philadelphia: Temple University Press.

Ireland, T. 1987. *Antonio Gramsci and Adult Education: Reflections on the Brazilian Experience.* Manchester: Manchester University Press.

Kidd, R., and Kumar, K. 1981. "Coopting Freire: A Critical Analysis of Pseudo-Freirean Adult Education." *Economic and Political Weekly, 16* (1, 2), 27–36.

La Belle, T. J. 1986. *Non-Formal Education in Latin America and the Caribbean: Stability, Reform or Revolution?* New York: Praeger.

Laclau, E., and Mouffe, C. 1985. *Hegemony and Socialist Strategy: Towards a Radical Democratic Politics.* New York: Verso, pp. 80–82.

Lajolo, L. 1985. *Gramsci un Uomo, Sconfitto.* Milan: Rizzolli.

Lange Christensen, E. 1996. *Freire and Liberation Theology.* AERC Proceedings. Tampa: University of South Florida.

Lawner, L. (Ed.). 1973. *Letters from Prison, Antonio Gramsci.* New York: The Noonday Press.

Livingstone, D. W. 1976. "On Hegemony in Corporate Capitalist States: Materialist Structures, Ideological Forms, Class Consciousness and Hegemonic Acts." *Sociological Inquiry, 46, 3* (4), 235–250.

London, Edinburgh Weekend Return Group 1979. 1980. *In and Against the State.* Bristol: Pluto Press.

Lovett, T. (Ed.). *Radical Approaches to Adult Education.* London: Routledge.

Lunacarskij, A. 1976. "La Cultura nel movimento socialista," in Caprioglio, S. (Ed.), *Antonio Gramsci, Scritti, 1915–1921.* Milan: Moizzi Editore.

Mancini, F. 1973. "Worker Democracy and Political Party in Gramsci's Thinking," (discussion paper). Bologna, School of Advanced International Studies, The John Hopkins University.

Marks, L. 1957. Biographical Notes and Glossary. *The Modern Prince and Other Writings.* New York: International Publishers.

Mayo, P. 1991. "Pedagogy and Politics in the Work of Paulo Freire." *Education* (Malta), *4* (1), 20–28.

Mayo, P. 1993. "When Does It Work? Freire's Pedagogy in Context." *Studies in the Education of Adults, 25* (1).

Mayo, P. 1994a. "A Comparative Analysis of the Ideas of Gramsci and Freire from an Adult Education Perspective." *Canadian Journal for the Study of Adult Education, 8* (2), 1–28.

Mayo, P. 1994b. "Gramsci, Freire and Radical Adult Education: A Few Blind Spots." *Humanity & Society, 18* (3), 82–98.

McLaren, P. 1989. *Life in Schools.* New York: Longman.

Meiksins Wood, E. 1986. *The Retreat from Class.* London: Verso.

Merrington, J. 1977. "Theory and Practice in Gramsci's Marxism," in *Western Marxism a Critical Reader.* London: Verso, pp. 140–175.

Morgan, W. J. 1987. "The Pedagogical Politics of Antonio Gramsci: 'Pessimism of the Intellect, Optimism of the Will.'" *International Journal of Lifelong Education, 6* (4), 295–308.

Morrow, R. A. 1987. "Introducing Gramsci on Hegemony. Towards a Post-Marxist Interpretation." Paper delivered at the Colloquium on the Fiftieth Anniversary of Gramsci's death, Edmonton, Dept. of Educational Foundations, The University of Alberta, 27 April.

Morrow, R. A., and Torres, C. A. 1995. *Social Theory and Education. A Critique of Theories of Social and Cultural Reproduction.* Albany: SUNY Press.

Retamal, G. 1981. "Paulo Freire, Christian Ideology and Adult Education in Latin America." *Newland Papers,* No. 5, Hull: University of Hull.

Ross, R., and Trachte, K. C. 1990. *Global Capitalism: The New Leviathan.* New York: SUNY Press.

Senese, G. B. 1991. "Warnings on Resistance and the Language of Possibility: Gramsci and a Pedagogy from the Surreal." *Educational Theory,* Winter, *41* (1), 13–22.

Shor, I., and Freire, P. 1987. *A Pedagogy for Liberation Dialogues on Transforming Education.* Massachusetts: Bergin and Garvey.

Showstack Sassoon, A. (Ed.). 1982. *Approaches to Gramsci.* London: Writers and Readers Publishing Cooperative Society.

Taking Liberties Collective. 1989. *Learning the Hard Way: Women's Oppression in Men's Education.* London: Macmillan.

Thomas, J. E. 1991. "Innocence and After: Radicalism in the 1970s," in Westwood, S., Thomas, J. E. (Eds.), *The Politics of Adult Education.* Leicester: NIACE.

Torres, C. A. 1982. "From 'The Pedagogy of the Oppressed' to 'A Luta Continua': An Essay on the Political Pedagogy of Paulo Freire." *Education with Production,* Review No. 2, Botswana, Spring, pp. 76–97.

Torres, C. A. 1990. "Adult Education and Popular Education in Latin America: Implications for a Radical Approach to Comparative Education." *International Journal of Lifelong Education, 9* (4), 271–287.

Torres, C. A. 1991. "The State, Non-formal Education, and Socialism in Cuba, Nicaragua, and Grenada." *Comparative Education Review, 35* (1), 110–130.

Torres, C. A. 1993. "From 'The Pedagogy of the Oppressed' to 'A Luta Continua', The Political Pedagogy of Paulo Freire," in McLaren, P. and Leonard, P. (Eds.), *Paulo Freire: A Critical Encounter.* New York: Routledge.

Torres, C. A. 1994. "Paulo Freire as Secretary of Education in the Municipality of Sao Paulo." *Comparative Education Review, 38* (2), pp. 181–214.

Torres, C. A., and Freire, P. 1994. "Twenty Years after 'Pedagogy of the Oppressed,' Paulo Freire in Conversation with Carlos Alberto Torres," in McLaren, P., and Lankshear, C. (Eds.), *Politics of Liberation, Paths from Freire.* New York: Routledge.

Viezzer, M. 1990. "La Poblacion Marginada, Objeto del Ano Internacional de la Alfagetizacion (interview with Paulo Freire)." *Convergence,* Vol. XXIII, No. 1, pp. 5–8.

Walker, J. C. 1981. "The End of Dialogue: Paulo Freire on Politics and Education," in Mackie, R. (Ed.), *Literacy and Revolution: The Pedagogy of Paulo Freire.* New York: Continuum, pp. 120–150.

Weiler, K. 1991. "Freire and a Feminist Pedagogy of Difference." *Harvard Educational Review, 61* (4), 449–474.

Williams, R. 1976. "Base and Superstructure in Marxist Cultural Theory," in Dale, R., Esland, G., and Macdonald, M. (Eds.). *Schooling and Capitalism.* London: Routledge and Kegan Paul, pp. 202–210.

Youngman, F. 1986. *Adult Education and Socialist Pedagogy.* Kent: Croom Helm.

Index